British Universities and Teacher Education: A Century of Change

Edited by

John B. Thomas

The Falmer Press
(A Member of the Taylor & Francis Group)
London · New York · Philadelphia

UK The Falmer Press, Falmer House, Barcombe, Lewes, East Sussex, BN8 5DL

USA The Falmer Press, Taylor & Francis Inc., 1900 Frost Road, Suite 101, Bristol, PA 19007

First published 1990

British Library Cataloguing in Publication Data

British universities and teacher education: a century of change.
1. Great Britain. Teachers. Professional education. Role of universities, history.
I. Thomas, J. B. (John Bernard), 1941–
370.730941
ISBN 1-85000-706-3
ISBN 1-85000-707-1 (pbk.)

Jacket design by Caroline Archer

Typeset in 10½/12 point Baskerville by
Bramley Typesetting Limited, 12 Campbell Court, Bramley, Basingstoke, Hants.

Printed in Great Britain by Taylor & Francis (Printers) Ltd, Basingstoke on paper which has a specified pH value on final paper manufacture of not less than 7.5 and is therefore 'acid free'.

Contents

Preface

This book is intended both as a contribution to the history of teacher education and as a contribution to contemporary debate on teacher training.

It was initially conceived as a centenary celebration of the opening of the first day training colleges in 1890, a landmark in the historical development of university involvement in teacher education. As such a celebration the first five chapters of the text describe the growth of teacher training in the universities of England and Wales. Two specialist historical chapters follow on Scotland and Northern Ireland. The remainder of the book is thematic with chapters looking at a number of specialist interests which make an important impact on present-day practice in university teacher education. The final chapter analyzes the present state of teacher education in the universities and is an important statement about professional theory and practice as teacher educators learn to live with the 1990s. In many respects the 1890s are not that far away and it is to be hoped that this edited collection will serve as an inspiration for the future as well as a memorial to the pioneers of our profession.

The universities have experienced a century of change and the present is as full of change and challenge as the past. The contributors to this volume speak from different universities and various professional interests, but are all united in a common concern to maintain and continue the high quality of university teacher education into the twenty-first century.

John B. Thomas
Loughborough University of Technology
December 1989

Acknowledgments

Editors are always indebted to their contributors and I must thank them all for their unfailing good humour in meeting deadlines and answering editorial queries. I also wish to thank Professor Ivor Goodson for his early encouragement and Malcolm Clarkson, Managing Director of Falmer Press Ltd for his unfailing support. I am grateful to Professor Brian Simon and Roger Osborn-King of the Carfax Publishing Company for permission to republish a paper which first appeared in *Studies in Higher Education*. Similarly, the chapter in this book by Professor Maurice Craft is a revised and edited version of the paper published in Verma, G.K. (Ed) (1989) *Education for All: A Landmark in Pluralism* (Falmer Press) and is reproduced here by kind permission of Professor Verma and the publisher. Thanks are due also to Professor Alec Ross and Professor Peter Gordon for help with the appendix to this volume. I am grateful to Marjorie Salsbury and Paula Cross who produced the final version of this book and to Mary Hodgkinson who dealt valiantly with many bibliographical enquiries. Finally I wish to thank my wife Betsi, and our daughter, Amy, for putting up with editorial panics. Without the two of them nothing would ever have been completed.

Chapter 1

Victorian Beginnings

John B. Thomas

Early Teacher Training

The formal involvement of British universities in the training of teachers is barely a century old. The formal training of teachers in specialist institutions designated for that purpose is older with the oldest teacher training college, Borough Road, commencing work of a rudimentary nature in 1808. Gestures towards teacher training were made in the eighteenth century by the Society for Promoting Christian Knowledge (SPCK) and by rare individuals like the Reverend Griffith Jones who provided short courses on the content of lessons for teachers in the 'circulating schools' of Wales. A system for training teachers only became necessary in the early nineteenth century with the growth in the provision of elementary schools to educate children to meet the labour needs of a newly industrialized society. The monitorial schools of Lancaster and Bell were an attempt to establish such a system using the best pupils in a school to teach the remainder. By 1820 about 200,000 children were being taught in over 1500 monitorial schools. Advanced as this was by eighteenth-century standards, the monitorial system was eclipsed by the Glasgow Normal Seminary opened in 1837 by David Stow. Stow demanded more maturity from his recruits and they had to learn a much more professional set of skills than the boy monitors with the result that 'the best of the Glasgow trainees were sought all over the world in preference to Bell and Lancaster robots' (Wragg, 1974). Elements of the Stow system, also incorporating practices from experiments in Holland, were incorporated in a national pupil teacher scheme devised by Kay-Shuttleworth and launched by the Committee of Council in England and Wales in 1846. This scheme combined the best elements of earlier attempts at training based in schools with training at residential training colleges (of which there were twenty in 1847) and was greeted with euphoria by inspectors of schools. The pupil teacher system did improve the efficiency and morale of the elementary schools, but depended for success largely on the quality of its recruits, as one successful pupil teacher later in the century, Abel Jones, records in his autobiography: 'he [the pupil teacher] learned young how to control a class, how to interest children, and how to achieve the maximum good results for his own as well as his children's efforts. He became a thoroughly efficient teacher, that is, of course, if he had any capacity for teaching'.[1] A much more cynical view of pupil teachers is given by some of the headteachers who supervised them and found 'indifference to lessons and inattention to duty'.[2]

The deficiencies of the pupil teachers were not the concern of the universities until the last decades of the nineteenth century. Those universities which existed in Britain in the first fifty years of that century were not concerned with elementary school teachers except where such people had studied at university for a degree though very few university students graduated and even in Scotland the 'learned dominie' was more myth than reality.[3] Universities concentrated on teaching content in academic subjects and ignored consideration of teaching methods, believing that 'the possession of a degree — especially if it were reinforced by holy orders — was an entirely adequate qualification for teaching in an endowed or public school' (Barnard, 1961). Such graduates could sometimes be found in elementary schools whilst the nineteenth-century profession of public school master operated in an elite world of schools which were an extension of Oxford and Cambridge and in some cases, in the last half of the century, were equivalent, if not superior to some of the Oxford colleges (Bamford, 1973). Secondary school masters in the middle class schools of Victorian Britain, influenced by the tradition of such public school masters, rejected the illiberal and mechanical model of elementary teacher training as shown in pupil teachers and residential colleges and during most of the nineteenth century remained uninterested in the matter of training for the profession. This lack of interest was one aspect of a watchful and hostile relationship between the middle class secondary teachers and the certificated elementary teachers; 'the status of the certificated master is far beneath that of the independent middle-class educators'.[4] Forty years on from the date of this quotation, an article in the *Fortnightly Review* of May 1899 continues the hostility:

> the elementary school teacher is not likely to be a person of superior type. He is, in truth, a small middle class person — with all the usual intellectual restrictions of his class. He is, in other words, unintellectual, knowing hardly anything well, parochial in sympathies, vulgar in the accent and style of his talking, with a low standard of manners. He is withal extremely respectable, correct morally, with a high sense of duty, as he understands it, and competent in the technique of his calling — What we want is educated ladies and gentlemen as teachers.[5]

The implication is that educated teachers did not need training and the elementary teacher would not be received into the cultured middle class world of the secondary school teacher. Training the secondary school teacher would reduce his social status by associating him with the trained teacher of the lowly elementary school. In a Victorian male world obsessed by social status it is perhaps not surprising that the first believers in training for secondary teaching were mainly women.[6] Women turned to the universities for training, and though Professor Tuck is correct in arguing that the University Day Training Colleges of the 1890s were 'founded as the second phase of the public provision of institutions for the training of teachers for elementary schools' (Tuck, 1973), the piecemeal provision in universities before that decade had much to do with secondary schooling and meeting the educational and training needs of governesses and women teachers.

Teachers for Secondary School

The nineteenth century universities had taught the content of the widening curriculum of the secondary schools but this had only benefited teachers in the better schools. The many private schools of Victorian England recruited teachers who were neither prepared academically or professionally for their work, whilst women were not allowed (until the last quarter of the century) the benefits of a university education. The training of secondary teachers began with these two classes of private and women teachers, pioneered by the College of Preceptors founded in 1846. This institution, described by R.W. Rich as 'a kind of Teachers University', was incorporated by Royal Charter and provided with funds for 'the founding or endowing of normal or training schools or instituting lectureships, on any subject connected with the theory on practice of education'.[7] With slender resources the College could do little to provide training but it did attract able teachers for its occasional lectures and in 1871 appointed Joseph Payne as a lecturer in education and then two years later as Professor of Education, a position which lapsed shortly afterwards though lectures continued to be given by distinguished visitors. The initiative of the College of Preceptors was part of a general spread in the 1870s of the idea that there should be provision for the training of secondary school teachers and the diplomas of the College were particularly useful to teachers in private schools. Equally valuable were the diplomas awarded by the University of Cambridge after it established a Teachers Training Syndicate in 1879. Cambridge made provision for lectures in the 'theory, history and practice of education' and conducted an examination system which offered the widest opportunity for secondary training by providing a certificate award which could be prepared for in local centres and thus awarded to external candidates. This became extremely popular, especially with women teachers in the developing private schools for girls, and acted as a model for developments in other universities, for example, the University of Durham Certificate for Teachers in Secondary Schools[8], the University of London Diploma in Education established in 1883, and the Oxford Diploma in Theory, History and Practice of Education dating from 1896. Secondary training departments were opened in other universities and by 1900 there were twenty-one in operation, (Rich, 1972).

The success of the Cambridge Teachers Training Syndicate was largely due to the energy of its first secretary, Oscar Browning, later first Principal of the University of Cambridge Day Training College, and to the quality of its early lecturers: the Reverend R.H. Quick in history of education and J.G. Fitch, formerly Chief HMI for Training Colleges, who provided a course on practical teaching. Success was also due to the foundation in 1885 of the Cambridge Day Training College for Women[9] supported by heads of important schools for girls such as Miss Buss of the North London Collegiate School and an immediate success under its first Principal, Miss E.P. Hughes. The services of the Cambridge Syndicate were used a great deal by the training colleges for women in late Victorian England; male teachers virtually ignored them, a fact commented upon by Henry Sidgwick in 1894, giving evidence before a Royal Commission, when he said of the Cambridge Training Syndicate that its scheme had 'remained almost inoperative up to the present time so far as the schoolmasters for whose benefit it was primarily instituted are concerned'[10]. The Syndicate and Hughes Hall also appeared attractive as a source of training for Catholic men and women but such hopes were frustrated by Cardinal Vaughan, (McClelland, 1975).

Courses for Pupil Teachers

The courses provided by Oscar Browning and his colleagues were courses of professional theory and practice. The universities were also increasingly involved in providing 'secondary education' in subject content for teachers in elementary schools, by adapting their courses to the needs of the pupil teacher curriculum. This was particularly true of classes organized for the University Extension Movement, the ancestor of the extra-mural and adult education departments of today, as provided by the Lord Lectures Syndicates at Cambridge and Oxford and especially impressive in their work in Hull and in London, and in the activities of the Victoria University and in the early history of the University of Reading (Marriott, 1981). The Victoria University Certificate was almost entirely supported by teachers and by 1901, when that University examined some 760 extension students, 90 per cent of the candidates were pupil teachers.[11] Other universities also attracted teachers to many of their classes. University College, Aberystwyth, had special Saturday classes for schoolmasters in 1877 at 10/- for two terms of part-time study, (Ellis, 1972). University College, Cardiff, tried to meet the professional needs of teachers from its first session in 1884 and noted the very large numbers of teachers taking evening classes in a variety of subjects; Greek, Latin, philosophy, English, physics, chemistry, biology, Welsh, French, German, music and mathematics.[12]

Piecemeal provision of university courses for teachers as outlined in the last paragraph served only by their uncoordinated nature to highlight the professional needs of those teaching in both the elementary and secondary schools. The opening of university day training departments from 1890 onwards, though designed primarily for teachers in elementary schools, reacted also in favour of training for secondary school teachers, as Barnard has pointed out.[13] These day training departments came about through the interaction of apparently chance but, fortunately, simultaneous developments in educational opinion and practice. The immediate cause was the acceptance by the Education Department in Whitehall of the recommendations concerning teacher training in the reports of the Cross Commission, but longer term considerations themselves influenced the Commissioners and their witnesses. Such considerations were the failure of the pupil teacher system, the results of the Education Act 1870, the nature of existing training colleges, the interests of the school boards, the growth of the civic universities, and the increasing interest in the academic study of education.

As Rich has pointed out[14], the work of the elementary schools had improved greatly as a result of the introduction of pupil teachers whose final government examination had also been the entrance examination for the residential training colleges, the successful candidates being known as Queen's Scholars. Such scholars were better candidates than these colleges had previously taught. However the deficiencies of the pupil teacher system which we briefly noted earlier, and which had been largely ignored in the Newcastle Commission on elementary education in 1861, were worsened considerably by the introduction of the Revised Code a year later. The Revised Code restricted the syllabus of teacher training to those subjects which students would have to teach in the narrow curriculum of the elementary schools. 'By 1866, the number of pupil teachers had fallen by a third and the standard of the Queen's Scholarships had to be lowered', (Barnard, 1961). There were increasing complaints about the lamentably poor educational standards of pupil teachers when entering training colleges and many of the school boards set up after the 1870 Education Act established Pupil Teacher Centres in an attempt to improve the quality of the pupil teachers in their employment. The 1870 Act, the first United Kingdom legislation to accept the principle of compulsory elementary education, had laid down that properly elected school boards should be established to manage schools for pupils aged 5–13 in areas where no voluntary schools existed or where the provision of elementary education was inadequate. The pupil teacher centres arose directly out of the rapid extension of board schools after the 1870 Act and were pioneered by the Liverpool and London School Boards. The practice spread rapidly to other areas and by 1890 most pupil teachers were being educated in pupil teacher centres. At the same time secondary education was developing, including in the pupil teacher centres themselves, and between 1870 and 1882 board school populations had increased by 258 per cent. The strain on the pupil teacher system was enormous and cries were being heard to abolish the system altogether, for example, Dr Crossley of the Birmingham School Board: 'I do not think that it is right to sacrifice the education of the working classes to an indifferent mode of preparing teachers'.[15]

Dr Crossley was providing evidence for the Cross Commission appointed in 1886 to examine the working of the elementary schools since the Education Act of 1870. The views of the Commission reveal evidence that Dr Crossley was not alone in his unfavourable opinion of the pupil teachers. They are revealed as in general unsatisfactory, many never having received any practical instruction during their teaching practice. Even a former admirer of the system, Matthew Arnold, who had viewed them affectionately in the report of the Newcastle Commission, was forced reluctantly to conclude that 'the time had come for substituting a higher order of teaching, and for relying more on adult and well-trained teachers'.[16] The pupil teacher centres, well organized as some were, had come to the scene too late — a fact increasingly demonstrated as both pupil numbers and the complexity of schooling increased — and the more progressive of the school boards were to become major supporters of radical change in teacher training.

Training Colleges for Teachers

That radical change was not likely to be found in the residential training colleges. An education at a training college had made the pupil teacher an elite member of the profession for even as late as 1900 the ratio of trained to untrained teachers was 1:12 and barely 44 per cent of qualified pupil teachers were admitted to a college.[17] At the time of the Cross Commission the teaching population in the elementary schools was made up of pupil teachers awaiting a place in college, those teachers who had successfully trained in college, and those who became certificated teachers by taking the examination conducted by the government from the Education Department in London. But the residential training college system was breaking down in spite of a rapid growth in college numbers and student places since 1850. In the four decades from 1850 to 1890 the number of colleges had risen from sixteen to forty-nine, with the number of student places rising from less than 1000 to 3679, numbers which almost doubled by the end of the century.[18] Unfortunately these increases saw little change in the quality of the training college course which remained unchallenging. The academic education in their teaching subjects provided for teachers was meagre and sterile and the theory and practice of education taught was excessively repetitive and formal with students using manuals of teaching method with such titles as *Introductory Textbook to Method and School Management* (by Gill, 1857, 1858, 1860 and 1891), *Practical Hints on Teaching* (Menet, five editions from 1867), and *The Philosophy of Education or the Principles and Practice of Teaching* by Thomas Tate, first published in 1854. Such books reflect the prevailing pedagogy of nineteenth century schooling and they were written in terms that 'appeared novel but sounded common-sensical. Insofar as they worked at the intersection of theory and practice they had to trade in earthly possibilities not utopian visions' (Hamilton, 1982). This meagre level of education in the training colleges arose partly from a view that had long been common currency in England, namely a conviction that such a low level of personal education was sufficient for the needs of the working classes. Briefly to be educated in a training college was to deny to such an elementary school teacher a cultured and liberal education and condemn him to remain a worker amongst the working class.

We shall return to the defects of this training curriculum below. Before we do so it is important to point out that not only were the colleges poor trainers of teachers but they were also insufficient in number and often of the wrong type and geographically in the wrong situations. In addition, and most importantly, they could not meet the statutory requirements of central government.

The training college system could not meet the needs of the great explosion of elementary education in England and Wales which followed the Education Act of 1870. As Bergen[19] has calculated, the percentage of school-aged children attending elementary schools rose rapidly, from 26 per cent in 1871 to 46 per cent in 1881. By 1891 the figure was 57 per cent. These figures, based on average attendance, underestimate the real growth and the number of students registered was much higher. There was correspondingly an increase in the number of schools from 9521 in 1871 to 19,508 in 1891. Similarly expenditure on elementary education increased more than fourfold over the same two decades. In 1871 teachers constituted less than one-tenth of 1 per cent of the workforce. By 1891 teachers had become five per thousand of the working population. These national statistics are also supported by local historical researches. The population of the city of Cardiff in 1891 was 129,000 compared to 82,000 a decade earlier and the number of schools had grown accordingly. By 1907, when the total population was approaching 182,000 people, the total register for elementary schools was 25,151 in council schools and 8842 in Church schools.[20] In Bristol average school attendance by 1900 had increased to 85 per cent from less than 50 per cent in 1870. In the intervening thirty years the Bristol school board had provided 29,000 school places, including sixteen new elementary schools in the three years 1898–1901.[21]

Such increases in school places brought a demand for an increase in numbers and quality in the training colleges. The school boards pressed for more college places outside the control of the voluntary societies. Success as a pupil teacher and in the examination for a training college scholarship did not necessarily guarantee a person entry to college. In 1888 for example there were 2800 successful candidates and only 1600 admissions to colleges, (Browne, 1971, p. 136). Enquiry by the school board among Birmingham teachers showed that only one-sixth had been trained in colleges and the city's pupil teachers had also performed better than average in the government examinations. The national situation was also extremely variable in terms of the entry standards of those colleges which existed. The great London residential colleges, according to HMI Oakley, 'have slowly but firmly made themselves known throughout the country as having trained many generations of highly qualified and efficient teachers', were highly sought after by London pupil teachers and difficult to enter with Westminster College for men and Southlands College for women being particularly difficult.[22] The problem in Bristol was one of poor standards in the local voluntary college at Fishponds. HMI Fitch delivered a broadside to the Council of the Diocesan College at Fishponds in 1889, complaining about poor results in certificate examinations, inefficient and poorly paid tutors, and the poor work of the matron. He complained of the succession of amateur principals who were graduate Oxford and Cambridge parsons with no experience of teaching, (Elmes, 1969). Conversely the high entry standard for Bangor Normal College in North Wales excluded large numbers of pupil teachers, a fact made worse in Wales because in an overwhelmingly non-conformist country two of the three training colleges, at Swansea and Carmarthen, were Anglican. Only Bangor was undenominational and, as William Williams, the Chief Inspector for Wales, wrote, 'for some years a number of the male pupil teachers from the board schools of this division, although they have occupied a fair position in the scholarship list, have been unable to enter a training college because there is no room for them in the only undenominational training college for males in the Principality.'[23] In addition, Wales suffered a great shortage of female teachers, worsened by the fact that 'there has been no increase in the training colleges for female teachers in the last twenty years, although the population has gone up some 40 per cent and the number attending the schools has more or less doubled'. These comments from a report of the Cardiff School Board quoted in Allsobrook (1979) have to be read not only in the light of the needs of the 1870 Education Act but also with the need for trained teachers to staff the large numbers of girls and mixed secondary schools in Wales under the provisions of the Welsh Intermediate Education Act of 1889. Teacher training supply in Wales was complicated by the rural geography of the country, as it could also be in parts of England. For example, as Tyson and Tuck (1971) have pointed out, there was no training college provision in Newcastle or north of the Tyne; the nearest colleges were the two Church of England colleges of Bede College and St Hild's in Durham, for men and women respectively. Only the pupil teacher system provided trained teachers for Newcastle and the county of Northumberland. The deficiencies of this system were especially noticeable in a largely rural environment.

The school boards, in debating the shortcomings of both pupil teachers and training colleges, decided that they themselves should provide additional training colleges free from any religious restrictions on entry and thus improve the quantity, quality, and type of teacher training provision. Various of the school boards, particularly Birmingham, advocated such a policy. Simultaneously the new civic universities of late nineteenth-century England and Wales, conveniently in the large expanding urban centres of Victorian industry and commerce needing more schools and thus more teachers, were advocating the closer connection of these universities with the training of teachers. They won the support of many of the school boards and strengthened their case by putting the academic arguments not only for better practical teaching but for teachers to study as properly professional students the newly developing science of education.

Arguments for the Universities

The illiberal and anti-intellectual nature of much existing teacher training prompted a variety of pleas for teachers to be educated in and exposed to the wider culture of the universities. This ideal of a liberal education[24] for elementary school teachers had been present earlier in the century but was largely unsupported, confined as the intellectual level of training was to government restrictions and the school curriculum. Those, like Joshua Fitch, attracted to residential training colleges for their moral importance, acknowledged intellectual narrowness as their chief limitation, and felt that 'the antidote for such narrowness was to educate intending teachers in the company of other young people preparing for a variety of different professions', (Hyams, 1981). Even a geographical proximity to the University College would benefit student teachers, as Sir Henry Lewis, a sponsor of University College, Bangor, records in his diary when that institution opened in 1884 as a place 'of incalculable advantage to the existing educational institutions . . . the young men in the Normal College would feel the inspiring influence of a University College visible to them every day. Their ambition would be stimulated and they would be early drawn into the struggle for high academic honours of which they would be constant witnesses'.[25] A similar sentiment is expressed by A.J. Mundella, Vice-President of the Committee of Council (and effectively a Minister for Public Instruction), speaking at University College, Cardiff, in 1887 when he argued that the Welsh needed to 'give a broader and more intelligent life to their teachers, and more breadth and culture to their minds, and it was the [University] Colleges of Wales that should produce not only the elementary teachers, but the future teachers of the intermediate schools.'[26]

The strongest views on the liberalization of training probably came from Scotland where the universities had already forged more links with schoolteachers than had developed south of the border. In Scotland the Free Church had begun offering bursaries to some of the most successful of their student teachers and in 1873 permission was given to selected college students to attend university during the winter sessions.[27] Chairs of education were founded in Edinburgh and St Andrew's universities and the respective professors, S.S. Laurie and J.M.D. Meiklejohn, became the first two professors in Britain of the theory, history and practice of education.[28] Both had strong views on the importance of teachers being educated at university if they were ever to be regarded as a true profession. Professor Laurie, who was the more influential of the two, was quite clear that a specialist training college did not answer the same purposes as a university. He saw the latter as giving an educational influence which specialist colleges could never exercise and argued that teachers ought to have the universities open to them to experience 'the broader culture, the freer air' which the universities could give them. Laurie used the status of his chair to argue his case throughout Britain, always asserting that a faculty of education in the university would raise the teaching profession to a higher level: 'it promotes the movement which has been steadily progressing for twenty years, the recognition of the large body of teachers as a great national institution, looking, as other professions do, to the university as its source and head, and drawing strength and self-respect from that connection'.[29] Similarly, in an address at Liverpool, he argued that 'the university trained schoolmaster imbibes some of the spirit of the university and goes forth as a scientific worker, and not as a mere craftsman' (Laurie, 1892). It could be argued also that the university colleges were better equipped to provide teachers for the needs of an increasingly scientific society, and Amos Henderson, the first Head of the Teacher Training Department at University College, Nottingham, was to argue that the 'residential training colleges could not fit up any single department like our physical, chemical or natural science'.[30]

Such arguments were increasingly attractive for the new civic universities founded in England and Wales to augment the university provision of Oxford, Cambridge, Durham and London. The university authorities, though sympathetic to the cases made by Laurie and others, were also governed by the pragmatic need to increase their numbers. All saw teacher training as a way of increasing student population and their academic prestige. The Welsh colleges were particularly in need of teacher training. Bangor had only 117 students in 1890, and Aberystwyth in the first eight years of its existence totalled only 313 and was threatened with closure (Davies and Jones, 1905; Rees, 1968). Lewis Williams, the energetic Chairman of the Cardiff School Board and supported by the Council of University College, Cardiff, argued for the funding of Queen's Scholarships at the Welsh university colleges (Trow and Brown, 1933). The representatives of English provincial universities like Leeds made similar pleas to the Education Department, urging the suitability of their institutions for the training of teachers. The universities had history on their side in a favourable political climate, as noted in a letter from Lord Aberdare, President of University College, Cardiff, to his Principal J. Viriamu Jones: 'I like your plan of having the College accepted by the government and see much in it that would be acceptable at least to a Liberal government, who are sometimes sore pressed by objections as to the denominational character of the great majority of the training colleges'.[31] In 1871 the Universities Test Acts had established in the public mind the idea of a university accessible to all denominations. Residence and study at university had become possible for women (witness Girton College in 1872) and by 1880, 56 per cent of the teaching force were women. The first public grants to the universities, made to the Welsh colleges in 1883, accustomed the government to thinking about aid for university growth from public money, while of course the school boards themselves, largely undenominational and secular in character, had accustomed people to public action in the educational sphere.

As a result of all these influences the school boards were willing to examine new approaches to the training of teachers in their employment, and some notable partnerships developed between school boards and the university authorities in their areas. Lewis Williams, the Chairman of the Cardiff School Board, and keen supporter of university training, had been greatly encouraged by Professor J. Viriamu Jones, the charismatic Principal of University College, Cardiff. Principal Jones had been first faced with providing courses for teachers in his earlier career as Principal of Firth College, Sheffield. He had developed a very strong opinion that elementary education throughout England and Wales could be greatly improved by bringing together the teachers and the universities. He concluded that the most efficient and effective way of doing this was in establishing departments for the training of teachers in the new university colleges. This idea was enthusiastically received by audiences of elementary school teachers in Wales in 1885 and he made proposals for the setting up of Queen's Scholarships in the University of Wales. The Cardiff School Board championed the idea, (Thomas, 1984). Similarly in Newcastle-upon-Tyne, the local school boards of Newcastle and Gateshead assured the University College (Durham College of Science as it was then called) that they would support the establishment of a department for the training of teachers and the Newcastle School Board assured the Principal of the College that it would be prepared 'under suitable conditions and proper supervision to permit the use of certain of its schools as practising schools for the students'.[32]

Education as an Academic Subject

The converging interests of school boards and the universities related to increasing opportunities for the practical training of teachers. The universities had an additional interest: the promotion of the study of education as an academic subject and as a newly-developing science. This concern was expressed at its most forceful by the Scottish professors mentioned above but earlier English support may be seen, for example, in a proposal of 1833 from a London philanthropist, John Morgan, that a chair of education should be established in the University of London, (Fitch, 1931). It was, however, from Scotland that the main impetus came for chairs of education, notably in an essay of 1864 published by James Donaldson, Rector of the High School in Edinburgh and later Principal of St Andrew's University. Donaldson argued for the establishment of professors of education in all the Scottish universities and makes special reference to the educational writings of Herbert Spencer and Alexander Bain. The latter author, in particular, was to influence developments in England because his classic 'Education as a Science' was a major influence on Laurie and Meiklejohn and constantly quoted by Laurie on both sides of the Scottish border. Similarly the tireless campaigns of T.H. Huxley on behalf of scientific method in education was influential in both Scotland and England. Bain, Professor of Logic at Aberdeen until 1880, published 'Education as a Science' in 1879 and it was widely translated many times and used as a teacher training text in Britain, the USA and Europe, (Humes, 1983).

Bain very much fostered the view that psychology was the basic science of education but both Laurie and Meiklejohn saw the theory of education as wider than this. S.S. Laurie argued in his inaugural lecture at Edinburgh that a theory of education was allied to psychology, physiology and sociology. Such a theory drew from the philosophies of the subjects and also from 'the practice of the school room and from the rich domain of history'. In addition theory of education related to educational systems abroad and to ethical questions. Meiklejohn, in promoting a similar theoretical curriculum, pointed up the urgent need for the universities to promote the study of educational science. He stressed that the literature of education was fragmentary: 'in the history of it we have not a single work; in the practice, entirely without thoughtful books which survey both historically and scientifically the whole field . . . professors of education have actually to create the literature of their subject'. Meiklejohn's complaint was to be echoed in 1901 when Professor Rein, the distinguished Professor of Pedagogy at Jena, commented in a lecture at Cambridge University that the universities had neglected only one branch of knowledge — namely education — and where could education as a science succeed if not in the universities? (Rein, 1901).

Opposition to the University Training of Teachers

There were some people only too glad to see education neglected in the universities and saw such institutions as singularly unsuited to the training of teachers. Association with teacher training was not seen as necessarily advantageous by some university staff largely because of the poor reputation of the residential training colleges and the social origins of their students. A suggestion that Owens College, Manchester, should incorporate a teacher training college in the 1850s was rejected by the Senate because it would bring into the university students of 'somewhat miscellaneous description' (quoted in Fiddes, 1937, p. 170) while one of the Queen's College history lecturers argued that 'the union of a training school with the college would bring down the latter to the level of the former' (Sadler, 1911, p. 24). It was the 'elementary' nature of the teaching profession that was part of the objection, and according to Miss E.P. Hughes, Principal of the Cambridge Training College, the fact that secondary *women* sought training in teaching was another source of bias from within the universities, (Patrick, 1986). There were many within the universities who believed that the elementary teachers of younger children did not need a university education, (Hyams, 1979). In addition such teachers were regarded as overambitious and already sufficiently trained and educated. Within the undereducated middle class, in particular, there was a great deal of antipathy towards teachers. The more you educated teachers the more they would want to be paid, and many school boards, especially in rural England, were anxious to keep education as cheap as possible.[33]

The residential training colleges themselves were not greatly in favour of closer links with the universities. This was sometimes because certain colleges had high reputations and saw no benefit to their students in a university connection. This was the case in Bangor Normal College which in the late nineteenth century provided Wales with some of her best teachers and scholars. The Principal of Battersea Training College had a quite clear attitude to the universities: 'I do not like to say anything offensive about university professors but I have not a very high opinion of them, I am bound to say, as teachers. I can conceive scarcely that they could teach more efficiently than we do'.[34] Many training college principals and some HMI felt that university colleges, lacking residential places, would lack force in moral training. Other HMI and principals felt the universities were too academic and not sufficiently vocational. There were also members of the teaching profession who were not in favour of greater university participation feeling that the teachers produced by the universities would come to have a disproportionate influence on the profession and thus disadvantage those teachers who were merely college certificated.

The Cross Commission

Views for and against the greater participation of the universities in teacher training were presented in the evidence to the Cross Commission, the Royal Commission on the working of the Elementary Education Acts.[35] Established in 1886 it was empowered, among other things, to enquire into the pupil teacher system and the efficiency of the training colleges. The commissioners worked thoroughly collecting evidence from all the interested parties: the Secretary of the Education Department, senior HMI, university representatives, training college principals, representatives of the churches and of the National and the British and Foreign School Societies, and the chairmen and secretaries of school boards. The volumes of evidence give a valuable cross-section of educational opinion in late Victorian Britain and have been used at various times in the present chapter. Reading these volumes would suggest that the evidence in favour of major changes in teacher training was overwhelming, but the report of the Commission cautiously endorsed the view that residential colleges were the best form of teacher training and that the pupil teacher system should not be abolished. Most significantly, from the point of view of the universities, the commissioners had spent a considerable time examining the views of Mr Patrick Cumin, Secretary of the Education Department, and he had produced a well argued and fully costed blueprint for the opening of day training colleges in the universities and university colleges. This strategy had become departmental policy while the Cross Commission was in session. As Professor Tuck writes: 'the decision seems to have been made on the grounds of cheapness rather than because the administration of the new day colleges would be more appropriately placed in the hands of academic institutions'.

By the end of 1888 it was apparent to the university authorities that the recommendation on the setting up of day training colleges was to be implemented and despite the caution of some university staff as described earlier, a major development in teacher education in universities took place in 1890 when the Education Department issued regulations permitting universities and university colleges to establish day training colleges. By 1900 there were 1355 students in the eighteen new institutions compared with 4179 students in the residential colleges (Ogren, 1953). These day training colleges are the ancestors of our modern departments and schools of education and their individual dates of foundation are as follows:

1890	Manchester, Newcastle, Cardiff, London (Kings), Birmingham, Nottingham
1891	Sheffield, Cambridge, Liverpool, Leeds
1892	Bristol, Aberystwyth, Oxford, London (University College)
1894	Bangor
1899	Reading, Southampton
1901	Exeter
1902	London Day Training College (now the University of London Institute of Education).

These dates of foundation are those provided by Tuck (1973) but many dates are contentious in this area and sources vary. Not all the colleges were coeducational at first. Manchester, Kings, Cambridge, Liverpool, Leeds, Oxford and University College were for men only, the last named closing for lack of support in 1894. Birmingham and Bristol were colleges for women only. Cardiff initially operated two separate colleges for men and women. One should add to the list two distinguished colleges for women which were not DTCs as defined by the Cross Commission: the Cambridge Women's Training College, pre-dating its DTC, and the Education Department at Bedford College, London, which opened in 1892 and closed in 1922 after training women for careers in secondary schools. In the second chapter of this book we trace the development of these collective institutions from their Victorian beginnings to the end of the 1930s, from day training colleges to departments of education.

Notes

1 See Jones (1943) p. 13. Short accounts of early training may be found in Dent (1977) chapters 1 and 2 and in Wragg (1974) chapter 1. Seaborne (1974) is an excellent account of the theoretical basis of these early schemes.

2 Quoted in the diary of Harry Payner, a Leicester headteacher. See Elkington (1981) p. 60.

3 Universities in early and mid-nineteenth-century Britain were the medieval

foundations of Oxford, Cambridge, Aberdeen, Edinburgh, Glasgow and St Andrews. Durham founded 1832 and London founded 1836. In Wales, St Davids College, Lampeter, founded to train clerics. See Bell in this volume for a discussion of the 'learned dominie'.

4 Quoted from *The Literarium* 1857 in Tropp (1963) on the suggestion that elementary school teachers be admitted to the College of Preceptors.
5 Tropp (1963) p. 159.
6 See the interesting discussion in Archer (1966) pp. 345–7.
7 College of Preceptors (1896) *Fifty Years of Progress in Education*, London, p. 9 quoted in Rich (1972) p. 250. See also Chapman (1985).
8 See Tyson and Tuck (1971) pp. 33–7 for details.
9 Now called Hughes Hall and still very closely connected with teacher education in Cambridge.
10 Quoted in Barnard (1961) p. 190.
11 Victoria University Extension Committee, *Annual Report*, quoted in Marriott (1981).
12 University College, Cardiff *Principals Report* 1884–1885.
13 Barnard (1961) p. 191. I anticipate here later discussion in the chapter.
14 Rich (1972) p. 139.
15 In evidence to the Cross Commission, quoted in Sadler (1911).
16 Cross Commission, Final Report, p. 270 quoted in Ogren (1953), p. 62.
17 Dent (1977) p. 51.
18 Figures from Birchenough (1914) p. 367.
19 See Bergen (1982) p. 3 and his various tables.
20 Figures from Magnus (1907) *Report on School System of Cardiff* quoted in Thomas (1984) p. 10.
21 Review of the work of the Bristol School Board in *Seventh Triennial Report 1889–1891* (Bristol 1892).
22 The quote from Oakley comes from *Committee of Council in Education Report 1892–1893*. See the implications for university teacher training places in Thomas (1986a).
23 *Report of Committee of Council 1893–1894*, p. 316 quoted in Thomas (1984).
24 See Hyams (1981) for an important paper on this concept.
25 University College of North Wales Belmont Papers MSS 67A (*The Diary of Sir Henry Lewis*) quoted in Thomas (1983) p. 123.
26 The Welsh Intermediate Schools were a national system of secondary schools set up under the Welsh Intermediate Education Act of 1889 and planned to link the elementary schools with the higher education provided in the university colleges of Wales. The scheme was coordinated by the Central Welsh Board. The Mundella quotation comes from Allsobrook (1989) p. 7.
27 Cruickshank (1970) p. 93 quoted in Hyams (1981). See Bell later in this volume for the universities and teacher education in Scotland.
28 For their important inaugural lectures see Laurie (1876) and Gordon (1980) which reprints the 1876 lecture of J.M.D. Meiklejohn.
29 Laurie (1876) p. 14.
30 *The Gong*, November 1897 p. 3 (the student magazine of Nottingham University) quoted in Thomas (1986b).
31 Quoted in Thomas (1984) p. 12.
32 Quoted in Tyson and Tuck (1971) p. 16.
33 See the many and interesting negative attitudes to teachers in Pugh (1982).

34 Cross Commission, Vol. I, p. 445 quoted in Rich (1972).
35 The following account is largely a summary of Tuck (1973) pp. 72–6.

References

ALLSOBROOK, D. (1979) *'The Department of Education'*, unpublished MS history of teacher training at University College, Cardiff.

ALLSOBROOK, D. (1989) 'A benevolent prospect of old — reflections on the Welsh Intermediate Education Act of 1889', *The Welsh Journal of Education*, 1,1, pp. 1–10.

ARCHER, R.L. (1966) *Secondary Education in the Nineteenth Century*, London, Cass.

BAMFORD, T.W. (1973) 'Public school masters: a nineteenth century profession' in COOK, T.G. (Ed) *Education and the Professions*, London, Methuen and the History of Education Society.

BARNARD, H.C. (1961) *History of English Education from 1760*, London, University of London Press.

BERGEN, B.H. (1982) 'Only a schoolmaster; gender, class, and the effort to professionalize elementary teaching in England 1870–1910', *History of Education Quarterly*, 22, 1, pp. 1–21.

BIRCHENOUGH, C. (1914) *History of Elementary Education in England and Wales from 1800 to the Present Day*, London, W.B. Clive.

BROWNE, J.D. (1971) 'The Act of 1870 and the training of teachers', *Educational Review*, 22, 2, pp. 131–40.

CHAPMAN, J.V. (1985) *Professional Roots: The College of Preceptors in British Society*, Epping, Theydon Bois.

CRUICKSHANK, M. (1970) *A History of the Training of Teachers in Scotland*, London, University of London Press.

COLLEGE OF PRECEPTORS (1896) *Fifty Years of Progress in Education*, London, The College.

DAVIES, W.C. and JONES, W.L. (1905) *The University of Wales and its Constituent Colleges*, London, F.E. Robinson.

DENT, H.C. (1977) *The Training of Teachers in England and Wales 1800–1975*, London, Hodder & Stoughton.

ELKINGTON, T.J. (1981) 'The pupil teachers of St Margaret's Boys School, Leicester 1863–1867', *Leicestershire Archaeological and Historical Society Transactions*, 57, pp. 57–63.

ELLIS, E.L. (1972) *The University College of Wales, Aberystwyth 1872–1972*, Cardiff, University of Wales Press.

ELMES, D.S. (1969) '*A study of the development of voluntary training colleges for teachers with special reference to Fishponds Diocesan College, Bristol, later known as the College of St Matthias*', unpublished MEd thesis, University of Bristol.

FIDDES, E. (1937) *Chapters in the History of Owens College and of Manchester University 1851–1914*, Manchester, Manchester University Press.

FITCH, M.G. (1931) '*History of the training of teachers for secondary schools in England*', unpublished MA thesis, University of London.

GORDON, P. (1980) *The Study of Education; Inaugural Lectures: Volume 1 Early and Modern*, London, Woburn Press.

HAMILTON, D. (1982) 'A note on masters of method and the pedagogy of nineteenth century schooling', *History of Education Society Bulletin*, 29, pp. 13–16.

HUMES, W.M. (1983) 'Science, religion and education: a study in cultural interaction' in HUMES, W.M. and PATERSON, H.M. (Eds) *Scottish Culture and Scottish Education 1800 to 1980*, to Edinburgh, John Donald.

HYAMS, B.K. (1979) 'Anti-intellectualism in the history of the education of teachers: England and Australia', *Journal of Educational Administration and History*, 11, 1, pp. 43–9.

HYAMS, B.K. (1981) 'Culture for elementary schoolteachers: an issue in the history of English education', *Paedagogica Historica*, 21, 1, pp. 111–20.

JONES, A.J. (1943) *I Was Privileged*, Cardiff, Abbrevia.

LAURIE, S.S. (1876) *Chair of Education, University of Edinburgh: Inaugural Address*, Edinburgh, Edmonston and Douglas.

LAURIE, S.S. (1892) *University Training College, Liverpool: Address by Professor S.S. Laurie on the occasion of the inaugural address delivered at University College, Liverpool, 15 July 1892*, Liverpool, Lee and Nightingale.

McCLELLAND, V.A. (1975) 'Herbert Vaughan, the Cambridge teachers training syndicate and the public schools 1894–1989', *Paedagogica Historica*, 15, 1, pp. 16–38.

MARRIOTT, S. (1981) 'The University extension movement and the education of teachers 1873–1906', *History of Education*, 10, 3, pp. 163–77.

OGREN, G. (1953) *Trends in English Teacher Training from 1800: A Survey and Investigation*, Stockholm, Esselte Aktiebolag.

PATRICK, H. (1986) 'From Cross to CATE, the universities and teacher education over the past century', *Oxford Review of Education*, 12, 3, pp. 243–61.

PUGH, O.R. (1982) 'The status of the elementary teacher in the 1890s: some evidence from the north west of England', *Paedagogica Historica*, 22, 1, pp. 147–56.

REES. L.M. (1968) '*A critical examination of teacher training in Wales 1846 to 1898*', unpublished PhD thesis, University College of North Wales, Bangor.

REIN, W. (1901) 'Outlines of the development of educational ideas during the nineteenth century' in ROBERTS, R.D. (Ed) *Education in the Nineteenth Century*, Cambridge, Cambridge University Press.

RICH, R.W. (1972) *The Training of Teachers in England and Wales during the Nineteenth Century*, Bath, Cedric Chivers.

SADLER, M.E. (1911) 'University day training colleges: their origins, growth and influence in English education' in ANON (Ed) *The Department of Education in the University of Manchester*, Manchester, Manchester University Press.

SEABORNE, M. (1974) 'Early theories of teacher education', *British Journal of Educational Studies*, 22, 3, pp. 325–30.

THOMAS, J.B. (1983) 'The beginnings of teacher training at University College, Bangor', *Transactions of the Caernarvonshire Historical Society*, 44, pp. 123–53.

THOMAS, J.B. (1984) 'The origins of teacher training at University College, Cardiff', *Journal of Educational Administration and History*, 16, 1, pp. 10–16.

THOMAS, J.B. (1986a) 'University College, London, and the training of teachers', *History of Education Society Bulletin*, 37, pp. 44–8.

THOMAS, J.B. (1986b) 'Amos Henderson and the Nottingham Day Training College', *Journal of Educational Administration and History*, 18, 2, pp. 24–33.

TROPP, A. (1963) 'The changing status of the teacher in England and Wales' in KING HALL, R., HANS, N. and LAUWERYS, J.A. (Eds) *Year Book of Education 1963*, London, Evans Brothers.

TROW, A.H. and BROWN, D.J.A. (1933) *Short History of the College 1883 to 1933*, Cardiff, Western Mail.

TUCK, J.P. (1973) 'From day training college to university department of education' in LOMAX, D.E. (Ed) *The Education of Teachers in Britain*, London, John Wiley.

TYSON, J.C. and TUCK, J.P. (1971) *The Origins and Development of the Training of Teachers in the University of Newcastle-upon-Tyne*, Newcastle, University Department of Education.

WRAGG, E.C. (1974) *Teaching Teaching*, Exeter, David & Charles.

Chapter 2

Day Training College to Department of Education

John B. Thomas

Introduction

The day training colleges (DTCs) referred to in the last chapter experienced only a modest scale of operation in their first decade. However by 1900/01 they were providing nearly 25 per cent of the training places available for teachers, a figure which rose to about 33 per cent by 1939. The latter figure represented a quarter of the nation's trained teachers in terms of output.[1] The DTCs were clearly an important factor in the arithmetic of teacher supply after only ten years of existence. They had also developed characteristics as institutions of teacher training which can be identified as essential elements of a modern day department of education. These elements may be observed in the history of one of the first day training colleges, Aberystwyth. The DTC at the University College of Wales, Aberystwyth, opened in October 1892 with thirty students (ten men, twenty women). By 1893 Henry Holman had been appointed Professor in the Theory of Education and a woman student had gained the Cambridge Teachers' Diploma with distinction, the germ of courses of special training for secondary schools. By 1895 the College had instituted full courses of secondary training and the University of Wales had recognized education as a subject of study within the undergraduate degree. In 1905 all King's Scholars (as Queen's Scholars became after the death of Queen Victoria) were admitted to a three-year course, the Board of Education accepting matriculation to the University in place of the King's Scholarship examination. In 1906 education was recognized as an ordinary degree, the honours degree being instituted six years later. The Board of Education recognized a secondary training department in 1907, to which eight students were admitted. In 1911 Aberystwyth changed to three-years of degree work plus one year of professional training for the diploma in education, the ancestor of the modern PGCE course. This potted account of one department[2] shows the main trends in the history to be discussed in this chapter; the organizational dependence on Whitehall and its slackening, the quality of students, the development of chairs in education and the quality of teaching, and the beginning of secondary training. The chapter concludes with a discussion of the 1925 Departmental Committee on the Training of Teachers and with an assessment of departments of education in the 1930s and their status in universities.

Organization of the DTCs and Practical Teaching

The new Education Code of 1890 had presented regulations for the administration of government grants to DTCs established in universities and university colleges. *Circular 187* of the Education Department laid down regulations as follows:

(1) Local Committees are to make arrangements for lecturers to give lessons on the theory and history of education, superintend school practice, give model lessons, and preside over criticism lessons.
(2) Candidates for Queen's Scholarships could opt for Residential or Day Training Colleges.
(3) For certification, students would have to take Education Department examinations in professional subjects. But in general subjects, college or university examinations would be accepted under the following conditions; the programme of studies was to be approved by the Education Department and examination answers sent to the Department to be adjusted to the residential college standards.
(4) The Local Committee was to send copies of arrangements concerning school practice, terms of admission, and the provision for lodgings within the department.
(5) The Day Training Colleges were to be responsible for the conduct of students.

Each Local Committee was thus to act as an executive committee for its day training college. All such committees established themselves very quickly and had distinguished members representing the needs and interests of the university, the community, the teaching profession and HMI, the latter interviewing the Committee on regular inspections. They bear a striking resemblance to the local committees which arise from the Council for the Accreditation of Teacher Education (CATE) in our present decade and the tensions between university, local and national governmental interests have been present throughout the historical development of university involvement in teacher education. The Local Committee of the Bristol DTC shows a typical composition: Professor Lloyd Morgan, Principal of University College, Bristol and Secretary to the Committee (1), representatives of the Bristol, Bedminster, and St George's school boards (6), the voluntary schools (4), Council of University College (3), staff of University College (3), Society of Merchant Adventurers (1), Council of Clifton College (1), governors of Bristol Grammar

School (1), Council of Clifton High School (1), Council of Redland High School (1). Ten co-opted members were allowed for. The Chairman was Mark Whitwell, also Chairman of the Bristol School Board, and other influential members included the industrialist Albert Fry and HMI Fitch.[3] The duties of local committees involved not only administering the regulations as described earlier but also to deal with such routine matters as admission of students, provision of finance, rooms and the routine administration.

The first duty of the local committees was the appointment of masters and mistresses of method following the instructions for DTCs issued by the Education Department in May 1890 (*Circular 287*) which stipulated that 'a normal master or mistress must be appointed to lecture on history and theory of education, to supervise teaching and to give a course of model lessons and preside at criticism lessons'. Such appointments, more commonly referred to as masters of method, were made in all the day training colleges. Our first professors of education were indeed masters of method and often held the two titles at the same time or succeeded to the former title after holding the latter one.[4] We shall mention their work as professors of education below but here we concentrate on their training functions where they were expected to prepare students for the two-year certificate examination of the Education Department. Unlike their counterparts in the residential training colleges, however, they had freedom on the academic side to follow their own autonomous university syllabuses provided that copies of the question and answer papers were sent to the Department. This is the origin of the concurrent course where students studied their professional subjects alongside the academic study of those subjects they were to teach in schools. The resulting curriculum appeared in the Education Code of 1891 as Part One and Part Two subjects, the former consisting of the professional subjects of practical teaching; the art, theory and history of teaching; singing, drawing; needlework (women) and elementary English and arithmetic. Part Two subjects included mathematics, the sciences, English, elementary geography and history, languages, political economy, and domestic economy for women. Part One required Education Department examinations whilst Part Two examinations could be set by a day training college and approved by the government. In 1891 a special one-year course was made available for graduates who wanted to teach in elementary schools. This system obtained until 1904, and traces of it remained until the 1920s.[5]

It was the duty of the masters of method to teach the professional subjects and to coordinate the academic work of their students. Thus they taught school management, history of education, ethics, psychology of education, practical teaching and related topics. It was for this reason, apart from reasons of scholarship and research, that early heads of departments and professors wrote introductions to the theory, history, and psychology of education, and why men as distinguished as Sir John Adams and J.W. Adamson produced their own manuals of method. The flavour of such manuals and the detailed nature of the professional syllabus is illustrated from the text written by Amos

Henderson, the first Professor of Education at Nottingham. Its chapters introduce teaching methods in reading, spelling, English, writing, drawing, singing, arithmetic, geography, history, and the object lesson. An analysis of the chapter on reading gives the flavour of the text, with its sub-divisions on aims of the lesson, word recognition, enunciation and pronunciation, reading with intelligence, phrasing, punctuation, intuition, simultaneous reading, pattern reading, silent reading, school reading books, the Reading Lesson.[6]

The practical nature of the work is seen also in the organization of teaching practice and in the development of model schools and criticism lessons. Judged by the standards of the 1980s the amount of teaching practice was surprisingly small, a month or little more in the schools over a two-year course, done in college vacations. In addition students attended schools each week for criticism lessons where students taught in turn before other students and the master of method. An account of a practice and criticism lesson is given by Professor A.W. Wolters, a former student in a Day Training College in 1902 at Reading:

> Each of us had to do three weeks practice each year and only one school was used. So all through two terms we were drafted by batches into school. I fear we were blind to the sufferings of that tortured school with its generations of youngsters butchered to make a training department — the criticism lesson was pretty generally disliked. I would gladly have taken the place of anyone present, for choice that of a pupil, for these events did much to brighten young lives. What is the supervisor to do when, knowing that the show must go on, he observes a young teacher put the equator around the earth from north to south.[7]

Both the student teachers and pupils benefited from the school visits and other educational experiences organized by some day training colleges. Reading organized a farm school for pupils where, as Wolters comments, 'a class in elementary surveying in a field owned by a fairly tolerant but very inquisitive bull added to one's educational insight in a way that no classroom exercise could', (Barnard, 1949). Similarly, Mark Wright at Newcastle built a deserved reputation for his field trips and camping expeditions and, for example, in 1910 organized a fortnight's boys camp school at Warkworth with 120 boys from Tyneside schools and taught by thirty day training college students.[8] Such expeditions were also held in Manchester where J.J. Findlay organized student school camps in Derbyshire with each day including an educational expedition. Findlay regarded such camps as a major contribution to the life of the pupils: 'in camp we find the best expression of a child's life in regard to his fellows: by taking scholars who are already friends in the day school away from the home; it intensifies their corporate life and, without their knowledge, satisfied their instinctive desires for independence and for friendship', (Findlay, 1908). It was certainly a change from some of the unsatisfactory schools some day training colleges were forced by circumstances to use, leading some, like Bangor, to open their own college demonstration schools because existing schools were 'by no means models to the young teachers in respect of their buildings, fittings and apparatus'.[9]

Teaching Staff and Scholarship

The staff who taught these students were few in number and not always in autonomous departments in their university colleges, for example, Nottingham DTC remained part of the general literature department for many years after its foundation. The staff came usually from existing residential training colleges, teacher pupil centres, or headships. Amos Henderson at Nottingham had been a normal master and held the Cambridge Teacher's Diploma with distinction, J.A. Green had been head of the pupil teachers centre in Hackney, and Mark Wright had been head of a higher grade school at Gateshead.[10] The day training colleges saw the first generation of professors of education — modest men like Henderson, brilliant historians like Foster Watson and J.W. Adamson, pioneering psychologists like J.A. Green and Sir John Adams, outstanding administrators and comparative writers like Sir Michael Sadler, polymaths like J.J. Findlay. Their importance as professors is the subject of a later chapter in this book. What is equally important and sometimes forgotten is the academic quality of the staff who never became professors. Some brief examples must suffice. James Fairgrieve, appointed to the London Day Training College in 1912 eventually became a Reader in Education and during his career was to be Vice-President of the Royal Meteorological Society and President of the Geographical Association. He published nearly two dozen school geography texts, contributed to academic geographical and educational journals, and may rightly be regarded as a major influence on geography in education and on geography teaching method (Burrell, 1963). H.T. Mark appointed master of method at Manchester in 1899 wrote *History of Educational Theories in England, Moral Education in America, Education and Industry in America, The Teacher and the Child,* and contributed articles in French and English on personality, child study, and logic. He was awarded a DLitt by London University for his work in educational psychology, and he appears to be the first holder of a British doctorate in educational research.[11] Sandiford, also at Manchester from 1906, was the author of *The Training of Teachers in England and Wales* (1910) and a later text on comparative education, as well as contributing papers to the *Journal of Educational Psychology*, in the USA.[12] At Oxford and Cambridge, both denied chairs, were M.W. Keatinge and Charles Fox respectively, the latter undeservedly little known as a pioneering psychologist (Tomlinson, 1968; Barnwell, 1981).

The number of able women staff in the day training colleges is noticeable, reflecting the new opportunities provided for girls who had chosen teaching by the opening of day training colleges for women, and reflecting also the importance of Newnham and the Cambridge Training College in establishing an elite profession of women teachers, some of whom were educated at schools approaching the established boys' public schools in status. Two of the most distinguished of female staff were Geraldine Hodgson at Bristol and Catherine Dodd at Manchester. The former was one of that band of women who had entered teaching as part of that Girls' Public Day School Trust (GPDST) tradition which pioneered so much academic education for middle class girls. A highly gifted teacher, a successful scholar and novelist, and a Dublin LittD, her major educational research was *Studies in French Education from Rabelais to Rousseau*. Works of literary crticism included studies of Wordsworth, Browning and Elroy Flecker. She retired as Vice-Principal of Ripon Training College in 1921 and should be remembered as one of the most distinguished academics in university teacher training before the First World War.[13]

Promotion prospects were naturally limited given the small size of the DTCs and their university colleges. Day training college staff went elsewhere in the teacher training system, back into schools, and sometimes emigrated to promotion abroad. Staff at the Bangor Day Training College provide examples of all these. Catherine Graveson, Mistress of Method from 1898 to 1901 transferred to a similar post at University College, Liverpool, and finally became Vice-Principal at Goldsmiths College, London. Celia Johnson, the earlier Mistress of Method at Bangor became Headmistress of a higher grade school in Halifax. Alexander Mackie, at Bangor from 1903 to 1906, and a distinguished graduate of Edinburgh, returned briefly to his native university and then went to Australia to the combined post of Principal of Teachers College and Professor of Education at the University of Sydney. An equally distinguished emigrant was William Mitchell from the short-lived DTC at University College, London, who eventually became Vice-Chancellor of the University of Adelaide, and was knighted for services to education and philosophy.[14]

The great contribution made by the DTC staff to the growth of study and research represents a major period in the development of educational scholarship in British universities. As Professors Laurie and Meiklejohn had predicted the staff of the day training colleges perforce created an original literature of education. The wider context of that creation is discussed later in this book by Brian Simon. Briefly here one would note the way in which the field of education was institutionalized, especially at Manchester where J.J. Findlay consciously created an academic study of education, well illustrated by the efforts of Michael Sadler in the history of education, educational administration and in comparative education.[15] Similarly, Professor J.A. Green, in addition to his impressive Pestalozzi scholarship, through his editorship of the *Journal of Experimental Pedagogy*[16] for the whole of its existence helped shape the discipline of educational psychology as part of the wider science of education and published such distinguished writers on education and psychology as Charles Spearman, Godfrey Thomson, William Boyd, and C. Lloyd Morgan, (Thomas, 1982b). The early teacher educators were as concerned with academic study and liberal education as with teacher training, and in the present circumstances of the 1990s, the faith of one early professor is worth reaffirming: 'it is not the business of a training department to give students a finished technique — that would indeed be the end of them. It is their business to show that technique depends upon devotion, upon knowledge — of subjects, and of pupils, and the history of both — upon a philosophical conception of the value of subjects in a scheme of general education, upon laborious and loving practice continued through a lifetime'.[17]

Students and Student Life

Such a lofty ideal was a challenge for the DTC students, especially in the early days of the 1890s. The concurrent course was no place for the weak student, and Professor Findlay of Manchester, Professor Foster Watson, other staff, and HMI reports mention the strain on all but the brightest students as they coped with educational theory and practice, academic subjects, and criticism lessons and teaching practice. Many weak students needed remedial treatment in the subjects of the school curriculum and staff from other university departments often willingly helped. The position of the weak student arose primarily from the poor quality of their school education and the training colleges were to find students improved as schooling improved, especially with the spread of secondary education in England after 1902. Thus, for example, Liverpool admitted matriculated students directly from school after 1907 as well as those who came up through the pupil teacher system, which by 1914 was almost extinct.[18]

There was, indeed, a great variation in the quality of students admitted to the day training colleges, as measured by their positions in the scholarship examinations. The examiners remarked early in 1891 that the university day training colleges would have initial difficulties in attracting the better pupil teachers. At King's College, London, the average place on the Queen's Scholarship list of students admitted in 1890 was 1030 and in 1891, 884. King's was competing with some of the best residential colleges in the country, those in London, a fact which effectively closed the day training college at University College.[19] However Mr Willis, the HMI, also commented in 1891 'I see no difficulty in preparing all students for a university degree at colleges which attract a good class of candidates'.[20] Not surprisingly, Oxford and Cambridge attracted good candidates. Oxford stipulated matriculation, a first class in the Queen's Scholarship, and competence in Latin. The historian M.W. Keatinge, an excellent teacher, was Director of the Oxford DTC and produced some excellent teachers, including one Fred Clarke who later became Professor of Education at Capetown and finally Director of the London Institute of Education until 1945. At Cambridge most students also took degrees and early students in 1898 included J.H. Clapham, later Professor of Economic History at Cambridge and Lytton Strachey, historian and biographer. A future Cabinet minister and life peer, Chuter Ede, left the Cambridge DTC in 1905 for a quiet life of teaching in Surrey and returned to Cambridge for an honorary doctorate forty years later, (Barnwell, 1981). In 1894 the average Queen's Scholarship position at Cambridge was fifty-six; at King's, London, 954. Provincial day training colleges like Manchester and Liverpool had little or no competition, and early students at the latter were carefully selected as strong candidates, (Dale, 1907). Foster Watson at Aberystwyth in 1894 was able to admire thc 'willing way in which the students set themselves to their double burden of academic and normal work'[21] and Professor Chapple in his account of Aberystwyth points out that even with low average entrants there were students of outstanding brilliance who obtained first class honours degrees and were also amongst the best in the professional classes. Similarly, of the two dozen men who entered the Newcastle DTC with Godfrey Thomson in 1900 were two future professors who both became FRS in future years.[22]

The increasing number of DTC students completing their degrees as the decades progressed is a measure of the effect of improved secondary schooling on the quality of student entry though this improved quality developed slowly. In 1901 a degree student at Bristol amongst the day training students was very exceptional, by 1909, fourteen of the fifty-two students were on degree courses. In Nottingham by 1898 only three of the ninety-eight student teachers had obtained a degree, by 1900 some seventy-five students were on degree courses out of its 152 men and women. It has to be admitted however that in most cases reading for a degree was too much for the majority of DTC students and, in recognition of this, in 1911 the Board of Education decided that it was asking too much. In future, day training college students were to take the now familiar four-year course; three years of undergraduate study for a degree followed by a one-year course of professional teacher training. This concession, it should be noted, did not benefit all DTC students because it applied only to universities and not to places like Nottingham and Exeter which were only university colleges working for the external degrees of London University. Such external students faced an especially onerous course of study and, for example, in Exeter, from 1904 to 1914 only four students graduated in each year, (Clapp, 1982).

The term *day* training colleges was something of a misnomer because very early in their history they developed halls and lodgings and became residential. This was largely a result of the geographical origins of their students though the need to chaperone their female students in the fashion of true Victorian morality was also part of the story. In Exeter, ten out of the first twenty-five students came from Wales, and this proportion was never less than 30 per cent for the next twelve years.[23] Bristol opened its own boarding house in 1897 and attracted students from all over the country. Life was very regimented and there was little privacy, with a roll call at 7.15 am and lights out at 10.30 pm. Social life was equally organized with newspaper clubs, rambling parties, evening social talks, concerts and staff garden parties. Staff were always present on all these occasions and there was none of the modern independence of students; this was especially true of girls. A future professor at Bristol recalled his student days as follows: 'any really intimate life with other students in a cultural sense occurred at a little cafe, a rather dirty little place kept by an Italian called Giacomelli where we ate poached eggs on toast on tablecloths which were changed once a month'.[24] The extent to which day training college students mixed with other students varied with the size of the parent university and its own cultural traditions. Thus the students described by Oscar Browning at Cambridge may not have been typical of student teachers in general: 'they belong to colleges, they row in college boats and play in college football teams, and they leave us with a measure of University spirit which will last them through their lives'.[25] Always, however, student teachers were expected to be decorous. Decorum, especially for women, was a difficult business and as late as 1915 the Nottingham DTC authorities were remarking that 'the girl who is seen talking in hall or corridor with a man is not regarded favourably'.[26] No wonder the future novelist D.H. Lawrence felt his fellow training department students were treated like schoolchildren.[27] Of course some college students were little older than children and it was 1910 before Nottingham stopped admitting students aged 16 and younger.

The Significance of the Day Training College

Professor R.W. Rich believed that the major influence of the day training college was in promoting the development of the study of education as an academic subject and encouraging the growth of research and scholarship (Rich, 1933). The nature of that scholarship has been described earlier in this chapter and it is further assessed by Brian Simon in a later chapter of this book. Clearly the relatively small size of training departments and the poor staff student ratio, in combination with the onerous demands of government examinations and training requirements, limited what research could be done. One should never, however, underestimate the cumulative effect, especially in historical and psychological studies, of the early pioneers of educational research on future developments.

Neither should one underestimate the importance of the day training colleges in the growth of the modern university and Armytage has pointed out their vital contribution, especially in stimulating increased numbers of students into arts faculties, (Armytage, 1955). Individual university historians support this view that without the student teachers there would have been very few students of arts and literature (for example, Shimmin, 1954). In Newcastle, the opening of the day training college, immediately revealed serious weaknesses in the teaching of the arts subjects which had to be provided for students preparing to teach these subjects in schools. The teaching of history, music, geography and several other subjects commenced in Newcastle with the opening of the DTC, (Tyson and Tuck 1971). The DTCs also encouraged a flow of science students, as shown at King's College, London, where in 1910, thirty-five of the fifty-two student teachers were science not arts men,

(Hearnshaw, 1928). Student teachers represented a major increase in numbers for the new universities and university colleges of late Victorian Britain. In Aberystwyth, one in four students were training to teach; in Bangor, in 1897, there were 258 students of whom ninety-eight were in the DTC; in Cardiff, the University College had 156 students when the day training college opened in 1890 and trainee teachers were a quarter of the student body by the end of the decade, (Davies and Jones, 1905; Thomas, 1983a and 1984). The historian of Exeter University tells us that 'before the establishment of the training department the college was merely a local institution for local students. Those who came from outside the city boundaries lived in adjacent parts of the country and went home at the end of the day's (or morning's) work. The students in training came from further afield' (Clapp, 1982). The wider geographical catchment from which DTC students came also benefited the growth of DTCs because the gradual provision of residential places and of approved lodgings for women allowed the training departments to admit graduates of other universities. This was to facilitate the growth of one year diploma courses for secondary training, a topic to be discussed in a further section of this chapter.

It should be remembered also that the day training colleges were a major step forward in the provision of higher education for women. The number of women students at Leeds University became appreciable only when it proved possible to provide facilities for them in teacher training from 1896, (Gosden and Taylor, 1975). In Bristol, in the session 1895–1896, 42 per cent of students in the faculties of arts and science were DTC girls, and they were 35 per cent of the students reading mathematics.[28] At Bedford College, London, where the students in training were never a major factor in college number increases, the majority of postgraduate students in the all-women institution came from the department of education, providing twenty-eight of the fifty-one postgraduates in attendance in 1919–1920.[29]

In summary, the day training college broke the monopoly control of the old residential training college tradition and henceforth a dual system of teacher training operated, stimulating the residential institutions into a review of their academic, professional, and social traditions and attitudes. In general, the training of teachers improved in the older colleges. The profession of teaching had entered university life in England and Wales, the DTCs helped develop coeducational higher education, and last but not least they led to a close connection between the new universities and the Board of Education. The struggles for university autonomy over the control of teacher training thus have a long history traced in their various forms throughout the present volume.

Secondary Training

The universities were involved in training for secondary schools because of a growing recognition in the 1890s that teachers for those schools should be trained. This recognition arose not only because of the success of the Cambridge Teachers Training Syndicate and secondary training colleges for women teachers (who were the more professional of the sexes when it came to training) but also out of increased public interest which was stimulated by the teachers registration movement and by important conferences on secondary education held at Oxford and Cambridge in 1893. There was general agreement that the university was the right body to concern itself with secondary training. In 1902 a Teachers Registration Council was established, the register to come into use in 1906. Professional views of such a register had been expressed in a memorandum of 1900 'that, after the expiration of five years from the commencement of the Board of Education Act, no new member of the profession should be qualified for a place in the Register of Secondary Teachers who has not undergone a systematic course of training'.[30]

The day training college system could clearly be extended to include secondary training. This extension had occurred before the memorandum. Indeed, in 1900 there were twenty-one courses of secondary training in the universities. However, to quote Professor Tuck, 'the early provision which was made was piecemeal, the number of students was small, and the secondary trained teachers were either trained in separate departments under only one tutor, or in separate groups in the same departments'.[31] At Leeds the University's attempts to train secondary school teachers began in 1904 where female graduates commenced a one-year course for a diploma in secondary school teaching. The course was criticized by the Board of Education three years later as being inadequately staffed and, in curriculum terms, being insufficiently differentiated from training for the elementary schools. Leeds strengthened the teaching staff but an attempt to extend the course for male students was abandoned in 1910, (Stephens, 1975). At Bristol, the appointed Head of the Secondary Training Department resented the administrative links with elementary training, and from 1902 there appeared a complete lack of coordination between training courses, (Thomas, 1988a). Though numbers of secondary students were low in universities (for example, 168 as opposed to 2132 elementary students in 1907[32]) there were some departments which successfully trained secondary teachers in viable numbers. The University of Wales had the stimulus of the 1889 Welsh Intermediate Act and Bedford College, London, had the advantage of being a single sex institution attracting able graduates on to a secondary training course. The staffing needs of the Welsh secondary schools were a stimulus to training at the Welsh DTCs and Cardiff provided training for both men and women wishing to teach in such schools. Alongside the Cardiff DTC another training department was established in 1890 for specialist teachers in cookery and domestic arts, directed by a special committee of the University College and granting diplomas recognized by the Board of Education. This development rapidly supplied Wales with a large number of qualified specialists in these subjects, (Phillips, 1979). The training department at Bedford College, London, opened in 1892. and trained only for secondary schools. The department admitted only graduates and awarded the London Diploma in Pedagogy or the Cambridge Diploma in the Art, Theory and History of Education. There were twenty students on the course in 1900, thirty in 1902, and 904 students had passed through the department before its closure in 1922, numbers having reached a peak of sixty students in the 1914/1915 session. The students were generally academically well-qualified. From 1912 to 1916 out of 126 students entering the department eighty-one had obtained honours in those subjects in which they wished to specialize as teachers, (Thomas, 1983b).

The growth of secondary training in the universities was, however, generally slow. The registration of teachers was never made compulsory with the result that few secondary schools were willing to accept the principle of training. In addition, with the exception of the Welsh schools mentioned above, few secondary schools were established from public funds until after 1902. Grants for secondary training courses only became available in 1908 and all candidates for one-year courses of teacher training had to hold degrees or equivalent qualifications.

Thus, before World War 1, the university training departments contained two types of students on two different courses. There were students on two and three-year elementary school courses for Board of Education examinations and other students on one-year courses of training, usually for elementary teaching. There were more students on the former courses than on the one-year courses, but 'gradually concurrent courses died out as more students became capable of graduating and desirous of teaching in secondary schools', (Gilbert and Blyth, 1983). The regulations issued by the Board of Education in 1911 recognized the four-year course, establishing that the first three years were devoted to undergraduate degree study and the fourth year to professional studies. Thus, by 1914 there was an increase in secondary training numbers, though average numbers still remained under 200 a year, of whom 160 were women. After the disruption of World War 1 and the resulting staff shortages in schools it became possible for suitably qualified elementary students to convert to teaching in secondary schools, and henceforth universities began to specialize in preparing graduates for work in secondary schools. The doubling of the secondary school population between 1918 and 1939 also encouraged the university departments to concentrate on secondary training, though one-year primary courses continued in places. The last two-year course in the universities did not close until 1951, though most of these elementary training courses disappeared in the 1920s, (Patrick, 1986). However, as Professor Tuck reminds us, writing about the decades between the wars, 'it would be impossible without a great deal of detailed enquiry to find out how many students from the university departments went into elementary and how many into secondary schools, and in the 1930s when unemployment was a real risk, many served in both, starting in elementary schools, and moving later into secondary schools'.[33]

New Departments and Joint Boards

Changes occurred in the map of university teacher training in the 1920s —

Bedford College, London, closed in 1922, under competition from the London Day Training College, where the London County Council wished to centralize the training of secondary teachers for the capital city. The two separate day training colleges at Cardiff became one department of education under Professor Olive Wheeler in 1925, whilst Helen Wodehouse, first holder of the chair of education at Bristol, appointed in 1919, successfully managed to integrate separate men's and women's departments there. Her task was no easy one, the respective heads of department, T.S. Foster and Amy Mullock, being difficult personalities. An acquaintance of all three commented that Professor Wodehouse saw Miss Mullock by appointment and Mr Foster by accident.[34] Four new university departments were opened between 1920 and 1940. The University of Wales opened a fourth department of education in 1921 at the newly-established University College, Swansea, and appointed F.A. Cavanagh as the foundation Professor of Education. Durham established a department and chair of education in the Durham colleges in 1922. The department of education at Leicester University was established in 1929, though its first chair appointment was J.W. Tibble in 1946. Hull opened a department in 1930, after some complex local politics with the Municipal and Endsleigh Training Colleges, and by 1934 had built up its PGCE course to sixty-two students. The first Professor of Education at Hull was R.W. Rich, the distinguished historian of teacher education.[35] Cambridge was to establish a chair of education in 1938, appointing G.R. Owst, whilst two universities were to manage education under jointly-named departments under joint chairs: Exeter, under S.H. Watkins as Professor of Education and Philosophy; Southampton, with A.A. Cock in a like-named chair.

This increase in the number of education departments was part of a general pressure on the universities to become more closely involved with teacher training, and during the 1920s the Departmental Committee report (the Burnham Report) on the training of teachers for the elementary schools was to draw universities and training colleges into a partnership for the examination of students in training. The Committee discovered a variety of existing relationships prior to 1925 when the report appeared. Some training colleges prepared for external degress of London University. Others organized four-year courses in association with their local university. A few colleges in the north-west had examinations organized by Liverpool University and not by the Board of Education. The total number of students involved in these links was very small.

The report of the Committee favoured 'a much larger number of graduate teachers in elementary schools'[36] but rejected incorporating teacher education into the universities on grounds of cost (extending a two-year course to three years plus a year of professional training) and educational politics. There was no great wish on the part of the universities to take over the teacher training system. The Committee believed that the universities would regard such a move as a lowering of academic standards and as a threat to their autonomy if they became over-involved in a state activity like teacher education. In effect the Board was anxious to give up the expensive administrative work of examining in the training colleges and the report established, between 1927 and 1929, nineteen joint boards based on the universities to conduct teacher training examinations in the colleges and construct the subject syllabuses and general regulations as the basis for those examinations. The university departments of education, which had previously been given most of the responsibility for their own examining, played a central part in these joint examining boards consisting of representatives of the universities and the training colleges. The two education departments at Oxford and Cambridge were not involved in these regional arrangements, the two universities claiming that their national reputation made it unsuitable for them to enter into local arrangements. Cambridge did, however, develop links with a single college — Homerton.

The changes in regulations changed little other than the administrative simplification. Closer links between colleges and universities did not develop to any great extent with the joint boards themselves as symbols of the different attitudes to training in the different sectors for the boards only examined training college students. The universities continued to examine their own students with HMI moderation for practical teaching and expressed little enthusiasm for their relationships with the colleges. A Board of Education discussion paper expresses this lack of interest in a number of telling phrases: 'the Manchester Vice-Chancellor is not greatly interested' and 'at Birmingham the part played by the University is very small'. The university connection was not a satisfactory one and the resulting discontent produced the McNair Committee set up in 1942, the decisions of which are discussed later in this volume. It is perhaps not surprising that there was no great breakthrough in teacher training as a result of the joint boards. After all, as Dent (1977) sensibly points out 'they had to weather first the world wide economic depression of the early 1930s, and they were hardly clear of that before the Second World War broke over their heads'. Considerable unemployment among newly-qualified teachers as a result of the depression also acted as a further demoralizing factor for the teacher training institutions, where by 1934 the number of training college and university training department students had been reduced by about 20 per cent.[37]

Advanced Studies and Research Degrees

The university departments had developed advanced studies and research degrees alongside their pre-service or initial training courses and although they never became a major aspect of their collective work before the Second World War there were nevertheless some important developments which laid the foundations for successful post-war initiatives. Distinguished leadership from a number of inter-war professors of education associated certain universities with particular strengths in educational scholarship which became the basis for nationally and internationally famous developments later. For example, C.W. Valentine at Birmingham established his department as a major centre for studies and research in educational psychology, a position it has maintained to the present day. In other cases individual professors changed the direction of their departments. Thus, at Newcastle[38] where Mark Wright had held the chair of education from 1895 to 1920 and achieved great success as a trainer of teachers, the appointment of Godfrey Thomson as his successor brought outstanding original scholarship to the department. Under Thomson the academic study of education took root in the department and the MEd degree was established in 1928. It was also possible for doctorates to be awarded and Newcastle produced two DSc degrees in education in 1928.

The general history of academic studies in education is outlined by Brian Simon in a later chapter of this volume and professors of education are studied by Peter Gordon in a further chapter. My present purpose is to hint at those developments of advanced courses which occurred in the 1920s and 1930s. One of the major providers of advanced courses was the department of education at Leeds which had students reading both for the MA and the MEd degrees in education, the latter instituted in 1920. Between 1919 and 1939, 128 MEd degrees were awarded, some of which were scientific in bias. The same department provided diplomas for teachers who wished to acquire additional qualifications through courses of study. Leeds awarded nearly 2000 between 1920 and 1939 and teaching for this diploma constituted the main activity of the department. With such a history it is not surprising that by 1969 Leeds had more advanced students of education than any other British university with the exception of the London Institute.[39] Bristol was another university which provided advanced degrees and courses, early developing a reputation for further professional studies. By 1920 education had been added as a subject for higher degree study. Students had to be a BA or BSc of the university of at least two years standing and have obtained a teaching diploma at least one year before entry to the MA and demonstrated efficient teaching experience in a written submission to the University. Bristol had also instituted a BA (Education) by research, first taken by a local teacher in 1920. These developments in research degrees at Bristol had originated in 1908 when the University had established a committee for educational research looking at the administration of schools, history of education, teacher training and the study of school children. This committee established a reference library and reading room for teachers employed by the Bristol Education Committee, (Thomas, 1988b).

Conclusion

Lest one appears too euphoric about the position of the university departments of education in the 1930s, one should remember that they were not held in high regard by some of their parent universities. They were viewed as occuping themselves in low level work of little academic status not advancing the study of education. The development of four-year courses probably strengthened the former view, cutting most of the departments off as it did from the academic undergraduate study of education when the concurrent courses of training were phased out. The content of courses changed little between the wars and the demands of training restricted the time available for research. The departments also suffered from the low status of the teaching profession and the fact that academic colleagues in the universities were not usually sending their own children into the state schools. Some writers, such as Patrick (1986) believe that the staff of education departments were intellectually inferior to those in other departments of the university. The evidence for that view is not easy to find and is also based on an unproven assumption that all academics in other departments were great scholars and researchers. It is more likely that the departments of education were forced by circumstances into a professional training role rather than the role of advancing educational research. The staff student ratio was high, students were on busy training courses, and the role of the professor of education was seen as administrative. He was, as the calendar for Aberystwyth read well into the 1960s, 'professor of education and head of the training department'. The ambivalence with which universities regarded education departments may be illustrated by reference to the book published by Sir Walter Moberly in 1949. He suggested that university academics, themselves untrained to teach, were sceptical about the value of teacher training and 'till lately at least, the bulk of academic opinion has had no real belief in teacher training and has been half ashamed of the university's part in it'.[40]

Marginal as some of the university departments may have appeared to the academic life of the universities it remains clear that these departments were a benefit to the universities. Teacher training brought in new subjects and new students and gave the universities closer links with the school system. Of special importance is the principle about training which Professor Tuck saw the departments of education establishing as a permanent feature of teacher education: that teachers should have their higher education alongside those students preparing to enter other professions and occupations. A special feature of this principle as it developed was that all universities became involved in teacher training, a pattern that was only broken when some of the universities established in the 1960s failed to develop departments of education or take part themselves in teacher training. In 1939, however, all universities were involved with the teaching profession, 'for all presumably recognized not only that there was a contribution which they alone could make, but also that in the long run there is value in an association between a seat of learning and the humblest elementary school in the land' (Tuck, 1973).

Notes

1 Percentages computed by Tuck (1973) from the Annual Reports of the Board of Education for this period.

2 Summarized from Chapple (1928) quoted in Thomas (1978) p. 255.
3 The Bristol details are from Thomas (1988a) p. 58.
4 For details of individual appointments see Thomas (1982a).
5 My summary is from Tuck (1973) pp. 78–9. A detailed description of such a curriculum in practice is given in Thomas (1979).
6 For Henderson see Thomas (1986a) pp. 25–7. Other manuals of method were Findlay, J.J. (1902) *Principles of Class Teaching*, London, Macmillan; Adams, J. (1903) *Primer on Teaching*, London, Heath D.C.; Raymont, T. (1904) *Principles of Education*, London, Longmans; Welton, J. (1906) *Principles and Methods of Teaching*, London, Chine W.B.; Adamson, J.W. (Ed) (1907) *The Practice of Instruction: A Manual of Method, General and Special*, London, National Society; Green, J.A. and Birchenough, C. (1911) *A Primer of Teaching Practice*, London, Longmans.
7 Quoted from Wolters (1949) 'Early Days' in Barnard (1949).
8 See the accounts by a former student and later professor at Newcastle, Sir Godfrey Thomson, in Thomson (1969) pp. 78–81.
9 *Report of Committee of Council 1896–97*, p. 208, quoted Thomas (1983a) pp. 142–4, for a full discussion of the school practice problems of one DTC.
10 Tyson and Tuck (1971), p. 20. Unless stated to the contrary, the sources for the detail in this section and the section on students comes from my case studies of day training colleges as listed in the references.
11 See Roscoe (1915) for Mark and other early educationalists.
12 Extracted from Findlay (1908).
13 See *Who Was Who 1929–1940*, the obituary in *The Times*, 7 December 1937, and the *British Museum General Catalogue of Printed Books* 12.
14 See the account of his appointment and career in Britain in Thomas (1986b).
15 See the two important papers by Higginson (1980 and 1982), and also Pickering (1982).
16 From 1911 to 1922. It eventually became the *British Journal of Educational Psychology*.
17 E.T. Campagnac, Professor of Education at Liverpool from 1908, quoted in Kelly (1981) p. 233.
18 See Kelly (1981) p. 160.
19 See Thomas (1979) and (1986b) for details.
20 Quoted from Education Department reports of examiners in training colleges in Thomas (1978) p. 257.
21 Quoted from Chapple (1928).
22 George Goldsbrough and Heslop Harrison, quoted in Thomson (1969) p. 43.
23 Clapp (1982) p. 30.
24 Tyndall A.M., 'Sixty years of academic life in Bristol' quoted in Macqueen and Taylor (1976) p. 128. Tyndall was Professor of Physics at Bristol from 1919 to 1948.
25 Browning O. (1898) 'The training of teachers at the University', presidential address to the Association of Principals and Lecturers in Training Colleges under Government Inspection, at Westminster Town Hall, 19 December 1898.
26 Quoted in Wood (1953) p. 157.
27 Wood (1953) p. 64.
28 Calculated from the figures in Council of University College, Bristol, minutes for 17 November 1897.
29 Bedford training department was not a day training college. The figures are found in *Report of Bedford College Council* 1919–1920.
30 Quoted on p. 273 of Rich (1933). The Board of Education Act of 1899 established

the Consultative Committee, one of whose duties was to establish and maintain a register of teachers.
31 Tuck (1973) p. 84.
32 *ibid.*, (1973) p. 89.
33 *ibid.*, (1973) p. 94.
34 The comment is recorded in Humphreys (1976) p. 7.
35 An entertaining and scholarly account of the history of the Hull department may be found in Armytage (1980).
36 Board of Education (1925) p. 27 quoted in Patrick (1986) pp. 247–8.
37 Figures quoted in Dent (1977) p. 105.
38 Details from Tyson and Tuck (1971) pp. 69–73.
39 Figures for Leeds from Stephens (1975) p. 283 and p. 292.
40 Moberly W. (1949) *The Crisis in the University*, London, SCM, p. 251 quoted in Patrick (1986) p. 250.

References

ARMYTAGE, W.H.G. (1955) *Civic Universities: Aspects of a British Tradition*, London, Benn.

ARMYTAGE, W.H.G. (1980) 'F.O. Morgans legacy — fifty years of teacher education', *Aspects of Education*, 24, pp. 1–8.

BARNARD, H.C. (Ed) (1949) *The Education Department Through Fifty Years*, Reading, The University.

BARNWELL, P.J. (1981) *The Cambridge University Schoolmasters Training College 1891*–1938, Cambridge, Cambridge Institute of Education.

BOARD OF EDUCATION (1925) *Report of the Departmental Committee on the Training of Teachers for Public Elementary Schools*, London, HMSO.

BURRELL, E.R. (1963) 'James Fairgrieve: his contribution to the teaching of geography', unpublished MA thesis, University of London.

CHAPPLE, C.R. (1928) 'The Department of Education and the training department', in MORGAN, I. (Ed) *The College by the Sea*, Aberystwyth, Students Representative Council.

CLAPP, B.W. (1982) *The University of Exeter: A History*, Exeter, The University.

DALE, A.W. (1907) *University College and the University of Liverpool 1882–1907. A brief Record of Work and Progress*, Liverpool, Liverpool University Press.

DAVIES, W.C. and JONES, W.L. (1905) *The University of Wales and its Constituent Colleges*, London, F.E. Robinson and Sons.

DENT, H.C. (1977) *The Training of Teachers in England and Wales 1800*–1975, London, Hodder & Stoughton.

FINDLAY, J.J. (1908) *The Demonstration Schools Record: Being Contributions to the Study of Education by the Department of Education in the University of Manchester*, Manchester, The University Press.

GILBERT, J.E. and BLYTH, W.A.L. (1983) 'Origins and expansion of PGCE primary courses in England and Wales before 1970', *Journal of Education for Teaching*, 9, 3, pp. 279–90.

GOSDEN, P.H.J.H. and TAYLOR, A.J. (Ed) (1975) *Studies in the History of a University*, Leeds, Edward Arnold.

HEARNSHAW, F.J.C. (1928) *The Centenary History of King's College, London 1828–1928*, London, Harrap.
HIGGINSON, J.H. (1980) 'Establishing a history of education course: the work of Professor Michael Sadler 1903–1911', *History of Education*, 9, 3, pp. 245–55.
HIGGINSON, J.H. (1982) 'Michael Sadler the researcher', *Compare*, 12, 2, pp. 143–52.
HUMPHREYS, D.W. (1976) *The University of Bristol and the Education and Training of Teachers*, Bristol, University of Bristol School of Education.
KELLY, T. (1981) *For Advancement of Learning: The University of Liverpool 1881*–1981, Liverpool, Liverpool University Press.
MACQUEEN, J.G. and TAYLOR, W.S. (Eds) (1976) *University and Community: Essays to mark the Centenary of the Founding of University College, Bristol*, Bristol, The University.
PATRICK, H. (1986) 'From Cross to CATE: The universities and teacher education over the past century', *Oxford Review of Education*, 12, 3, pp. 243–61.
PHILLIPS, E.R. (1979) 'The history of the development of the teaching of domestic subjects between 1870 and 1944 with particular reference to Cardiff', unpublished MEd thesis, University of Wales.
PICKERING, O.S. (1982) *Sir Michael Sadler: A Bibliography of his Published Works*, Leeds, University of Leeds Department of Adult and Continuing Education.
RICH, R.W. (1933) *The Training of Teachers in England and Wales During the Nineteenth Century*, Cambridge, Cambridge University Press.
ROSCOE, J.E. (1915) *The Dictionary of Educationists*, London, Pitman.
SHIMMIN, S.N. (1954) *The University of Leeds: The First Half Century*, Cambridge, Cambridge University Press.
STEPHENS, W. (1975) 'The curriculum', in GOSDEN, P.H.J.H. and TAYLOR, A.J. (Eds) (1975) *Studies in the History of a University*, Leeds, Edward Arnold.
THOMAS, J.B. (1978) 'The day training college: A Victorian innovation in teacher training', *British Journal of Teacher Education*, 4, 3, pp. 349–61.
THOMAS, J.B. (1979) 'The curriculum of a day training college: The logbooks of J.W. Adamson', *Journal of Educational Administration and History*, 18, 2, pp. 24–33.
THOMAS, J.B. (1982a) 'A note on masters of method in the universities of England and Wales', *History of Education Society Bulletin*, 30, pp. 27–9.
THOMAS, J.B. (1982b) 'J.A. Green, educational psychology, and the Journal of Experimental Pedagogy', *History of Education Society Bulletin*, 29, pp. 41–5.
THOMAS, J.B. (1983a) 'The beginnings of teacher training at University College, Bangor', *Transactions of the Caernarvonshire Historical Society, 44, pp. 123*–53.
THOMAS, J.B. (1983b) 'Teacher training at Bedford College, London 1891–1922', *Durham and Newcastle Research Review*, 10, 50, pp. 59–64.
THOMAS, J.B. (1984) 'The origins of teacher training at University College, Cardiff', *Journal of Educational Administration and History*, 16, 3, pp. 10–16.
THOMAS, J.B. (1986a) 'Amos Henderson and the Nottingham Day Training College', *Journal of Educational Administration and History*, 18, 12, pp. 24–33.
THOMAS, J.B. (1986b) 'University College, London, and the training of teachers', *History of Education Society Bulletin*, 37, pp. 44–8.
THOMAS, J.B. (1988a) 'University College, Bristol: pioneering teacher training for women', *History of Education*, 17, 1, pp. 55–70.
THOMAS, J.B. (1988b) 'A note on the beginnings of teacher training for men at University College, Bristol', *History of Education Society Bulletin*, 41, pp. 40–5.
THOMSON, G.H. (1969) *The Education of an Englishman*, Edinburgh, Moray House.

TOMLINSON, L. (1968) 'Oxford University and the training of teachers; The early years 1892–1921', *British Journal of Educational Studies*, 16, 3, pp. 292–307.

TUCK, J.P. (1973) 'From day training college to university department of education' in LOMAX, D.E. (Ed) (1973) *The Education of Teachers in Britain*, London, John Wiley.

TYSON, J.C. and TUCK, J.P. (1971) *The Origins and Development of the Training of Teachers in the University of Newcastle-upon-Tyne*, Newcastle, University of Newcastle-upon-Tyne Department of Education.

WOOD, A.C. (1953) *A History of the University College, Nottingham, 1881–1948*, Nottingham, The University.

Chapter 3

The Area Training Organization

John D. Turner

Origins

Area training organizations were established immediately after the 1939–45 war, with the purpose of improving the quality of teacher education and planning the provision of such education on a regional basis. They were abolished legally in 1975 but *de facto* at an indeterminate later date. They may yet have to be reinvented.[1]

One of the most surprising features of government during the 1939–45 war was the number of important committees which were established to consider the social reorganization of the country in the years following the war. Amongst them was a committee appointed by the President of the Board of Education to consider the supply, recruitment and training of teachers and youth leaders, appointed as early as March 1942 in the darkest days of the war and reporting in 1944. The terms of reference of the committee were, 'to investigate the present sources of supply and the methods of recruitment and training of teachers and youth leaders and to report what principles should guide the Board in these matters in the future'.

The preparatory note of the Report[2] reminded readers that 'the Committee of Council on Education first defined the conditions under which training colleges could qualify for grant in 1843–44, exactly one hundred years' prior to the publication of the Report. During the following thirty years, thirty-four colleges were recognized, which accommodated 2500 students, while during the next thirty years an additional twenty-seven colleges were recognized, the sixty-one accommodating 6000 students. In 1944, the number had risen to 100 institutions, a number which included university training departments. At the outbreak of the war there were 15,000 students, including those in university departments, in attendance at training institutions recognized by the Board of Education.

The perennial nature of the problems surrounding teacher supply is well illustrated by the news item in the *Daily Telegraph* on 4 May 1944, describing the publication of the Report. 'The Committee's suggestions', the *Telegraph* summarized, 'include substantial increases in teachers' salaries, new methods of recruiting and training teachers, abolition of the "marriage bar" and the attraction into teaching of people who have already proved their quality in commerce and the professions'.[3] Apart from the recommendation that no local education authorities should oblige women to resign their posts on marriage, the recommendations have a peculiarly modern ring.

It is particularly interesting that the Report recommended recruitment of mature adults from 'industry, commerce and the professions'. 'We have no doubt that there are intelligent men and women still comparatively young who, after a spell in some other occupation, . . . would adopt teaching as a profession if a clear way into the profession were available and made known'. It was even recommended that such entrants might have a shorter course. 'The course must be one which in point of length and character is tolerable to them having regard to their maturity and experience'. This recommendation cannot be said to have been pursued with vigour, though the return of ex-servicemen and women from the war served a similar purpose of admitting to the teaching profession a large number of adults with wide and varying experience.

Perhaps the most important single recommendation, however, was 'that the Board of Education should recognize only one grade of teacher, namely the grade of "Qualified Teacher" and that, subject to the Board having discretion to accord such recognition to persons with good academic or other attainments, a Qualified Teacher should be a teacher who has satisfactorily completed an approved course of education and training'. The abolition of distinction between different types of teacher opened the way to a steady improvement of all categories of teacher which led eventually to the establishment of an all-graduate profession. Unfortunately, the retention by the Board of discretion to recognize non-trained persons as Qualified Teachers led to the admission as Qualified Teachers of any graduate, a practice which did not cease for many years.

At the time of the Report, there were some sixty-two two-year colleges, which provided the minimum two-year course of general education and professional training conducted more or less concurrently, which led to a student's recognition as a certificated teacher. There were eleven domestic subjects colleges, offering a three-year course, which was the minimum for the combined qualification of Certificated Teacher and Teacher of Domestic Subjects. There were also six colleges of physical education, which gave three-year programmes. In addition, there were twenty-two university training departments, including two each at the Universities of Durham and London, and one at each of the four constituent colleges of the University of Wales.

The two features of the training colleges which were indicated by the Report as leading to their low status, were poverty and small size. 'What is chiefly wrong with the majority of the training colleges is their poverty and all that flows from it'.[4] Of the eighty-three training colleges in 1938, sixty-four had fewer than 150 students and twenty-eight of these had fewer than 100. Conditions in many of the colleges were clearly very poverty-stricken.

In 50 per cent of the colleges, the laboratories, studios, workshops

> and gymnasia are inadequate. In more than 25 per cent of the colleges, the assembly halls, libraries, lecture rooms or dining accommodation are inadequate. Nearly 60 per cent have no cinema projector, and more than 30 per cent have no broadcasting reception equipment for teaching purposes, and these figures do not mean that the remainder are adequately equipped in these respects.

It was even indicated that washing and sanitary accommodation in some colleges was insufficient or unsuitable in kind, and that in many ways, the kitchens and kitchen equipment were out of date. There was clearly tremendous room for improvement. In short, 'the existing arrangements for the recognition, the training and supply of teachers are chaotic and ill-adjusted'.

When they came to look at the structure which would be most likely to improve the nature of the colleges and the status of teachers, all members of the Committee were agreed that it would be helpful to group the colleges together into geographically coherent areas. This common conviction may have been due to the fact that, since 1926, the colleges had been arranged in groups and brought into an examination relationship with the universities by the establishment of joint examination boards, each consisting of representatives of the university and of the colleges concerned. The Report noted, however, that, 'The fact that the several colleges of a group are all represented on the same joint board has not in general resulted in their having any closer relations with one another, save in the matter of examinations, than they had when they were more directly under the Board of Education. There is no cooperation between them about staffing, nor do they share amenities'

It was clear that members of the Committee thought that this lack of the cooperation, which had, at least in theory, been made possible by the previous groupings, had been a wasted opportunity and their recommendations went far to remedy this. They were quite clear that it was desirable to draw together the various colleges into a close relationship on an area basis, but they were totally unable to agree about the place of the universities in such an arrangement.

They therefore found it necessary to adopt the very unusual procedure of presenting two alternative scenarios in the main body of the Report, each supported by five members of the Committee.

The two different viewpoints were alike in believing that it was necessary that all teacher training institutions should be brought together in groups to provide 'an integrated service for the education and training of teachers', a service which would break down the clear lines of demarcation between the provision of teachers for primary and secondary schools, and would further reduce the power to control education which belonged to the Board of Education, and which had been initiated in 1926 when the responsibility for examining students passed from the Board of Education to the examining boards.

The main point at issue between the two groups was the role of universities in the education of teachers, and in particular in their relationship to the colleges of education. One group favoured the creation of university schools of education, and was opposed 'to a single centralized training service . . . We reject anything approaching permanent central control over the training of teachers. Centralization of power and authority has potential dangers in every sphere of education and nowhere are those dangers so great and subtle as in the training of teachers'.[5]

This proposal involved an oversight by the university of the training of the colleges in their area, and placed the training of graduates and non-graduates under the same authority, thus rejecting the idea 'which is sometimes suggested that the universities should concern themselves only with the education and training of older children'. The group was not prepared to go so far as to suggest that all teachers should be university graduates, but did believe that 'the education and the training of anyone fit to seek recognition as a Qualified Teacher are the proper concern of the university'.[6]

This part of the Report was surprisingly prescient. It recognized the important influence which university teachers could have in raising the standards of work in the colleges. It recognized the difference between quality of work and breadth of work, and hinted that students from colleges might take some programmes which were genuine university courses even though they were not seeking to take a university degree. Above all, it recognized that a college of education might cooperate 'with other educational institutions in the area, for example technical colleges, schools of arts, and agricultural institutes, in such a way that it became the centre of cultural interest for the neighbourhood and was not merely an institution for the training of students isolated from the community'.[7]

The concept of a higher education institution which cooperated with and influenced a wide range of different institutions within its own area, even where these institutions were not of full degree level, was a far-sighted one and one which has been adopted in a number of other countries; it never became effective in Britain, however, in spite of the McNair Report.

The Report was also remarkable in recognizing that these reforms may well take many years to become effective.

> We believe that in years to come it will be considered disastrous if the national system for the training of teachers is found to be divorced from the work of the universities or even to be running parallel with it. We are not looking a few years but twenty-five years ahead, and such an opportunity for fundamental reform as now presents itself may not recur within that period.

Finally, the authors of the university school of education section were determined to break down the difference between training and education. Universities should properly be concerned with the education of the professions and it was in no way different to prepare teachers for their profession than to prepare engineers for theirs.

The other group, however, advocated the building of the new area groups on the joint boards which, until that time, had been concerned mainly with the examination of students.[8] There were two major reasons for this view; the first we must regard as spurious. It was impossible for the group to deny that universities were in fact already involved in the education of the professions. They believed, however, that the main duty of universities 'consists and properly consists in teaching basic subjects and in the advancement of knowledge . . . For a variety of reasons, historical and others, they also participated in the provision of training for certain professions, but this is a subsidiary function . . . the universities cannot undertake all kinds of professional training'. Secondly, there was a fear that if universities determined standards, teachers would adopt an excessively academic outlook; the members of the group clearly felt that the human qualities of teachers were more important than their academic development.

> The predominant qualities required in addition to a good general education, are an interest in and understanding of children and a desire to live one's life with them and help them to develop themselves on the right lines — qualities which have no necessary connection with university standards at all and are apt not to receive due recognition and encouragement in an academic atmosphere but will be adequately safeguarded in the training colleges.

This is a foreshadowing of the anti-intellectualism of many subsequent writers on teacher education.

In addition, there was the objection that if the universities became responsible for the training of all teachers there would tend to be an undue concentration of new training colleges in the universities' cities and towns. This would not only be undesirable in itself but would also make it difficult to find teaching practice places. This would also lead to the teachers having 'an unduly urban outlook' which would be detrimental to the rural schools.

After the publication of the Report, universities were asked to consider the extent to which they would be able to assume the responsibilities outlined in it. The prompt and enthusiastic response ensured that the school of education scheme was adopted in preference to the joint board scheme.

Establishment and Organization

Seventeen area training organizations were established, thirteen of which were integral parts of universities or university colleges, and four of which were not but were financed directly by the Ministry of Education. The term, school of education, proposed by the MacNair Committee, was in fact adopted by only two of the new organizations. The great majority used the title 'institute of education', though the title 'delegacy for the training of teachers' was also used. The Ministry of Education used the neutral title 'area training organizations' to describe all these bodies. As new universities were founded and colleges of education multiplied in number, new area training organizations were developed which in some cases divided excessively large ATOs and to some extent rationalized the geographical area for which the ATOs were responsible. Eventually there were some twenty-three area training organizations, of which all but the Cambridge Institute of Education were integral parts of their universities. Each ATO included amongst its members the departments of education in their university and in due course also education departments of polytechnics and of other colleges such as colleges of art, as well as teacher training colleges.

In the last resort, the responsibility for the provision of an adequate number of teachers of an appropriate standard remained with the Department of Education and Science, as it later became. It therefore had to approve the constitution of each area training organization to ensure that it was properly constituted. It also retained the award of qualified teacher status, and the overall planning of numbers and levels of training within the profession. In these respects, however, it generally took advice from area training organizations and only allocated qualified teacher status to those students who were guaranteed by the area training organizations to have reached an appropriate standard and to be of a suitable character to enter the profession.

The government was always very careful to safeguard the rights of the area training organizations and not to trespass upon their prerogatives, and allowed them to retain their complete independence from the DES in their sphere of work.

The committee structures by which the various ATOs did their work were not identical and evolved gradually during their thirty years history. The governing body of the ATO was normally known as a 'delegacy', and consisted of representatives of local education authorities, of the university and of the colleges of education, and later also of the teaching profession. In later years an attempt was made to ensure that there was roughly one-third of the Delegacy from the local authorities, representing the employers, from the members of the colleges and the universities as the providers, and from the teaching profession itself. The Vice-Chancellor of the university or his representative normally chaired the Delegacy.

The position of the local education authorities was a difficult one. In a big urban authority such as Manchester, there might be several different LEAs with membership of the Delegacy. Several of these LEAs, however, might have parts of their authorities falling under a number of different ATOs, which might have had different policies. Not only did this make it difficult for such LEAs to play a full role in the governing of several ATOs, but it also subjected the teachers from the authority to a number of different sorts of provision which in some cases became remarkably divergent.

The Delegacy was advised by an expert committee, generally known as the 'Professional Board' or the 'Academic Board'. This Board would normally consist of representatives of the University Senate, the Director and academic staff of the ATO, and the Principal and other representatives of each of the constituent colleges or departments of the ATO. Many such boards would also include representatives of the teaching profession, of students and of LEAs, and assessors appointed by the Department of Education and Science.

These professional committees were in turn advised by a large number of sub-committees. In most cases each subject taught in the colleges had its own board of studies which was responsible for advising on curricula and standards in its subject. There would also be a Committee of Principals and an Awarding Committee; the latter was responsible for supervising the examinations and other arrangements for the award of certificates and degrees, while the Committee of Principals considered issues relating to broader policy and the governance of the colleges. For large ATOs, it is likely that there would be thirty or forty different sub-committees, dealing with the programmes of study and the examinations of several thousand students.

It should be noted that the ATOs were also responsible not only for the initial, but for the oversight of the in-service, education of teachers in their area. Most ATOs had separate units which offered a large variety of short and long courses which were taken by many thousands of teachers serving in the area's schools, and a typical ATO would also have a library which was accessible to all serving teachers in the area and a teachers' centre which included rooms where teachers could hold their own meetings. The ATO was therefore at the heart of the development of the teacher education system.

Under the guidance of the ATOs, the colleges changed out of all recognition. A tremendous expansion in numbers took place to meet the needs of a growing population, but the increase in the quality of provision was even more significant. The ATOs were concerned to improve the quality of the staff in the colleges of education and made available to them a wide variety of diplomas and advanced degrees in educational studies. It gradually became the rule rather than the exception for lecturers in colleges of education to engage in educational research and enquiry.

By the early 1960s, the ATO pattern was firmly established. The ATO lay in the centre of a great network of relationships. It related to the Department of Education and Science, since it was responsible for carrying out the policy of that Department with regard to the preparation of specified numbers of teachers for schools and ensuring, through in-service work, that teachers were able to meet changing school requirements. The DES kept itself informed of the progress of the ATOs through assessors who normally were members of Her Majesty's Inspectorate, who sat on, but rarely participated in the discussions of, the main committees of the ATOs.

The local education authorities, which were also represented on the committees of the ATO, increasingly established their own programmes of in-service teacher education and many of them provided teachers' centres and in some cases excellent libraries of professional literature. The teachers and their unions also played an increasing part in the work of the ATOs and were also concerned with providing courses for their teachers and ensuring their professional progress.

The Robbins Report and the ATOs

On 8 February 1961, the government established a Committee under the chairmanship of Lord Robbins,

> to review the pattern of full-time higher education in Great Britain and in the light of national needs and resources to advise Her Majesty's government on what principles its long-term development should be based. In particular, to advise, in the light of these principles, whether there should be any changes in that pattern, whether any new types of institution are desirable, and whether any modifications should be made in the present arrangements for planning and coordinating the development of the various types of institution.[9]

The Robbins Committee held 111 meetings and deliberated for two years, its Report eventually being published in October 1963. The Report was extremely influential for the development of the higher education system during the following twenty years. It will, however, be necessary here to concentrate specifically on its recommendations relating to the area training organizations.

The Report traced the developments which had taken place during the first twenty years of the ATOs.[10] Whereas in 1958/59 only three of the 140 colleges had over 500 students, by 1962/63 twenty colleges had more than 500 students and these catered for a quarter of all the students in training. The certificate course had been lengthened from two years to three years for those who entered college in 1960 and after, and the teaching staff had increased from less than 1000 before the war to nearly 5000 in 1962/63, of whom some 58 per cent were graduates. The staff-student ratio was 1:11. Of the 146 colleges in England and Wales, ninety-eight were LEA colleges and forty-eight were provided by voluntary bodies, mostly religious denominations.

The Robbins Report made two important recommendations about the ATOs and their member colleges. Firstly, they looked at the future needs of the colleges and came to the conclusion that, by 1980, the number of students in the colleges should increase from the then total of 50,000 to about 130,000. They saw that this would enable the average size of colleges to be raised and indicated that they were convinced 'that in the long term a college with less than 750 students should be regarded as exceptional'.[11]

Secondly, the Committee looked at the nature of the awards given in colleges and asked whether the courses should lead to a degree and if so how long that degree should be. They decided that, for the time being, it was not appropriate that all students should take a degree level course and were quite clear that the existing certificate course could not simply be renamed a degree. They did believe, however, that a number of students in colleges should have the opportunity of taking a full degree programme and that such a programme, including, as it would, both academic and professional training, should last for four years. It recognized that, 'though the academic standard of the degree must be broadly related to what is customary in universities, the nature of the course and the approach to the various subjects should be such as to suit the needs of future teachers'. Nevertheless, 'such a degree should be accepted as a suitable qualification for registration in universities for a higher degree'.[12]

The Committee suggested three possible modes for such a degree: the first would be distinct from the certificate course from the beginning of the programme, while the second would overlap with the certificate programme, providing an initial common course for all students and dividing them later into a degree stream and a non-degree stream. They also mentioned the possibility of students transferring to the university in order to complete their degrees. They stated that the new degree should be called a BEd and that 'by the middle of the 1970s provision should be made for 25 per cent of the entrants to training colleges to take a four-year course'.[13]

The Committee also looked very closely at the future administrative arrangements for this sector of higher education which they envisaged as increasing almost threefold during the successive fifteen years. Again it considered a number of different models. First, it considered the representations that had been made for the continuation and enlargement of the existing system, but ultimately rejected this because it did not believe that control by local authorities sufficiently reflected the colleges' development as national institutions which drew their students from far beyond their own localities and sent them out to serve anywhere in the country.

The second possibility was to separate the colleges completely from the universities. A number of submissions had been received by the Committee which were broadly critical of the amount of influence which universities had exerted on the colleges. It was indicated that the colleges were not in the mainstream of university life, hardly any of their students would get degrees, and in many cases their students and staff could not share in the activities of the university. 'At the same time their semi-dependence on the universities had in the eyes of some people inhibited the leading colleges from developing to the stature that they might have achieved under different circumstances'.[14] If, as a result of these criticisms, the system was adopted which would separate the colleges from the universities and put them under the control of a central body on the model of the National Council for Technological Awards, this would enable the leading colleges to become autonomous either on their own or as a constituent part of a university. 'It has been claimed that under such arrangements the colleges would have the best chance of developing vigorously and maintaining their characteristic approach to their work, and that in particular the leading colleges would be able to strike out more freely by themselves and to rise to a greater stature than they could do under any evolution of the present system'.[15]

Later in the Report, the Robbins Committee did indeed make the suggestion that the existing National Council for Technological Awards should be replaced by a Council for National Academic Awards (CNAA) covering the whole of Great Britain. It would be different from the existing Council in awarding degrees at honours level as well as at pass level and in covering areas of study outside the field of science and technology. This recommendation proved to be an extremely important one, not least for the field of education. Nevertheless, the Committee rejected the proposal for the total independence of the colleges and their separation from universities and instead proposed a solution which it believed to be in line with the proposals of the MacNair Report.

University schools of education would be developed which would take over all the functions of the ATOs and would also establish arrangements for the award of the new Bachelor of Education degree. The most important change from existing ATOs that they recommended, however, was that 'academic and administrative responsibility should go hand in hand'. The colleges themselves should become more responsible for their own governance, having independent governing bodies related federally to the school of education, and through the school of education to the university.

In particular, the financial support of the colleges should not now come from the LEAs but from a special earmarked grant made available to the schools of education by the University Grants Committee (UGC). The schools of education would have their own well-qualified administrative and financial officers who would relieve the central administration of the universities from a considerable burden.

These proposals were extremely far-reaching. They recognized the growth in autonomy which was needed for individual colleges to develop their own programmes of study and mode of operation but at the same time brought them fully into the centre of university life and activity. It is interesting to speculate what would have been the outcome if they had been adopted in full. The Committee realized clearly that the discontent in the training colleges as they aspired to a higher status was not just a matter of getting degrees taught in the colleges but of having their whole status raised by virtual incorporation into the university structure. They emphasized 'that our proposals form a whole, even though agreement on some parts of them may be possible more speedily than on others'.[16]

In the event, the government agreed with the institution of the BEd degree but rejected the advice on the restructuring of the college system. The universities responded rapidly and with some enthusiasm to the creation of the new degrees and these were being taught in all ATOs within a remarkably short time.

In some ways, however, this separation of high level academic achievement from the government and financial provision of the colleges was a totally unsatisfactory solution to the problems which the Robbins Committee had identified. It is very difficult to separate the financing of programmes of study from the academic implications of such programmes, and this led to increasing problems between ATOs and LEAs. Moreover, the aspirations of the colleges to attain a higher status and more control over their own affairs was also frustrated, and this in turn led to continued dissatisfaction and further proposals for change.

Two other recommendations of the Robbins Committee were implemented. The colleges were renamed 'colleges of education' rather than 'teacher training colleges', thus emphasizing the importance of education in the preparation of teachers. Similarly, the government of the colleges was greatly liberalized as a result of the Weaver Report on the Government of Colleges of Education, which gave detailed consideration to some of the proposals in this field of the Robbins Committee.[17]

The years which followed the publication of the Robbins Report were years of great development and progress. The raising of the level of teaching in colleges from certificate to degree level was accompanied by the doubling of the number of students in the colleges and a consequential massive building programme. The principals and staff were concerned simultaneously with developing new courses of study, recruiting increasing numbers of teachers and students, developing structures capable of dealing with financial and administrative problems of an unfamiliar size and complexity, and planning library, laboratory and other plant for purposes not previously undertaken in colleges of education. This was a remarkable achievement and the involvement of the universities in these changes was not less remarkable at a time when they too were undergoing great change, seeing the formulation of the binary system, the creation of the polytechnics, and an increasing demand for higher education for the increasing numbers of qualified school leavers.

If, therefore, one were to draw up a balance sheet of the position of ATOs in the years following the publication of the Robbins Report, one would find both achievements and failures. The achievements have been largely outlined in the last paragraph. The creation of the new degree programme emphasized the sound structure of the ATO. The existence of groups of subject committees which allowed colleagues in the same discipline in the member colleges to participate in the discussion of programmes with colleagues in their parent university, was an outstanding strength. It led to the development of a number of innovatory programmes which managed to break new ground in the relationship of academic study to the practical needs of the teacher, while at the same time achieving a genuine university degree level. Moreover, the association in these board of studies or subject committees of colleagues with similar interests led to the development of research and enquiry, even though, at a time of rapid expansion, the amount of time available for such research was strictly limited.

Problems

There were, however, also problems which were clearly beginning to emerge and which were emphasized by the growth of the system. Perhaps the most important of these was the divergence of practice between ATOs which seemed quite inappropriate in a national system. Perhaps the most controversial example of this was the attitude of different universities to the creation of a

Bachelor of Education degree with honours. Some universities initially refused to give an honours degree at all, others refused to classify such a degree, whilst still others gave a full honours classification. Some universities insisted on students taking a fifth year to complete the honours programme, while others gave an honours programme in four years.

Such divergence was clearly extremely unsatisfactory for students, not only those at the beginning of their careers but also those serving teachers who wished to supplement their existing certificates with study for an in-service BEd. In some LEAs which had a part of the authority in three or four different ATOs, the difference with which their teachers were treated by different ATOs was quite intolerable. If universities were not able to cooperate in the national interest, perhaps, it was said, they ought to lay down their control of the teacher education system.

Moreover, the exclusion of the colleges from the central fabric of universities was beginning to reap its reward. The larger colleges, of around or in excess of 1000 students, began to ask why they should be treated as subservient institutions who were unable to exercise control over their own academic processes, and bitterly resented the cavalier attitudes adopted by some of the university colleagues with whom they worked. It was indeed aggravating, to take an extreme case, for an experienced college of education head of department, who may have a doctoral degree and be an established writer, to have to submit his work for approval to a newly-qualified young lecturer in the university department who knew considerably less about the topic than he did. Very often the awareness by university staff of their own lack of expertise in teacher education served to harden their attitudes to their college colleagues.

At the same time, the colleges were beginning to receive a certain amount of criticism from the schools which they served and from the general public. The school system had been growing rapidly while the curriculum and social environment had been changing. The schools were encountering entirely novel problems as they regrouped into comprehensive systems and examined their relationship with technical colleges and other post-secondary institutions, while problems of growth were subjecting schools, colleges and higher education to unparalleled strain.

The James Report and the ATOs

In response to the mounting criticisms of the teacher education system, many of them grossly ill-informed, the Secretary of State for Education, Mr Short, initiated an enquiry at the beginning of 1970, into the teacher education system. He drew attention to the fact that 'there has in recent months been widespread debate about the content of teacher education and there has been pressure for the institution of a comprehensive enquiry'.[18] He expressed the view that 'many of these criticisms were misconceived and based on inadequate evidence' and expressed his doubt whether such a general enquiry would be the best course. Instead, he considered it appropriate 'for all area training organizations themselves to review their present structures and activities and the content of the courses for which they are responsible'. He particularly asked that the ATOs should examine their structure from the point of view of involvement of the teaching profession itself in the overall surveillance of teacher education.

Unfortunately, Mr Short's intention to use the ATO machinery for a thorough review of the problems of teacher education was frustrated. The Labour government of which he was a member had been replaced by a Conservative government before the date for the submission of the ATO reports had arrived, though most ATOs continued to develop their responses and eventually published them. Mrs Margaret Thatcher, the new Secretary of State for Education and Science, lost little time in appointing a special committee under the chairmanship of Lord James of Rusholme, with very comprehensive terms of reference 'to enquire into the present arrangements for the education, training and probation of teachers in England and Wales'[19]. The Committee was asked to begin its work early in 1971 and to report within twelve months.

The James Report proved to be a watershed document. Its 133 recommendations covered the whole field of teacher education and made a number of important recommendations which continue to deserve detailed study. Perhaps the most important aspect of the Report was its advocacy of the necessity of a life-long education for the teacher. It divided the education of teachers into three parts or cycles. The first cycle would consist of the personal higher education of the student, which would be either a full degree programme or a two-year course of study leading to the award of a Diploma in Higher Education. This was a new diploma which, while it was proposed specifically in the context of teacher education, was not intended to be restricted to those wishing to enter teaching but was to be generally available to any students for whom a full three-year degree programme did not seem to be a desirable aim.

The second cycle would consist of the teacher's initial professional education on a two-year programme of studies, the first year of which would be undertaken in a college of education, a university department of education, or the education department of a polytechnic, and the second year in schools. At the end of the first year, the student would become a 'licenced teacher', a term which has recently been revived in a different context, and would teach as a full member of a school staff while undertaking the second year of the second cycle of studies. During this year the licenced teacher would be released for attendance at special professional centres for the equivalent of not less than one day a week of further training. Successful completion of the second cycle would lead to the award of 'registered teacher' status and also of the degree of BA(Ed).

The third cycle of training would extend from that stage for the rest of the teacher's life. This cycle would cover

> a wide spectrum at one end of which are evening meetings and

> discussions, weekend conferences and other short-term activities with limited and specific objectives and taking place usually but not always in the teacher's own time. At the other end are long courses leading to higher degrees or advanced qualifications and requiring the release of teachers for full-time attendance at suitable establishments.[20]

A particularly important recommendation was that full-time in-service study should become a matter of right rather than privilege. Initially the teacher might expect to receive one term on full pay in every seven years of service, but it was hoped that eventually the entitlement would reach one term for every five years of service.

A design of this complexity covering the professional education required by a teacher over his or her whole working life naturally involved a very large number of other reforms to the system. Amongst the many beneficial changes which resulted from the report were an increase in the number of teachers' centres and the establishment in many schools of 'professional tutors' to be responsible for staff development including in particular the final year of the second cycle training.

Amongst the most important changes from our point of view, however, was the reorganization of the whole structure of teacher education which was necessary to provide a framework for the oversight of the second cycle of training, which, as has been indicated, would be partly in colleges and university departments and partly in schools, and for the granting of the awards.

The Report therefore proposed that ATOs should be abolished and replaced by a series of Regional Councils for Colleges and Departments of Education, above which would be a national body, perhaps called the National Council for Teacher Education and Training. A whole chapter of the Report is taken up by a detailed account of the organization and membership of these bodies and with a plea that they should be established at least on an interim basis well in advance of the reorganization of local authorities which was to take place in April 1974.

The James Report has already been described as a watershed document. One of the detrimental ways in which this was the case was its anti-intellectual approach to teacher education, in its criticism of 'educational theory'. 'It must be doubted', said the Report, 'whether such studies [for example, studies of educational theory], especially presented through the medium of lectures to large groups of perplexed students, are in terms of priorities a useful major element in initial training'.[21] In another chapter we read that, 'In an attempt to make the college courses academically "respectable", students are sometimes fed with a diet of theoretical speculation based on researches, the validity and scholarship of which are not always beyond question'.[22]

This elimination of major theoretical study from initial training and subsequently, though this was contrary to the intentions of the James Committee, from in-service education and training, has accelerated during the years since the publication of the Report.

Another watershed element of the document relates to the brief statements in the Report about the future of the colleges. Until the time of the James Committee, teacher education had been constantly expanding; the colleges were becoming larger and had a greatly improved quality of staff and students. The Report itself can be read, and indeed was probably intended to be read, as signalling a continuation of the same trends, with colleges continuing to expand and becoming a steadily more important part of the higher education system. In one paragraph, however, the Report foreshadows the possibility of wholesale change. Reference is made to the possible amalgamation of colleges with universities or polytechnics, to groups of two or three colleges amalgamating, and even to the closure of certain colleges, some of which might be made over to other educational uses.[23] This was a cloud no bigger than a man's hand in a sky which was otherwise unclouded. In the following years, however, the importance of this statement became clear and the issue of the size of the teacher education system became the dominating theme of educational planning.

Although James had insisted on the necessity for a rapid response to his Report and the early establishment of the national and regional bodies for which he had called as the first step in the total redevelopment of the system, it was in fact a full twelve months before the Secretary of State responded to the document, after a lengthy period of consultation, in a White Paper ironically called *Education: A Framework for Expansion*.[24] This document covered the government's intentions for the whole educational system, but in particular looked at the recommendations of the James Report.

The very first paragraph of the chapter on the James Report drew attention to the growth of the system from less than 40,000 students in 1961, to nearly 120,000 at the time of the White Paper.[25] Its seventeenth section contained the bombshell that, 'On present trends the best estimate which the government can make is that the number of initial training places required in the colleges and polytechnic departments of education by 1981 will be 60,000 to 70,000, compared with the 1971/72 figure of about 114,000'.[26]

The numbers issue dominated the following years with the numbers in the public sector of teacher education being constantly reduced. In January 1976, the 60,000 places were shown to include 12,500 for induction and in-service education, while in November 1976 the DES proposed a further reduction in the number of teacher education places outside the universities to 45,000 including 10,000 for induction and in-service education. The effect of these reductions on the teacher education system was dramatic and is well-documented elsewhere.[27]

This startling decline in the number of students in the system virtually ruled out the possibility of developing elaborate new national and regional structures to supervise and give awards to a new system of teacher education. In chapter 11 of the White Paper, the Secretary of State noted that, 'The radical recommendation of the James Committee that these organizations (ATOs) should be replaced and all their present functions assumed by new bodies virtually divorced from universities, has caused wide misgivings which the government share'.[28]

The functions which needed to be discharged in relation to teacher training were identified as (i) academic validation; (ii) professional recognition; (iii) coordination; and (iv) higher education supply. The White Paper proposed that, 'after further consultation, the Secretary of State should establish in place of the existing university-based ATOs new regional committees to coordinate the education and training of teachers, composed in such a way as to properly reflect these three sets of interests' (for example, of LEAs, training institutes and the teaching profession).[29] While a study of the issues involved and in particular the teacher supply problem was proceeding, 'the Secretary of State hopes that the ATOs will continue to discharge their existing responsibilities for both initial and in-service training'.[30]

This chapter sounded the death knell of the ATOs and the sentence was carried out in the further education regulations which came into operation on 1 August 1975. *Circular 5/75* of 18 July, which accompanied these regulations, noted that amongst the most important provisions of the previous regulations which then lapsed were those relating to the constitution and functions of ATOs. Nevertheless, pending the establishment of new regional advisory machinery, the Circular hoped 'that universities responsible for ATOs will continue their existing coordinating activities in relation to in-service education and training of teachers until new regional committees are established'.[31]

A great deal of discussion continued to take place spasmodically about possible ways of establishing new regional organizations. Perhaps the most thoroughly developed proposal was that of the Council of Local Education Authorities (CLEA), which recommended the creation of a series of committees which would: (i) subsume the functions of the existing Regional Advisory Councils for Further Education; (ii) advise on the provision of courses of initial education and training for teachers; and (iii) be responsible for the promotion, coordination and review of in-service training for teachers and an improved system of induction. *Circular 5/75* stated 'that the Advisory Committee on the Supply and Training of Teachers had already recommended that interim regional committees should be established as soon as possible for the third of the above functions'.[32]

Nevertheless, such regional advisory machinery was never established and the ATOs continued to exercise some of their functions into the 1980s especially with regard to the organization of special HMI regional courses for serving teachers which were provided with special finance from the DES. The RACs, which planned on a regional basis the non-teacher education provision of the public sector institutions, both polytechnics and colleges, and liaised with universities in their region, also continued in operation, though the removal of polytechnics and colleges of higher education from local authorities and their transfer to the Polytechnics and Colleges Funding Council (PCFC) on 1 April 1989 made them redundant as far as the regional planning function was concerned. It must also be assumed that the function of ATOs with regard to coordinating in-service education and training of teachers 'until new regional committees are established' has also become redundant.

Importance of ATOs

The area training organizations were devised for distancing the academic control of teacher education from the direct influence of government. In this they succeeded admirably, largely because the government also believed that academic independence was an important route to the development of high quality teacher education. The combining of initial and in-service teacher education was also an important feature of the ATOs which was several decades ahead of its time.

The success of the university-linked ATOs in raising the aspirations of the colleges of education and their staff members was startling, and there is no doubt that to maintain and indeed substantially improve the quality of teacher education during a period of unprecedented expansion was a quite astonishing achievement. It was also an achievement that was widely imitated in other parts of the world as a way of coordinating teacher education and raising academic standards, and there was widespread dismay in other Commonwealth countries when the government abolished its own ATOs.

The ATOs enshrined a number of important principles. The first of these was that the standard of teacher training awards should be guaranteed by universities, with degree levels equivalent to other intra-university degrees. The second was that all the groups responsible for the work of the schools should be involved in the determination of teacher education policy and practice. Another important principle was the devolution of the control of teacher education to local areas which were big enough to include a number of different LEAs but small enough to facilitate an easy interchange of people and ideas and to ensure the involvement in policy matters of all those engaged in the teacher education process.

The fourth principle was that there should be a separation between the awarding body and the employers of teachers, whether these were conceived of as LEAs or as the central government which provided for local authorities a great deal of the cost of the education service available.

The fifth principle was the stress on the unity of the teaching profession. For the first time, primary education had parity of esteem with secondary education and the different sorts of special education provision were also regarded as being of comparable importance.

Finally, there was the close relationship between initial and in-service education which was subsequently emphasized by the James Committee Report.

The tendency of the Thatcher government has been towards centralization of educational policy-making and control. The creation of the Council for the

Accreditation of Teacher Education (CATE) in 1984 centralized the control of the content and many of the procedures of teacher education, while the Education Reform Act of 1988 increased the powers of the Secretary of State for Education and Science and gave him/her and the Department a greater executive role than they had ever previously had. One may be doubtful whether these changes will result in the continued improvement of the qualifications and enthusiasm of the teaching profession and their sound deployment throughout the regions of the country.

Notes

1 For example, the DES Green Paper on *Future Arrangements for the Accreditation of Courses of Initial Teacher Training*, issued in May 1989, proposed a local committee structure remarkably similar to the ATO delegacies for the education of teachers.
2 Board of Education (1944) *Teachers and Youth Leaders*, London, HMSO.
3 *Daily Telegraph* and *Morning Post*, 4 May 1944. Article by 'Daily Telegraph Reporter' entitled 'Drastic Reforms Urged to Improve Teaching'.
4 Board of Education (1944) *op.cit.*, para. 34.
5 *ibid.*, para. 169.
6 *ibid.*, para. 173.
7 *ibid.*, para. 174.
8 *ibid.*, paras. 183–196.
9 *Higher Education* (1963) London, HMSO.
10 *ibid.*, paras. 70–9.
11 *ibid.*, para. 319.
12 *ibid.*, para. 327.
13 *ibid.*, para. 339.
14 *ibid.*, para. 348.
15 *ibid.*, para. 349.
16 *ibid.*, para. 360.
17 *Report of the Study Group on the Government of Colleges* (1966) London, HMSO.
18 Letter from Rt. Hon. Edward Short, Secretary of State for Education and Science to ATOs, February 1970.
19 Department of Education and Science (1972) *Teacher Education and Training*, London, HMSO.
20 *ibid.*, para. 2.
21 *ibid.*, para. 316.
22 *ibid.*, para. 22.
23 *ibid.*, para. 537.
24 *Education: A Framework for Expansion* (1972) London, HMSO.
25 *ibid.*, para. 54.
26 *ibid.*, para. 150.
27 For example, Hencke, D. (1978) *Colleges in Crisis*, Harmondsworth, Penguin Books.
28 *Education: A Framework for Expansion*; (1972) *op. cit*, para. 88.
29 *ibid.*, para. 95.
30 *ibid.*, para. 96.

31 Department of Education and Science Circular 5/75 (1975) *The Reorganization of Higher Education in the Non-University Sector: The Further Education Regulations 1975*, London, HMSO, para. 11.
32 *ibid.*, para. 10.

Chapter 4

The Universities and the BEd Degree

Alec Ross

Introduction

The BEd degree of the universities in England and Wales is to be distinguished from the BEd in Scottish universities described by R.E. Bell elsewhere in this volume. Within England and Wales a distinction has also to be made between a degree of that title validated by the university but taught wholly or almost wholly in colleges of education (now usually colleges or institutes of higher education) affiliated to the validating university making the award, and BEd degrees (though now most have become BA or BSc degrees) taught internally within the university. In both cases (external and internal) the degree programme includes a teaching qualification when offered to initial teacher training students and normally lasts for three or four years of full-time study. A further variant must be noted: the BEd degree for already qualified serving teachers, shorter in duration, frequently planned as a part-time degree and offered both in the university itself and in its affiliated colleges. This BEd degree does not include initial training but seeks instead to provide opportunities for the further professional and academic training of already qualified, usually non-graduate, teachers practising in the schools.

The Robbins Committee's Recommendation

The case for creating a new distinctive four-year degree, called BEd, to be equivalent to the BA, was argued cogently in the Report on Higher Education (Chairman Lord Robbins) published in 1963.[1] This was seen as the logical extension of the argument which had, by 1960, lengthened the course in the teacher training colleges from two to three years. There can be no doubt that the concept behind this proposal challenged the universities. They had accepted their regional responsibilities as major partners in the university-based ATOs which coordinated teacher training in each region and they had played a full and enthusiastic part, academically as well as professionally, in creating the new three-year certificate courses for entrants to the teaching profession. However certificates were not degrees and in any case the concept of a *professional* degree, notwithstanding the precedents in law, medicine, engineering and even, in some universities, commerce, was not welcome to some guardians of the academic traditions. Niblett *et al.* (1975) report that the universities were divided in their views of the radical Robbins proposal. By March 1964, however, 'every Senate (except London, Sussex, Oxford and Cambridge) was reported as having accepted the proposals in principle, although in one or two cases with doubts; only half were reported to be definitely in favour'.[2] Each university conducted its own seminar on the proposal. Will the charter allow us to do this? If so, would we wish to do so? Will this development call into question the quality of other degrees awarded by the university? Can a university offer a degree which includes a subject it does not teach itself? Once the initial training BEd had been launched there were even more difficult questions concerning part-time in-service degrees. With over twenty autonomous universities separately debating these and many other issues, it was inevitable that varying reactions emerged. The compromise reached in most universities reflected many traditional, local and personal factors. The soundness of the existing relationship with the colleges, the tenor of the university Senate, the standing of the professor who spoke for education and above all, the lead given by the Vice-Chancellor were all significant elements. The much cherished university autonomy meant that no one body could 'deliver' in the way that later the Council for National Academic Awards could commit the whole of non-university validation. Organizations such as the Committee of Vice-Chancellors and Principals (CVCP) and the Universities Council for the Education of Teachers (UCET) could advise but not direct. The point appears clearly in a note added to a UCET advisory note, dated 22 January 1970, on the BEd for Serving Teachers. 'This is a policy statement from UCET for the benefit of its members in deciding on their own policy in these matters ... It does not, of course, commit any of its members to the policy outlined here.' The debate was certainly thorough and all the issues fully explored. It would, however, be wrong to exaggerate the difficulties. Radical though the BEd proposal was, five universities moved quickly enough to be able to award BEd degrees in the summer of 1968. Given that the proposal was made in 1963 and the BEd programme was scheduled for four years, this is evidence of the ability of parts of the university system to respond with speed to an entirely new situation. By 1969 no less than twenty-one universities awarded the degree to 1388 candidates. The BEd thus, in a remarkably short period of time, had become an accepted part of the university validation system.

From the Robbins Report to the James Report

Nevertheless provision remained uneven; honours degrees were not always available and the problem of affording serving teachers equivalent opportunities became more serious. These and other matters led to repeated calls for a national enquiry into teacher training. However, the Department of Education and Science (DES) had for years 'resisted repeated calls from responsible bodies for an investigation into teacher training'.[3]

This was the opinion of the MP, Mr F. Willey, who chairerd the Select Committee of the House of Commons on Education and Science when it decided to break the deadlock by itself undertaking such an enquiry into the Parliamentary session 1969/70. This reluctance on the part of the DES may well have been part of a wider principle of heading off external enquiries; in the event the Select Committee was able to extract from senior officials an embarrassing admission that despite the requirements of the law they had allowed the Central Advisory Councils to fall into desuetude.[4] Be that as it may the Select Committee proceeded and took evidence amounting to six printed volumes which reviewed the whole teacher training scene at the time. The BEd degree was something which could not be ignored and received much attention throughout the proceedings.

The evidence presented by UCET concentrated on the principal form of university training, the one-year postgraduate certificate course and certain alternatives to it which UCET was preparing. The initial training BEd received little mention principally because it was by then an established part of the system but there was a detailed addendum providing an *Interim Policy Statement on the Provision of BEd (or equivalent) courses for Serving Teachers* (Select Committee, 3 February 1970). This statement reported that three universities (Hull, Lancaster and London) had already made arrangements for suitably qualified teachers to study for the BEd degree and expressed the hope that all universities would follow this lead. The paper recognized that in practical terms wholly part-time courses were needed and that, as with initial training BEd degrees, it was desirable that an honours classification should be available. It then went into detail concerning entry qualifications, qualifying examinations, recognizing post-experience qualifications such as diplomas, patterns of degree courses, administrative and financial arrangements. The considerable detail provided is a demonstration of the extent to which those bringing forward such proposals had to work their way through a complexity of problems involving local authority and other employers, colleges, the particular university, the DES and the UGC.

For a full account of the BEd as it stood at that time one has to turn to the evidence presented to the Select Committee on 15 April 1970 by the Association of Teachers in Colleges and Departments of Education (ATCDE). This pressed for teaching to become an entirely graduate-entry profession and as a step towards that aim, called for less regional variability in the provision of BEd courses so that every student teacher shown to be of degree calibre within the first two years of the initial training course would be able to proceed to a degree; the degree should be available at honours level in all universities. The ATCDE tackled the BEd degree along the lines of the UCET policy statement and then went on to make the case for the colleges playing a major part more generally in the expansion of higher education. When the Chairman asked Mr Stanley Hewett, General Secretary of the ATCDE, to summarize the college views on the BEd he replied as follows:

> The first thing one would like to say is that the colleges appreciate very much indeed the speed with which the universities moved in setting up the BEd courses. The universities are often accused of being slow. Robbins was not published until 1963. Five universities were able to offer BEd to students who entered in 1964. Twenty-one universities offered a BEd to students who entered in 1965. I cannot think of any other means which would have given BEd in so short a time. There are twenty-one universities now offering a BEd.[5]

The ATCDE accepted the Chairman's invitation to provide supplementary evidence and later submitted data giving the academic qualifications of college students. In 1969, 65.7 per cent of the men and 64.7 per cent of the women had 'A' level qualifications, the figures for two 'A' levels being 38 per cent (men) and 38.2 per cent (women).[6]

The Select Committee felt that it had now made it impossible for the government to avoid a national investigation but the DES made one more attempt to avoid a general enquiry. In 1970 the Secretary of State, Mr Edward Short (later Lord Glenamara), asked each ATO to carry out its own investigation of the arrangements for teacher training, including the BEd degree. The now familiar ground was reworked but before this exercise could be analyzed and general conclusions drawn a general election intervened and a Conservative government took office on 18 June 1970 with Mrs Margaret Thatcher as Secretary of State for Education and Science. At the hustings, in answer to a question, she had said she would instigate an enquiry into teacher training and so she did. The DES had, at last, to concede the point and set up a small 'Committee of Inquiry' chaired by Lord James of Rusholme charged with completing the task within a year. For the third time since 1969, the various interests marshalled their data and gave evidence. The report *Teacher Education and Training* (1972) was delivered by December 1971 and is known as the James Report. This included a major challenge to the whole concept of the BEd degree as developed, mainly by universities in consultation with their affiliated colleges, in the previous seven years.

The James Report

The James Report appeared early in 1972 and will be referred to in other chapters of this book. Amongst its proposals was the recommendation that the BEd degree should be abolished. 'It has been strongly affirmed that the BEd in its present form is not well suited to its purposes.'[7] The whole concept of the concurrent study of academic and professional matters which had informed the certificate course and the BEd degree which had evolved from it was rejected. Instead, students would take a two-year general academic course for a new award (a Diploma of Higher Education) before starting a two-year 'sharply focused' period of professional training, the second year of which would be school-based. (Those with an ear for the resonances would ring down the years may wish to note that before entering the school-based part of the course the student had to be recommended (to the Secretary of State) as a 'licensed teacher'; in 1989 the *Education (Teachers) Regulations* use the same terms for an entirely school-based form of training for people with a minimum of two years of higher education.) In the James plan, at the end of the second year of the professional 'cycle' the teacher would be eligible for the award of 'a general degree of BA (Education)'.[8]

The James Committee had obviously concentrated upon the difficulties encountered in the initial period of setting up the degree. It challenged the basic principle of a 'concurrent' degree blending academic with professional work and proposed a 'consecutive' model with the degree being awarded on the basis of the final period of school-orientated work. It expressed doubts as to whether universities were capable of encompassing this further challenge to traditional views of what constituted a university degree. Two of the members did not fully agree and in a 'note of extension' declared:

> We are more sanguine than our colleagues that a number of universities, given adequate financial support, will wish to undertake the new tasks described here. Universities have shown their concern for teacher education both by their response to the McNair Report in the 1940s and to the Robbins Report in the 1960s.[9]

The main report, however, summed up against the BEd as then offered.

> There is no doubt that the establishment of the BEd degree has been the result of devoted work by many people in universities, colleges and elsewhere. On the other hand, it is also true that much of the evidence has expressed a widespread disappointment with the degree: with the very limited extent to which it is available; with inconsistencies between different areas in such matters as entry standards, arrangements for the selection of students and the status of the award (general, classified honours or unclassified); with its adverse effect on the pattern of courses for students not proceeding to the degree and on the staffing ratios applying to these courses; and with the fact that, although designed as a degree for professional teachers, it has kept students away from the professional situation for periods well in excess of a year before their entry into teaching and, by its compulsory inclusion of an academic subject, has often been inappropriate for many non-specialist teachers.[10]

This virtual vote of no confidence in the universities caused not a little resentment in those many universities which had put considerable time, energy and resources into launching the new degree. It has to be recalled that the BEd debate in the period between the Robbins and James Reports took place against the background of a wider debate about the nature of higher education as the country sought to come to terms with the concept of what some commentators had begun to call 'mass' higher education. For the validating universities this was not a theoretical discussion; practical questions had to be analyzed, debated and answered. Evidence could be found somewhere for each of the James criticisms but the total picture painted was regarded by the validating universities as almost a caricature. However, as Lord James knew well, the university monopoly of degree-giving had been broken and the Council for National Academic Awards (CNAA) now offered an alternative which, as the writers of the note of extension to the James Report declared[11], displayed a liberal attitude. On the part-time side, serving teachers could turn to the Open University which began to provide, from January 1971, a BA (Educational Studies). Indeed there were some representatives of the more reluctant universities who felt that the combination of CNAA provision with that of the Open University offered an opportunity for universities to withdraw entirely from the field. The colleges, represented collectively through their professional body, the Association of Teachers in Colleges and Departments of Education, were not slow to seize upon the possibilities made available in the new situation. The links between the universities and the colleges they validated were close enough to provide for the ATCDE to nominate a member to each of the committees of the Universities Council for the Education of Teachers. The James Report was barely in the hands of the public when an ATCDE representative, Mr Norman Payne, at a UCET meeting, stated that

> as a Principal, his responsibilities were to the university, to the Area Training Organization, but most of all to the students. He had to consider the implications for his students not only at the moment but in twenty to twenty-five years time. How could he describe what would be best for them until he knew what the universities' answer to James was going to be? If the universities were going to insist on a university-validated diploma (DipHE) and say that only a few exceptional students might get two years' remission, he might well feel he should ask CNAA what they would offer a diploma holder. CNAA and the Open University both appeared quite willing to take on the job of validation.[12]

The first CNAA initial training BEd degree had been validated in 1971 and it was now clear that henceforth a college was free to seek validation from its local university or from the CNAA. An open market having been created, the need for central coordination, at least to the extent of establishing a common framework within which individual decisions could be made, was essential. A further implication was that the area training organizations, in which much of the BEd debate had been conducted, were approaching the end of their existence.

The debate following the James Report of 1972 brings to an end the first stage of the development of the BEd degree. The degree as it had evolved was an enhanced and extended certificate course often spoken of as having a 3 + 1 structure. Because of the difficulty of managing a system which put a student at the end of the third year in the position of having to decide to take a proffered post or decline it in order to stay a further year for the degree course made possible by achievements in the terminal certificate examination, there was a strong trend towards a 2 + 2 pattern with the certificate/degree decision being taken at the end of the second year. The degree was still seen by both universities and the CNAA as something reserved for the selected few. On the in-service side it had taken a little longer to get the degree launched but by the early 1970s there was widespread provision. Table 4.1 gives the picture as it existed in 1974.

Table 4.1 Universities awarding BEd degrees up to 1974

	Initial		**In-Service**	
	1968	*1974*	*1973*	*1974*
Universities awarding BEd in the year stated	5	23	23	23
Candidates sitting in that year	234	4961	377	768
Percentage of relevant certificate intake (ITT only)	1.0	14.0	N/A	N/A
BEd degrees awarded in the year stated	219	4747	372	751
Percentage of above gaining good honours	31.5	53.6	66.4	63.5

Source: Lancaster University School of Education Delegacy, 30 November 1974.

The higher percentage of good honours degrees awarded in the in-service category indicates the high quality of the serving teachers who though already qualified and experienced submitted themselves to the rigours of returning to study in mid-career. The overall picture at this point is one of careful, perhaps cautious, exploration of the new territory. The challenge of Robbins had been met and standards had undoubtedly been maintained. BEd graduates with high honours had been admitted to PhD programmes and experienced serving teachers had found their graduate qualification of value in developing their careers. The degree was still, however, something taken by the minority and the goal of an entirely graduate-entry profession still seemed to be a long way off. That situation was to be changed in the course of the 1970s.

Reorganization and Coordination

The debate on the James Report turned out to be as short-lived as it was intense for it was rapidly followed by a strong initiative from government in the form of a White Paper, *Education: A Framework for Expansion* (1972, Cmnd. 5174,

HMSO). This confirmed what had become known for some time, that the birth rate had reached a peak as long ago as 1964 and that what many thought was a mere dip in an undulating pattern had now become a strong and continuing downward trend. The information was given little attention by the James Committee though the report does have one noteworthy sentence:

> To put it bluntly, the supply of new teachers is now increasing so rapidly that it must soon catch up with any likely assessment of future demand, and choices will have to be made very soon between various ways of using or diverting some of the resources at present invested in the education and training of teachers.[13]

The White Paper of 1972 also had major recommendations to make concerning the area training organizations and these are dealt with elsewhere in this volume though it should be noted that an incidental effect was to loosen the ties between a university and its local affiliated colleges.

As regards the BEd degree itself, the paper supported the idea of a DipHE as recommended by the James Committee and called, for demographic reasons, for the number of teacher training places to be nearly halved in the next decade. Clearly the DipHE was seen as providing alternative work for the colleges. On the James proposal for abolishing the BEd degree, the White Paper decided that 'there is now greater support for those wishing to commit themselves to teaching at an early stage than there appeared to be when the (James) Committee were engaged on their task'.[14] It then made the suggestion that there should be introduced as soon as possible:

> new three-year courses incorporating educational studies which are so designed that they will lead both to the award of BEd degree and to qualified status. The degree would normally be an ordinary BEd degree with the assumption that a proportion of students who attain a sufficiently high standard in the three-year course could, if they wished, continue for a fourth year to take an honours BEd degree. The normal entry requirement would be the same as for universities and the academic content no less rigorous than that of existing degree courses. The length of the college of education year would also permit the inclusion of at least fifteen weeks' supervised practical experience in a three-year course.[15]

The White Paper displays a determination to meet the point about maintenance of standards. Since 40 per cent of college entrants had the two 'A' level minimum entry standard specified for normal entry to the BEd that would produce too few teachers so it recommended that the certificate programme (for less well-qualified students) should continue[16]; it did not disappear until 1980. There was no guidance as to the acceptable (in Treasury terms since students awards were involved) proportion to be entered for the honours year. Such advice was never given, this being regarded as a matter for academic and professional judgment best left to the colleges and the validating bodies. In practice the proportion steadily increased and many colleges had, by the eighties, eliminated their ordinary degree stream. Four-year programmes became the norm.

The CNAA, having validated its first BEd degree in 1971, was well embarked on the validation of colleges which had decided to leave university validation. The authors of the White Paper were able to report[17] that the CNAA had declared its willingness to validate this new three-year degree which was to include the professional qualification. It now became important not only to seek a measure of agreement across the universities but also across the so-called binary divide, i.e. between the universities on the one hand and the CNAA on the other and steps were taken to achieve this.

The New BEd

The White Paper of 1972 had pressed the case for the two-year Diploma of Higher Education which the James Committee had proposed. A transbinary conference held in January 1973 set up a study group to produce guidelines for this new award. On 18 June 1973 the work of that study group was received at a further conference convened by Sir Kenneth Berrill, then Chairman of the UGC, and Dr Edwin Kerr, the then Chief Officer of the CNAA. It was at this second conference that another study group was set up to produce guidelines for the new BEd degree. By the end of the year guidelines were available and were endorsed by a conference comprising representatives of the University Grants Committee, the Council for National Academic Awards, the Open University, the Association of Teachers in Colleges and Departments of Education, the Committee of Directors of Polytechnics and the Association of Principals of Technical Institutes. Mr Arthur Luffman, Chief Inspector for Teacher Training, was present as an observer. There can be no doubt about the historical significance of this event; though based upon consensus it represented the first move towards the centralization of decisions about the overall structure and balance of content of the BEd degree.

The agreement, headed 'A New BEd Degree', was issued under the joint auspices of the UGC and the CNAA and provided the blueprint for the next generation of BEd degrees. The guidelines called for a fully integrated concurrent degree programme and not one based on the old three years (certificate) plus one year (degree) sequence. An honours variant and adequate provision for serving teachers was also specified. Whilst standard entry qualifications were to be required there should also be special arrangements for mature students and for less well-qualified students admitted to the certificate course but judged to be capable of being switched to the more demanding degree course. Some members of the group thought that given the longer college year it might be possible to offer an honours degree programme in three years but the majority view was that for an honours award a further year's study was required. The decision to proceed to an ordinary degree (one year more) or honours (two years more) should normally be taken at the end of the second year. The White Paper suggestion of at least fifteen weeks of teaching practice was endorsed. So was established what is recognizably the BEd degree of today. The certificate course was (with one or two minor exceptions) withdrawn in 1980 and once the new pattern was established many colleges, with the agreement of their universities, withdrew the three-year ordinary degree version and recruited only students capable of tackling the full honours degree programme.

This intervention was to lead to other initiatives from the centre which further shaped the degrees in education being validated by universities and the CNAA. The failure of the attempt undertaken in the dying days of the Labour government in 1970 to create a professional body to control standards in the teaching profession left a vacuum gradually filled by succeeding Secretaries of State operating under the powers implicit in their responsibilities to ensure an adequate supply of teachers. In 1973 the Secretary of State created an Advisory Council on the Supply and Training of Teachers (ACSTT) which, though concentrating initially on the statistical exercise needed to reduce dramatically the number of teachers in training, also began to consider questions of degree content which formerly might be thought to have belonged more properly to the validating bodies. This wider sphere of interest was made clearer in the title given in 1980 to ACSTT's successor body, the Advisory Council on the Supply and Education of Teachers (ACSET). These bodies, serviced and advised by the DES and HMI, were used to bring forward, in discussion with university, CNAA and union representatives, views about the BEd degree being evolved within the DES as it responded to the ever-growing concern within government about the content of teacher training courses. The representative nature of these advisory bodies obviously put limits to the extent to which more radical policies could be developed under their *imprimatur* and when ACSET came to the end of its life it was replaced, in 1984, not by a further representative body but by a small body of people nominated in their personal capacity by the Secretary of State, called the Council for the Accreditation of Teacher Education (CATE). When that body came to the end of its life in 1989 it was reformed on the same lines and on a permanent basis. CATE has the power to recommend to the Secretary of State whether a BEd degree programme is suitable for the preparation of teachers. Universities are well used to dealing with professional bodies and their requirements for professional recognition; the difference here is that CATE is not a professional body but consists of the nominees of the politician who happens *pro tempore* to hold the post of Secretary of State. We have yet to experience what this unusual system will produce when a change of government involving a different political party takes place. For present purposes it is sufficient to record that the minutes of university Senates in the 1980s rarely record discussions on the BEd as detailed or as frequent as those which occurred in the 1970s. Though responsibility for standards remained with the validating bodies, questions of shape and content were now being determined elsewhere.

Further Developments

The White Paper of 1972 had major implications for the colleges in which the validated BEd was being taught. The story of the rationalization of the 1980s is told elsewhere. Most BEd colleges 'diversified' into providing other academic and professional programmes. In part this was a device to help colleges cope with the considerable reduction in their teacher training numbers but it was also a means of extending higher education opportunities at a relatively low unit of cost. The development of college-taught BA, BSc, and other non-teacher education degrees led to the creation of larger academic subject departments staffed by lecturers who had not necessarily taught in schools. This made it possible for such colleges to respond well to demands from CATE for BEd degree programmes to contain substantial amounts of 'pure' subject knowledge. Smaller colleges unable to diversify in this way sought to meet the demand for more 'subject' teaching by turning to their validating university for assistance with the teaching. There are instances now of college students spending up to a year of their four-year programme resident in their validating university, often reading their subject alongside the university's internal students.

For universities, college diversification into providing non-teacher training degrees raised a question as to whether the service developed because of the historical links and the special position of education should be extended to include the validation of degrees in other fields. Lord Boyle of Handsworth, who had played a significant part in developing the validation of BEd degrees in his own University of Leeds, had no doubts. 'It was of course essential, following the James Report, that if universities were to continue to validate college courses they had in principle to be prepared to award not only BEd degrees but also BA degrees.'[18] This was the view generally taken and, contrary to the expectations of some, the universities have remained a significant force in the validation of the BEd and other degrees. By 1982, of the seventy-five polytechnics and colleges offering the BEd (three and four-year schemes), thirty-nine were being validated by universities and the same number by the CNAA. Thus, though the university monopoly had been broken, the universities retained an important place. In 1978 Dr William Taylor, then Director of the University of London Institute of Education, told a conference sponsored by UCET and CVCP that university validation maintained a wider university influence especially in the education of the nation's teachers, offered an alternative to the CNAA, preserved the long-standing associations valued by many colleges and blurred the divisions imposed by the binary system of higher education.[19]

Some idea of the current scale of the university contribution can be obtained from a survey by the Council of Validating Universities in December 1988 which included Scotland and Northern Ireland as well as England and Wales. No less than 30,937 full-time equivalent students in public sector institutions were reading for university awards. Of these 11,772 were reading

full-time for the BEd degree; many of the other awards bei
in the field of education (for example, 2450 reading for the P
were significant numbers in other categories (for example,
the BA or the BSc). It is clear that comments on university v
the mid-1970s onwards refer to much more than validation of the BEd d

University validation was said to have a particular approach. A DES sponsored study (McNamara and Ross, 1982) noted the contrast between

> university styles (local, less bureaucratic, in some cases more relaxed as regards course adjustments but highly dependent upon the personal relationships established) and the CNAA style (national, more bureaucratic, more demanding in documentation but leaving more autonomy once the course has been approved).[20]

This more relaxed approach did not find favour with a 1985 Committee of Enquiry[21] into academic validation. This reported that the twenty-seven validating universities in England and Wales had responsibility for 9160 initial training BEd students and 2864 in-service BEd students.[22] The Committee's impression was that

> at its best university validation can be a highly effective means of maintaining and improving the academic standards of public sector degree courses. But the very features which can make it so effective — the close, personal relationships combined with the minimum of formal control — also have the potential in certain circumstances to lead to complacency and lack of rigour and challenge.[23]

To promulgate best practice in the field of university validation, the CVCP produced, as part of its response to this enquiry, *University Validation of Courses in the Polytechnic and Colleges Sector: Code of Practice* in May 1987 and this has become the basis for regular monitoring by the CVCP of validation practices. University validation, based as it is on independent activities of separate chartered institutions, can never be compared directly with that of the CNAA which operates under one charter. The untidiness which it presents to the eye of the seeker after uniformity does, however, also permit the development of the new relationships called for in an ever-changing situation. Two contrary tendencies in university validation can be identified as the final decade of the century unfolds: one is for a greater measure of autonomy to be extended to the colleges whilst the other is for an even more intimate relationship in which the validated institution increasingly operates virtually as an internal faculty of the university.

Within the Walls

This chapter emphasized the work of universities in validating BEd degrees taught in the colleges associated with them. However, as mentioned at the tset, the universities have also had internal experience of providing four-year programmes of study leading 'concurrently' to the award of a degree and a teaching qualification. This older tradition (Edwards and Lloyd, 1980), particularly strong in the University of Wales, was given new life when in 1951 the newly-created University College of North Staffordshire (later the University of Keele) offered a programme involving two honours degree subjects and a subsidiary subject together with the study of education theory and practice. Other universities developed similar patterns especially when, as a result of mid-1970s rationalization, colleges were merged into universities. The traditional concurrent BA or BSc courses have continued throughout the period but when colleges were absorbed into the universities their BEd degrees were gradually modified and in most cases were given the title of BA or BSc. When the subject teaching was done entirely in the faculty of education large departments ensued; Exeter and Warwick both of which absorbed colleges now have the largest university schools of education outside London. Where subject teaching was allocated to the existing university subject departments (Durham is an example) those departments had the advantage of increased student numbers. Mergers with colleges, leading to an increased university presence in BEd (or equivalent) provision, continue to occur: in 1988 Goldsmiths College became a School of the University of London and in 1989 Bulmershe College was merged into the University of Reading. These colleges were not included in the 1988 first destination survey of university trained teachers (Universities Council for the Education of Teachers, 1989): without them the universities produced 413 four-year trained teachers and this figure will rise steadily as the increased intakes of the late 1980s being to emerge. In April 1989, the DES allocated to the Universities Funding Council (for distribution between universities in England and Wales) a total of 1252 admissions to four-year initial training courses. Though the validation of externally taught BEd degrees remains an important part of the university contribution, there is also a significant growth in that older — perhaps too long neglected — tradition of offering within the university opportunities to those who are ready at entry to commit themselves to a career in teaching.

Conclusion

From 1963 (the Robbins Report) to 1973 (the agreement on the 'new' BEd degree) the validating universities interacted with their colleges to provide a variety of solutions to the problem of creating a new professional degree. At the same time the CNAA began to develop alternative provision. The 1973 agreement marked the start of a second phase of increasing standardization linked to a growing tendency for validation to take place within an ever-more detailed prescription laid down by government and its agents. The Council for the Accreditation of Teacher Education (1984, renewed 1989) marks the culmination of this centralizing process. Bottom-up (with its variations) has been replaced by top-down (with its uniformity). The main achievement is that within a generation teaching has (with a few exceptions) become a graduate entry profession. The validating universities together with the CNAA can rightfully claim a measure of praise for their contribution to this notable achievement.

Notes

1 Department of Education and Science (1963) *Report on Higher Education* (The Robbins Report), London, HMSO, chapter 9.
2 Minute of Conference of Institute Directors, 23 March 1964, quoted p. 231 of Niblett *et al* (1975).
3 Willey and Maddison (1971) p. 8.
4 Select Committee, 21 April 1970, Q 1244ff.
5 Select Committee, 15 April 1970, Q 1202.
6 Select Committee, 15 April 1970, p. 414.
7 Department of Education and Science (1972) *Teacher Education and Training* (The James Report), London, HMSO, paragraph 3.36.
8 *ibid.*, para. 3.34.
9 *ibid.*, p. 78.
10 *ibid.*, para. 3.36.
11 *ibid.*, p. 78.
12 Universities Council for the Education of Teachers Ms Minutes Standing Committee A, 3 February 1972.
13 DES (1972) *op cit*, para. 6.21.
14 White Paper (1972) *A Framework for Expansion* (Cmnd 5174), London, HMSO, para 74.
15 *ibid.*, para 75.
16 *ibid.*, para 79.
17 *ibid.*, para 76.
18 Committee for Vice Chancellors and Principals (CVCP) (1978) *The Universities and Teacher Education*, London, CVCP, p. 48.
19 *ibid.*, p. 17.
20 McNamara and Ross (1982) p. 54.
21 Department of Education and Science (1985) *Academic Validation in Public Sector Higher Education* (Cmnd 9501) (The Lindop Report), London, HMSO.
22 *ibid.*, p. 16.
23 *ibid.*, p. 19.

References

EDWARDS, P. and LLOYD, G. (1980). *An Evaluation of the Concurrent Sandwich Degree and Certificate in Education at the University of Bath*, Bath, The University. Occasional Paper.

MCNAMARA, D.R. and ROSS, A.M. (1982). *The BEd Degree and its Future*, Lancaster. The University.

NIBLETT, W.R., HUMPHREYS, D.W. and FAIRHURST, J.R. (1975). *The University Connection*, Windsor, NFER.

UNIVERSITIES COUNCIL FOR THE EDUCATION OF TEACHERS (1989), *First Destination Survey of Students completing University courses of initial training for the teaching profession in 1988*, London UCET.

WILLEY, F.T. and MADDISON, R.E. (1971), *An Enquiry into Teacher Training*, London, University of London Press Ltd.

Chapter 5

The James Report and Recent History

Peter Gosden

The James Report

The main characteristics of the history of teacher education during the last two decades have been strong criticism of the system for failing to produce the sort of teachers and teaching which the critics have thought were needed; various reforms and changes — both institutional and curricular — designed to meet these criticisms; and an acute need in the earlier years to reduce drastically the number of teachers entering employment. The appointment of the James Committee owed much to the first of these characteristics. In retrospect its positive recommendations did little to meet the criticisms from which its appointment sprang and it did not face the issue of contraction. On the other hand the publication of the Report served to mark the end of a series of policies going back over some years, and finding expression in both the McNair and Robbins Reports, which had associated colleges devoted to training teachers ever more closely with the universities in both an administrative and academic sense.

While the government announced its acceptance of the recommendations of the Robbins Report in 1963 within a day of its publication, the administrative and organizational arrangements which it put forward were the object of a good deal of opposition from the Ministry of Education. The Committee envisaged a Ministry of Arts and Science incorporating the existing Science Ministry and looking after the universities and higher education. The training colleges or colleges of education were to receive their grant-aid through the UGC and thus become part of the university sector. Sir Herbert Andrew, the Permanent Secretary at the Ministry of Education, argued strongly that his Ministry should take over those functions regarding science and higher education and they passed to the renamed Department of Education and Science in 1964.[1] The Department by that time did not share the Robbins Committee's vision of the universities being so central to higher education. The unpublished belief within the office was that the universities were so strongly wedded to a form of first degree consisting of single subject honours that they were very unlikely to provide the diversity of courses which it was thought the nation really ought to require of its higher education system. It was largely for this reason that the policy of the 'binary system' was developed and public sector institutions built up. Their purpose was to provide courses in line with what the Department saw as national needs.[2] Thus by the 1980s student numbers had come to be divided roughly equally between the universities and public sector institutions instead of being overwhelmingly in universities as recommended by Robbins.

It followed from this that the policies pursued in the 1920s and 1930s and taken still further at the time of the McNair Report of bringing colleges increasingly into the university sphere of influence could not be continued indefinitely. By the end of the 1960s strong criticism of the schools as expressed archetypically in the Black Papers[3], led to even stronger criticism of the training institutions which were identified in the minds of critics as the source whence flowed poorly prepared and inadequately educated teachers. Within the Department there was a feeling that once the rapid expansion of the colleges to meet the bulge in the number of pupils was over and things settled down, quality would improve and a committee of inquiry was not necessary. When Margaret Thatcher replaced Edward Boyle as Opposition spokesman on education, she reflected the more radical and critical attitude which was gaining ground in her party so that when she became Secretary of State after the 1970 election, an enquiry into the training of teachers became very probable. She wanted 'a quick report' covering the content and organization of courses and recommendations on the roles of colleges of education, polytechnics and universities although they were also to assume that 'local authority maintained institutions will continue to play a major part in higher education'.[4] The choice of Chairman for the enquiry of one who had been a leading critic of the teacher training system as it had been developed, made it the more likely that the removal of universities from the administration of the training system would be recommended along with the assimilation of teacher training into public sector higher education generally, thus completing the division required by the binary policy. The manner in which the Committee took its business made it unlikely that any evidence or representations would have much impact. It spent the first few months evolving its own views before receiving outside evidence. When the evidence came to be considered, it seems to have been regarded as confirmation of attitudes and conceptions which had been already refined.

Apart from the Chairman, the Committee had six members, one of whom was drawn from the universities. In examining the existing system it found that in concurrent courses which the great majority of teachers followed, much of the theoretical study of education was irrelevant and that the inclusion of theoretical study in initial training courses was 'often at the expense of adequate practical preparation for their first teaching assignments'. Concurrent courses also suffered from a confusion of objectives and a tension between the personal education of students and their professional preparation. The criticism of the theoretical aspects of initial courses had been made by Black Paper critics and has continued to be voiced by recent Secretaries of State, Keith Joseph and Kenneth Baker. In a speech to the North of England Conference in 1989, the latter was reported to have singled out study of theory in general and the history of education in particular as being a misuse of time. It followed that far more emphasis needed to be spent on practical work in schools.

Against this context the Report recommended that teacher training be divided into three stages or cycles. The first should consist of a course of study leading to a higher education award, either a degree or, it was proposed, a two-year course leading to diploma in higher education, a DipHE. Admission to the second cycle was to be open to those who had attained a degree or DipHE and was to consist of pre-service training and induction, this would cover two years, the first training and the second largely school-based training as a 'licensed' teacher. Successful completion of two years in this cycle would carry with it the award of a 'professional degree of BA (Education)'. The BEd should cease to exist as an initial qualification although it might continue as an in-service award. The third cycle was to cover in-service training. All teachers were to be entitled to leave with pay for one term in seven years, the scale being improved to one term in five years in due course. The university-based ATO system (discussed previously in this volume) should be abolished, fifteen Regional Councils for Colleges and Departments of Education should be set up. Above these RCCDEs there was to be an NCTET (National Council for Teacher Education and Training). This would have the power to award the BA (Education) and all in-service professional awards to be dependent upon its recognition and approval. On the pressing issue of the numbers taking initial training courses, the Committee provided no data or recommendations, but did comment that the supply of new teachers was increasing so rapidly that choices would have to be made between various ways of using or diverting some of the resources invested in the education and training of teachers.[5] While the Committee's terms of reference did not require it to report on numbers, in retrospect it was odd that it did not and turned away from this issue. This serves to confirm that the setting up of the Committee was in a political sense the product of increasingly severe criticism of the schools' level of achievement. Administratively it provided an opportunity to seek to make complete the application of the binary system.

Education: A Framework for Expansion

The James Report was completed in December 1971 and published early the next year. The controversy which it stirred was considerable and it was nearly a year before the government's response appeared as part of the White Paper, *Education: a Framework for Expansion*, in December 1972. The government did not wish to see a virtual end to concurrent courses but rather wished to see the ordinary BEd awarded after three year courses and the honours BEd after four years of initial training, such degrees carrying qualified teacher status. At the time no more than 40 per cent of entrants to colleges of education had the minimum entrance requirement of two 'A' level passes proposed for entry to BEd courses and in the short term it seemed that there would not be enough suitably qualified applicants to meet the needs of the schools. For this reason certificate courses would need to be offered for a while. The second cycle degree of BA (Education) was not acceptable.[6] As for organization, there were four functions to be considered. Academic validation should continue with universities or the CNAA as might be decided at the institutional level. Professional recognition of the newly-qualified was to be decided by members of the teaching profession acting through the training institutions whose staff were themselves members of the profession. On coordination at the regional level the White Paper stated that the government intended to set up suitable regional machinery but hoped that ATOs would continue to discharge their existing responsibilities in this respect in the meantime. The fourth and final organizational activity, supply, was a matter for the central government and the Secretary of State had it in mind to set up an Advisory Committee on the Supply and Training of Teachers to help with advice from the other partners in the system when considering questions related to numbers to be trained and supply generally.[7]

Of the other recommendations in the James Report, the government welcomed the proposal for two-year courses leading to a Diploma in Higher Education. This was hardly surprising for it was the DES which had tried in the late 1960s to persuade universities to offer two-year degree courses in an effort to offer higher education to larger numbers on a cheaper basis. Thus the White Paper welcomed the recognition by the James Committee of the potential of two-year courses and went on to suggest that they should serve a much wider purpose than that envisaged in the Report, claiming that recent consultations showed that there was sufficient support for their introduction. It proposed that this new option should be offered in both sectors of higher education and that both generalized and specialized courses should be made available. Students taking these courses were to qualify for mandatory awards on the same basis as degree students. The courses were to be validated by existing degree award bodies. The CNAA had already indicated its willingness to undertake this, the government believed that a number of universities would wish to offer the diploma themselves and be prepared to validate courses 'where colleges do not seek validation from the CNAA'. These proposals for a two-year diploma came to very little because they seemed to offer a second best form of higher education.[8] Since universities were in general unwilling to offer the diploma, there seemed little point in 'leaning on' the more 'socially responsive' public sector institutions to make very much of this initiative.

Perhaps the most widely agreed, and certainly the most necessary, of the James Committee's recommendations had been for a large increase in the amount of in-service and continued education for teachers.[9] The government accepted the thrust of this and firmly set as its aim a substantial expansion of in-service training beginning in 1974/75 with the achievement of the target of releasing the equivalent of 3 per cent of the total teaching body for continued professional education by 1981.[10]

By the time the White Paper was published events had moved at such a rate that it was essential to face the numbers issue and to give some indication of likely policies for dealing with the reduction in the demand for newly-trained teachers. This matter was taken up as part of the expansion and development of public sector higher education. The case for more places in polytechnics and colleges of higher education was set out. It was then forecast that as against the 114,000 initial training places in colleges and departments of education in polytechnics in 1971, no more than 60,000–70,000 would be needed by 1981. The reduction in teacher training places would enable some of those places to be used for students of arts subjects and the human sciences, some colleges would be expected to combine with polytechnics or other colleges of higher education. But many of the 160 colleges were comparatively small or inconveniently located for development into larger institutions; of these some would need to continue as teacher education colleges with increasing attention to in-service work. 'Some must face the possibility that in due course they will have to be converted to new purposes; some may need to close'. Any fusion of a college of education with a university was not completely ruled out, but it was made comparatively unlikely by the requirement that a university's numbers thus enlarged would have to form part of the total target numbers for university students as set out elsewhere in the White Paper.[11] Teacher education for the next decade was to be dominated by issues arising from contraction rather than by the recommendations of the James Report.

In-service Education for Teachers

The only James recommendation to be fully achieved was to abolish the university-based area training organizations for which Eric James himself had so little time. Their abolition as obstacles to the fulfilment of the binary policy's structure was achieved in 1975. Efforts to set up some sort of alternative machinery for the coordination of initial and in-service training at the regional level had by that time been unavailing and in the teacher education field they have never been replaced. In fact in some regions former ATO arrangements have continued to coordinate in-service provision and to facilitate the coordination of teaching practice arrangements. Proposals to replace the ATOs became intermingled with regional coordination arrangements for public sector higher and further education. Universities saw in the public sector regional machinery for this a threat to their autonomy and they have not been prepared to subject themselves to it. The initial proposal from the DES was for regional committees for teacher education to include employers, teachers and training institutions, funded directly by the DES. This led to a counter proposal from local authorities for Further Education Advisory Councils for the Region which would have placed the coordination of INSET in a sub-committee of a public sector regional council concerned mainly with further education and was unacceptable to the universities. This is not the place to study the governance of public sector higher education, but some ten years after James, the increasing central government control over higher education led to the setting up of the National Advisory Body (NAB) by the DES (WAB in Wales established by the Welsh Office.) Through these bodies the two government departments attempted to handle public sector initial teacher training places.

Arrangements for the regional coordination of INSET have varied a good deal across the country. Local cooperative arrangements have been worked out in some regions but the voluntary nature of many of these arrangements mean that any institution which was determined enough to offer a course or courses without local agreement was free to do so and to attract students as best it could.

While the government accepted a target of releasing 3 per cent of the teaching body for INSET each year with a reasonable proportion taking courses of more than three months it looked as though demand for courses would increase greatly. Yet six years after the White Paper barely 1 per cent were in fact receiving secondment.[12] At the same time government policy encouraged the colleges and polytechnics to make increasing provision of INSET courses, partly to take up some of the slack. The development of in-service diplomas in teacher education had been one of the fruits of the university institutes set up under the ATO system. The university schools of education, into which most of the institutes merged, continued to offer diplomas and they also offered on an increasing scale one-year full-time as well as part-time higher degree courses. Competition for the teachers being seconded by local authorities intensified noticeably. As the pupil rolls fell in schools, some local authorities felt able to take a more generous attitude towards the secondment of teachers. The greater part of the cost could be charged against the 'pool' to which all authorities contributed. The operation of the pooling system meant that those authorities who released the largest numbers of teachers gained the greatest benefit. Thus the falling rolls pressure and the pooling incentive led especially to a noticeable increase in the number of secondees taking higher degrees in education. By 1983/84, 1970 teachers spent the full year taking a higher degree, overwhelmingly in universities, whereas ten years earlier the total number had only been 407. In contrast the total number of full-year secondments to all courses in colleges and universities over the same period had only increased from 3142 (1973/74) to 4637 (1983/84).[13] The significant factor in this expansion of masters' degree students was undoubtedly the development of this provison by university schools of education as a response to the increasing competition from public sector institutions offering diplomas and certificates.

Government pressure to end any form of pooling which appeared to encourage public expenditure led to the ending of the pool for teacher secondments after 1986. The Advisory Committee on the Supply and Education of Teachers had reported on in-service arrangements in 1984 and it was against this background that the changes were made. In line with general government policy, the ACSET Report was based on the idea that in-service training for employees was the business of individual employers. Thus local authorities were to be offered grants for in-service training and each authority was to develop its own policies with much less direct 'steering' from the DES. All INSET courses lasting for less than one-term full-time were to have their directly attributable costs met through fee income: institutions were to charge on top of that whatever contribution to overheads the market would bear. The Committee urged that every school's needs should be reviewed each year.[14]

The adoption of the subsequent GRIST (Grant-Related In-Service Training) system has in practice had the effect of almost ending full-time secondment for as long as a year and has therefore left the full-time masters' degree courses in university schools of education largely denuded of UK students although often well supported by overseas students. In like manner full-time diploma courses are often no longer viable. A much larger number of teachers have come to work for higher degrees and diplomas on a part-time basis. Local authorities sometimes reimburse the fees they pay but quite often do not do so. The resources made available to local authorities have been spent on providing short — often very short — courses on some aspects of the curriculum. In spite of repeated representations the government has declined to take any steps to ensure that some provision might still be made for the longer courses. Critics have suggested that the new policy was more suited to instructing operatives in new production techniques rather than to developing the potential in members of a professional group.[15]

In 1971 45,600 students embarked on courses on concurrent training for BEd degrees or certificates in public sector institutions. The number so admitted in 1980 was 8700. The detailed story of this enormous reduction is no part of the concern of this chapter save that the great majority of the students in 1971 would have been preparing for university awards through the ATO system. That was no longer the case for the entrants of 1980. The general expectation of the White Paper had been that with the ending of the colleges of education as a sector of higher education and their assimilation to the polytechnics and public division, the students preparing to teach would in general take CNAA awards. The situation did not turn out quite as planned. Many teacher education colleges succeeded in maintaining their links with universities while a perhaps surprisingly large number of universities took steps to sustain their links with the colleges and to set up new machinery to facilitate that after the demise of the ATOs.

University Validation

The fall in the number of teacher training places led not only to college closures but to very sharp reductions in the permitted entry in remaining institutions.

Those colleges which were not closed were expected to diversify and to offer courses in the arts and social science areas as part of the total national provision for higher education generally. Thus the existing ATO machinery, restricted as it was to the award of teachers' qualifications, had in many universities to be replaced by arrangements which offered validation across a much broader spread of schemes of study and degrees. The alternative for universities which were unwilling to continue with the new wider forms of validation was to withdraw and end their connection with colleges. This latter course was that chosen by some universities such as London and Newcastle. Many of the universities founded since the Second World War had, for historical reasons, never had an ATO, but in the conditions of flux which existed, some of them, such as Surrey, came to undertake validation for the first time. Among the remaining colleges, some have followed the line which higher education officials within the DES had expected and gone to seek validation of their courses from the CNAA. Many others preferred to maintain and to build upon the existing links with universities while yet others moved their validation arrangements from one university to another.

In order to help themselves in dealing with the issues which this form of activity involved, representatives of universities concerned with it began meeting together. In 1980 there was a 'conference of universities validating awards in former colleges of education' at Leeds University and the Conference and Council of Validating Universities (CVU) emerged as a more formal basis as a result of the conference arranged in 1982. The CVU's purpose was to enable universities collectively to 'register and maintain their interests as validating bodies within the context of the new organizational framework which is emerging for the planning of higher education in the public sector'. The establishment of the NAB and WAB as the funding and planning agencies for the public sector and the possible difficulties this might have led to probably served to be something of a catalyst at the time. By 1989 slightly less than half of the total number of universities were undertaking some form of validation of awards for students in public sector institutions. On 31 December 1988 there were rather more than 28,000 students on full-time courses under these arrangements and of these nearly 15,000 were taking courses of preparation for entry to teaching.[16]

In 1986, on the initiative of the Inspectorate, the future allocation of teacher training places to a number of smaller colleges was made dependent upon the establishment of satisfactory schemes of association with 'more broadly-based higher education institutions'. The was part of the effort which the Inspectorate was making to strengthen the study of the main academic subject in first degree courses carrying qualified teacher status. Of the five colleges, Bishop Grosseteste became associated with the University of Hull, Charlotte Mason with Lancaster and North Riding with Leeds. The suggestion was made against the statement that permitted intakes of students for 1988 and beyond would be reviewed in the light of the progress made in establishing forms of association. Although there are variations in the pattern of the courses set up, essentially they provide for a year of full-time study of their academic subject by students in the appropriate department or school of the university with which their college is associated. It is essentially a practical arrangement designed to bring an academic enrichment to the students' courses beyond that which could be provided from the resources of the smaller colleges standing entirely on their own.[17] The early years of operation of these schemes has so far proved to be successful and beneficial.

UDEs and the PGCE

The collapse in the number of places for initial training had its most marked effect in the university sector on those institutions with which former colleges of education merged. Examples of this were Durham, East Anglia, Warwick and Exeter. More recently, and against a rather different context, Bulmershe College has merged with Reading University. Traditionally university departments of education had seldom been involved in offering three or four-year concurrent initial training courses — certainly not since the early years of the twentieth century. The mergers meant that for the first time the university sector now came to have a significant stake in the teaching of undergraduate courses leading to the BEd. Courses which led only to teaching in three or four years time when employment possibilities in the schools appeared to be so uncertain were bound to find recruitment more difficult than courses leading to a BA or BSc whose graduates could either turn to some other occupation or qualify to teach by taking a one-year PGCE course. The application of the normal 'A' level undergraduate course entry requirements to the BEd following the 1972 White Paper had served to make the recruitment problem more acute. Moreover it was, of course, the very subjects whose graduates found a strong demand for their services elsewhere which had most trouble in recruiting through the BEd. The famine in mathematics and the sciences worsened while very large numbers seeking to specialize in physical education applied for admission. In some universities it was felt that the image of the BEd was itself a deterrent to recruitment so that it came to be replaced by forms of the BA which were arranged in such as way as to be concurrent initial teacher training courses carrying qualified teacher status.

In retrospect the total number of places on PGCE courses in university departments of education has remained remarkably constant at around 5000 during the years of upheaval and contraction for teacher training which followed the James Report. There are a number of factors which produced this stability. The first impact of the fall in school rolls in the 1970s was in the primary schools and the great majority of those who taught in those schools entered teaching through concurrent courses. University-based PGCE courses were overwhelmingly secondary school oriented. Moreover, even when the smaller age cohorts passed into the secondary schools in the 1980s, it was the university sector which produced most of those qualifying in such shortage subject areas as mathematics and science. Even if it had not been fully appreciated earlier, the need to adjust the supply of teachers fairly rapidly made the one-year PGCE course more attractive than the three and four-year concurrent courses when the administration was only too well aware of the need to react quickly to demographic change. In the final major round of cuts in 1982 a reduction of up to 20 per cent was made in the university planning figures while a bigger reduction was made in the public sector. But by 1982 the emphasis in government policy was beginning to move away from numbers towards issues concerned with quality — the quality of courses themselves and the quality of the entry being recruited — and this was to prove helpful to the university sector.

In the later 1970s UCET (the Universities Council for the Education of Teachers) undertook a reexamination of the PGCE and in so doing it reflected a widespread desire in university schools and departments of education to improve and reform the staple course which they offered. The argument was that PGCE courses were too theoretical, too far removed from the problems confronting practitioners in the schools, that they were in the jargon of the time 'irrelevant'. The Report[18] which was published in 1979 found UCET over-optimistic in one respect for it suggested that the one-year PGCE would much more often be followed immediately by serious induction training. But the core of the Report was centred on a discussion of the relationships of education theory and practical issues. Since teaching methods and successful classroom practice were 'theory-loaded' activities, professional preparation for teaching was bound to involve significant theoretical study. But experience showed that if theoretical study and understanding were to have any influence, they must be related to teaching in the school situation. To offer students two terms of the study of theory and one term or its equivalent of school practice in the hope that students would themselves succeed in relating the two was ineffective and inefficient. It was necessary for professional training 'that within the course itself the educational theory included be put to work by students in the analysis of practice and in making practical judgments'. The UCET Report came towards the end of the period when the spread of the comprehensive form of secondary school organization with its very wide sweep of pupil ability and inability had come to make greater demands on teachers.

CATE and HMI

The demographic crisis had hit teacher training at a time when there had been no advisory committee demanding projections of pupil and teacher numbers with the consequence that less attention was being paid in the DES to monitoring the situation that was both desirable and necessary. The Advisory Committee on the Training and Supply of Teachers was set up for a five-year term from 1973/78. Its replacement was delayed by the General Election of 1979 but the Advisory Council on the Supply and Education of Teachers began its five-year term in 1980. To begin with it followed its predecessor and was greatly preoccupied with numbers. But Sir Keith Joseph's critical attitude to the service for which he now held responsibility as Secretary of State had a direct effect on the Advisory Council's affairs. It found itself caught up in the train of events which led to the production of the various criteria to which teacher training courses have been required to conform before they could receive the necessary 'imprimatur' from the Secretary of State. Under the influence of the Rayner Enquiry into its efficiency, the Inspectorate became a good deal more active and in 1982 published a report of its enquiries in the schools on how well newly-qualified teachers were dealing with their tasks. HMI rated over half of all newly-trained teachers as well or very well-equipped for their task and three-quarters as adequately equipped or better, yet the presentation of these findings in the Introduction to the published report and in the press release put the focus of attention on the weaknesses. The summary of findings in the Introduction began 'The overall picture presented by the survey is a mixed one. Many newly-trained teachers are dissatisfied with some aspect of their training; nearly one in four are in some respects poorly equipped with the skills needed for teaching . . .' or again 'many, in both primary and secondary schools, are engaged in teaching subjects in which they have themselves little academic background . . .'[19]

HMI were, of course, closely involved in the work of ACSET and steered through that body the planned criteria for courses for which the criticisms in *The New Teacher in School* prepared the way. In March 1983 a White Paper[20] set out the criteria which included more rigorous selection of students, much more emphasis on the subject content of courses (at least two years of subject study) or, in the case of PGCE entrants, on ensuring their degree was in a subject related to the school curriculum and that training institutions should take steps to secure substantial recent successful school-teaching experience among their staff. The criteria were further refined in ACSET and enforced through a newly appointed Council for the Accreditation of Teacher Education (CATE). The Council, which consisted of the Secretary of State's nominees, was to undertake a review of all existing courses of initial teacher training and to examine any proposals for new courses for which an allocation of students had been made. Courses of initial training could continue or be established only after being recommended by the Council to the Secretary of State for approval. In considering courses, the Council was to draw on all relevant information including submissions by institutions, visits made by its own members of working parties 'and in all cases the findings of HMI visits'.[21]

The criteria which required change in the arrangements in most university PGCE courses were the minimum length of 36 weeks in place of the existing 30 to 32 weeks and the establishment of a programme of regular school teaching experience for members of staff. Apart from their length, many courses needed some other modifications. Courses designed to prepare students for primary work often needed to have more time allocated to preparation for the primary curricular subjects. But perhaps the most obvious intrusion was the procession of visiting parties of inspectors going to university schools and departments of education. The autonomy of universities was respected by the state in a formal sense in that the HMI could only visit by the invitation of the appropriate university authorities, but it was made quite clear that no course would be approved without such an invitation to carry out an inspection. Thus universities which wished to stay in teacher training had no choice in the matter. The value of the visits in a professional sense to the university departments involved was often worthwhile. Assessment through discussion and interchange of ideas proved helpful in various ways, as did the timely support which the visitors were able to give in some instances to the requirements of education for more resources within their institutions. The Inspectorate has a long tradition of seeking to maintain a degree of independence of judgment, but it is very difficult to sustain a claim to independence when HMI are so clearly deployed as part of the checking mechanism of the funding body of the universities, the DES.

The increase in the length of the teaching year resulted in the UGC making additional financial provision for PGCE students in the grant and this has undoubtedly been essential in meeting the additional requirements at a time when universities have been under severe financial pressure, and the cuts in university funding which began in 1981 have had their impact in schools and departments of education as elsewhere. The severe cuts imposed in the summer of 1981 led to the closure of education departments at Aston and Bradford universities. It also produced the proposal from the Vice-Chancellor of Bristol to close education in that university. This latter proposal aroused a great deal of opposition and was not put into effect. But education generally in the universities has had its funding cut and has had to seek early retirements among staff as an economy in the same way as others have had to do. Where it has been possible to secure funds from various sources for short-term and part-time appointments, the financial squeeze has to some extent had the effect of destabilizing staffing arrangements and making it more difficult to undertake longer term planning.

As the 1980s drew to their close, the enactment of the National Curriculum provided a bench-mark against which to make more precise forecasts than hitherto of the likely demand for teachers in the different subjects. The government took the decision in the early 1980s not to follow the demographic decline fully for fear of eliminating training resources which would be needed a few years later with the larger age cohorts which by then were clearly on the way. The target entry figures for the universities and the public sector for the three years up to 1989 showed an increase in the primary output to meet an expansion in pupil numbers while the output of secondary teachers was thought to be in excess of short-term demand, the need for more from the early 1990s was apparent in 1986, before the National Curriculum introduced further more complicated requirements. The actual intake figures are given in table 5.1.

Table 5:1 Initial teacher training intakes England and Wales

	Universities				*Public Sector*			
	Concurrent (BEd/BA)		PGCE		Concurrent (BEd/BA)		PGCE	
	Primary	Secondary	Primary	Secondary	Primary	Secondary	Primary	Secondary
1986	321	242	827	4048	5992	1366	1880	2269
1987	328	294	946	4447	6588	1657	2188	2658
1988	484	315	1068	4350	7162	1691	2659	2454

Source: DES Statistics Branch

Most recently, at the time of writing, ministers have now been convinced of the need to increase the numbers to be admitted to courses by a further 10 per cent. They are also anxious to try to draw in untrained graduates and non-graduates who have had two years of higher education in an effort to meet the likely shortages in some subjects and in certain parts of the country. These persons would be called 'licensed' teachers and their employers would be supposed to train them while on the job.[22] It is for historians a matter of some interest to note that only six years ago, in 1983, Keith Joseph as Secretary of State accepted the advice of ACSET that the admission to teaching of mathematics and science graduates should no longer be permitted without their taking a full course of initial teacher training. Exemption of other graduates from training had been ended from 1973 so that pupils in maintained schools had at least been protected from the ministration of the untrained trying to begin to learn how to teach on the job. One of the reasons given for ending the exemption in 1983 was that 'there is some evidence that intending teachers who would otherwise have trained are dissuaded from doing so by the existence of the training exemption'.[23]

Notes

1 Lord Boyle (1979) 'Government, Parliament and the Robbins Report', Joseph Payne Memorial Lecture, p. 16.
2 Department of Education and Science, Administrative Memorandum 7/65 (6 May 1965), Text of Secretary of State's speech at Woolwich.
3 *Black Paper One: The Fight for Education,* 1969 and subsequent *Black Papers.*
4 AEC, A1098, Margaret Thatcher to William Alexander, 13 August 1970.
5 Department of Education and Science (1972a) *Teacher Education and Training,* London, HMSO, pp. 67–77.
6 Department of Education and Science (1972b) *Education: A Framework for Expansion,* London, HMSO, p. 21.
7 *ibid.,* pp. 26–7.
8 *ibid.,* pp 32–3.
9 Department of Education and Science (1972a) *op cit,* pp. 5–17.
10 *ibid.,* p. 18.
11 *ibid.,* pp. 41–5.

12 Department of Education and Science (1980) *Statistical Bulletin,* 9/80, London, HMSO.
13 Department of Education and Science, *Annual Reports,* 1973–4, p. 12, and 1983–4, p. 39. London, HMSO.
14 ACSET, Report submitted to the Secretary of State, 23 August 1984.
15 *ibid.*
16 Council of Validating Universities: survey of student numbers as at December 1988.
17 Department of Education and Science (1986) Press Release 111/86, 'Sir Keith plans high-quality, cost-effective system for 1990s' and accompanying Parliamentary Answer, 14 May 1986.
18 UCET (1979) *The PGCE Course and the Training of Specialist Teachers for Secondary Schools,* London: UCET.
19 Department of Education and Science (1982) *The New Teacher in School,* HMI Series: Matters for Discussion, London, HMSO, p. 1.
20 Department of Education and Science (1983) *Teaching Quality,* (Cmnd 8836), London, HMSO.
21 Department of Education and Science *Circular 3/84.*
22 Department of Education and Science News 22/89, *Kenneth Baker sets out new initiatives on teacher recruitment,* 27 January 1989.
23 ACSET (1983) 'The entry to teaching of untrained mathematics and science graduates', 20 January 1983.

Chapter 6

The Scottish Universities and Educational Studies

R.E. Bell

Nineteenth Century Beginnings

Edinburgh and St Andrews were, in 1876, the first universities in the English-speaking world to establish chairs of education. Such pioneering by Scottish universities is not difficult to explain. In curriculum they had always been closer to German and other North European models than to English ones and since the beginning of the century there had been no lack of distinguished Scottish advocates of educational studies at a university level. A career structure which made easy the transition from headships to university chairs produced an array of such advocates even in the Senates of all four ancient universities and their campaign was strengthened by the fact that in Scotland there was but one teaching profession with a prestige that might be increasingly threatened but still figured prominently in the national mythology.

The Educational Institute of Scotland, set up in the 1840s to guard such prestige, managed in a remarkable way to combine the roles of trades union and learned body. It not only fought for better working conditions and training but also awarded fellowships and commissioned essay competitions, attracting into membership not only the elementary teachers of the urban poor but also the masters of the secondary schools and members of the Inspectorate as well as university professors in a wide range of subjects. Above all it retained the loyalty of the parish schoolmasters who for centuries had served a national system of schools with its roots far back in the reformation settlement.

By the 1870s there was, of course, no possibility that such a national system, designed for the predominantly rural society and economy of the seventeenth century, could adequately meet modern Scotland's needs. Even in their heyday the reformers' plans had never been fully implemented in some of the country's less prosperous and less enthusiastic areas and the system had certainly proved inadequate to cope either with the demographic changes of the industrial revolution or with the scattered nature of the meagre population in some of the enormous Highland parishes. Even the setting up of a rival national system by the Free Church following the Disruption of the Kirk in 1843 still left many areas of the country without adequate schooling while the teaching standards or personal learning of many parish schoolmasters still fell short of the standard which the national education myth so persistently suggested. Nevertheless in many parishes the system still worked well, particularly in those areas of the north-east where the schools were financially supported and the teaching inspected by the trustees of the Dick Bequest. It was still possible to find village schools with high academic objectives, setting out to prepare promising boys for university entrance and teaching non-elementary subjects such as Latin and higher maths to the mass of their pupils in a way that could still horrify Lowe and other parsimonious and educationally elitist English ministers.

Thus the myth of the learned dominie still had sufficient reality in it to be a potent and flattering ingredient in the Educational Institute's recipe for professional renewal and advancement and great political emphasis came to be laid on the fact that, although it was increasingly a custom more honoured in the breach than the observance, such village schoolmasters had traditionally attended university and even though they rarely graduated (very few Scottish students did bother to take the full degree course or to go through the ceremony before the changes of the late nineteenth century), they had nevertheless been exposed to the cultured atmosphere and ordered set of intellectual excitements considered appropriate for the training of this mainstay of the Scottish teaching tradition.

Public and Parliamentary support for such a view was certainly sufficiently great following the Scottish Education Act of 1872 for the government to adopt a policy permitting the more able male students in the training colleges of Edinburgh and Glasgow to attend university classes at the state's expense and in the decades which followed such attendance become so common that men with university experience began increasingly to dominate the profession, an outcome made easier by the fact that women teachers remained a minority in Scotland with young non-graduate females becoming a major presence in the training colleges only in the 1930s. Eventually therefore it began to seem so natural for the universities to undertake responsibility for the general education even of elementary teachers that by the early 1920s government was able to insist on actual graduation for all male and secondary teachers save those teaching 'practical' subjects.

Against such a background it is easy to understand therefore why the EIS from the very beginning sought a firm academic foothold for their professional concerns within the universities and how two of those universities came to establish chairs of education before any of their English or North American counterparts. Yet the story seems less simple when we remember also that Scotland's two other ancient and equally teacher-orientated universities, Glasgow and Aberdeen, failed to establish any such chairs until three-quarters of a century later, long after many much smaller and much younger establishments elsewhere in the United Kingdom had done so and that even in the twentieth century no Scottish university, with the very recent and experimental exception of Stirling, has ever been allowed to undertake the professional training of teachers.

The origins of such apparent paradoxes are to be discerned in the actual circumstances surrounding the creation of the first two chairs themselves for they resulted not from any simple programme of curricular improvement on the part of enlightened Senates intent on the public good. Rather they were a product of that continuous search for profitable business that necessarily obsessed much of Scotland's university community throughout the nineteenth century for it just happened that in the early 1870s it was the world of schooling that promised particularly rich pickings.

Unlike the 1870 Act in England and Wales, designed merely to 'fill the gaps' in elementary education, the 1872 Act in Scotland was intended to produce a state education system far more complete and coherent than that south of the border. Unlike the English Act it established school boards to cover every district and not merely those in need, while the two major churches, the Established Church of Scotland and its large Free Church rival, handed over all their schools to the new system and to the mercies of a highly authoritarian Scotch (sic) Education Department which oversaw every aspect of school life to an extent unknown in England where a degree of local and church autonomy endured even in the worst days of payment by results. Moreover, the new Scottish state system embraced both elementary and secondary schooling of the prestigious high schools of Edinburgh and Glasgow joining the schools of the poor under their local school boards in a country where there were still few private institutions and most of those in the care of public bodies of one kind or another.

Such a new and broadly-based system could not fail to affect and attract the universities financially. For many years the professors had themselves provided secondary education of a kind in their so-called junior classes, an 'access' facility that often proved cheaper for potential undergraduates than attendance at an actual secondary school. Such professorial concerns were the natural outcome of an arrangement whereby the total earnings of each chair depended on the number of students its holder could attract, with the actual fee, in notes and coins, being placed directly in the professor's hand at the opening of each session. Moreover, as Principal Grant of Edinburgh was fond of pointing out, while the colleges of Oxford, Cambridge and Dublin received an average annual income of as much as £200 from each student, in Scotland it was a mere £12. No wonder therefore that the universities sought to swell their income in any way that seemed reasonable, never rejecting any idea on the grounds of mere tradition or current notions of academic respectability. Enterprising Senate members continually sought rich patrons for promising new ventures. As early as 1831, for example, the Edinburgh Professor Leslie was to be found proposing to a rich Scottish Canon of Westminster that he should endow a Chair of the Theory and Operation of Commerce the activities of which, he wrote . . . 'could be made a delightful class, crowded by students of all ranks, from boys to young lawyers to great proprietors' and successful searches of this kind usually attracted extra government endowments under a Scottish system of university grants that predated any University Grants Committee and, indeed, had originated in pre-union Scotland.

In the aftermath of 1872 it did not take long for Edinburgh University, the youngest and in recent years the most innovative of the four, to see the possible rewards of servicing the new education system. There were plenty of academically respectable German models for such activity in the field of pedagogy and Edinburgh had little difficulty in organizing a submission to the government by all four universities outlining an elaborate system of mass teacher education that they were now prepared to undertake. The government, however, remained unconvinced, preferring to keep the supply and training curriculum of state teachers firmly under its own control. It was willing only to allow the attendance of the more able teacher trainees at university classes in certain subject areas, partly as a political gesture to the dominie myth but partly also, no doubt, because it could mean a saving on training college budgets.

Some observers felt however, that if the universities were to appoint their own experts in pedagogical matters, the Scotch Education Department might eventually view things a little differently. With this in mind, Cook, the Factor of Edinburgh University and a lawyer of some financial influence, saw an opportunity. He happened also to be the most active of the executors of a Trust Fund under the will of the same Canon of Westminster from whom the commerce chair endowment had been fruitlessly sought in 1831. This Canon was in fact none other than Andrew Bell, the creator of the Madras monitorial system, who had left many thousands of pounds intended to spread his educational doctrines throughout Scotland. In the period up to 1872 these funds had been used mainly to establish elementary schools, and such a task was now clearly no longer one for private benefactors. Cook therefore persuaded his fellow executors that Bell's aims could now be better served by the establishment of a chair of education in Scotland's capital and the task was put in hand with the confident expectation that the promised Bell endowment would soon be augmented by funds from Whitehall, where all Scottish government was still firmly situated.

If Edinburgh at this time had a naturally keen interest in augmenting its income, St Andrews University was even more urgently concerned with the business of actually staying in existence. Its student body had shrunk to less than 300 and in the absence of a local training college it could not even hope to play the servicing role in teacher education now being played by the universities of the two major cities. A chair designed to provide actual professional training seemed therefore essential if the university was to profit at all from the post-1872 developments. As luck would have it, St Andrews was both the birthplace and the *alma mater* of Andrew Bell and in due course the Executors received favourably a request that the arrangement in Edinburgh should therefore be extended also to Scotland's oldest and most threatened university. Thus the two institutions were able to make a joint request to government for further funding.

At first this was received very favourably by Aberdare on behalf of a Liberal government and it seemed as if the education chairs would be given a routine supplementary endowment in the style of the recent Edinburgh chairs of engineering and geology but before things could be finalized the General Election of 1874 intervened and for political reasons the new Disraeli government was to prove far less sympathetic.

The origins of this unexpected problem lay in Glasgow where a group of churchmen had set their face firmly not only against both of these particular chairs but against the whole idea of university involvement in pedagogical matters, believing that professional training should remain firmly in the hands of the existing colleges which, they felt, were more likely both to safeguard Christian standards and to be answerable to government than were the universities.

By a quirk of the Scottish legislation, though the Presbyterian churches had handed over their schools to the state, they had been allowed to keep a monopoly of teacher training for elementary schools and this, for many churchmen, provided just that safeguard for the faith that the English bishops had sought by remaining proprietors of actual schools. If university professors were now to be allowed to train elementary teachers then there was no guarantee that even atheism could be excluded from the curriculum let alone the doctrines of rival Presbyterians, Episcopalians or Catholics.

In fact this church control of the training system very soon revealed itself as something of a sham as colleges became more and more dependent on public money and exercised less and less control over the doctrinal purity of their entry and staffing. Even so defence of the faith was still a vigorous rallying cry and could provide those who opposed the introduction of pedagogical studies into the universities on academic grounds or in the belief that good teachers were born and not made with a politically acceptable rhetoric and the chance of some useful alliances.

In the days before there was a Scottish Office or a Secretary for Scotland, Scotland's educational affairs at Westminster were handled by a variety of ministers including the Lord Advocate and the Home Secretary while even the Chancellor of the Exchequer could at that time become personally involved and be directly canvassed over what would now seem the trivial matter of the augmentation of a Scottish chair. All of the ministers answering in the House were embarrassed by a situation which necessitated going back on promises already made and at first they were intent on compromise. At one stage, for example, the St Andrews promise appeared to be dropped in order to save the far more important Edinburgh proposal and although for political reasons, this had to be quickly reinstated, the Chancellor in assuring the House that it had all been 'just a slip of the pen', went on, to express the view that the proposed chairs 'ought to be of a purely scientific nature' and that he understood the Bell money was to be used for teaching the theory and science of teaching and that it was 'not connected with any practical work' and except for a few short years at the turn of the century, such a view was henceforth to be built into all official pronouncements on the chairs and their function. This was to affect their development in a most profound way, the irony being that even after such a fundamental and enduring modification of the chairs' potential role (involving, as it did, a quite misleading interpretation of the trustees' aims) the extra endowments were not forthcoming after all and the two universities, out of deference to the Bell Trustees, were morally obliged to appoint professors whom they did not have the funds to finance even on the modest scale then usual in the Scottish arts faculties.

The new professors, Laurie at Edinburgh and Meiklejohn at St Andrews, were therefore faced with both acute financial difficulties and official disapproval of the mass training programme from which the planners of the chairs had hoped to derive such profits. True, they could, if they wished, train graduates from whom little in the way of training was as yet demanded as well as recruits to the tiny Scottish private sector but, in practice, they were to be entirely dependent on that small band of voluntary students who had an academic enthusiasm for their subject. Later when education had been accepted as a credit-worthy subject in the generalist ordinary degree the task of attracting students would become easier but, for the moment, such an underfunded venture could not even provide the St Andrews professor with a lecture room and he and his tiny classes were forced to seek refuge in his drawing-room.

Any attempts to modify government attitudes, once the heat of the endowment debate had died down, met with further difficulties, the greatest of these arising undoubtedly from the absence of similar chairs in the two other universities. Whenever the professors demanded further training rights they were simply reminded that Edinburgh and St Andrews could hardly be given privileges that could not also be accorded to chairless Glasgow and Aberdeen, a hypocritical enough response given that the universities in the two major cities were already encouraged by government to open their doors to state-financed 'concurrent' students while the two smaller universities still had no nearby colleges to provide such an intake.

Aberdeen in fact had always been anxious to establish its own education chair. The city and its region provided recruits to the teaching profession out of all proportion to the size of their population and for a further century its Arts faculty was to depend largely on future teachers for its students. But the Bell fund sent no funds in its direction and, like St Andrews, it was too small to move without assistance. Glasgow, on the other hand, eventually did have wind of local Bell money but rejected the idea. The University as such had played little if any part in the Glasgow campaign of opposition to the East of Scotland chairs and financial caution provides a better explanation for their lack of keenness. It had recently rebuilt itself at great expense on a green field site following the not entirely satisfactory sale of its medieval location to a city centre developer and at a time when the professor of physiology could earn only £8 in one year, having to pay from private funds for the equipping of his own laboratory, it was hardly the moment to embark on the costly experiment of setting up a probably under-endowed chair in a hitherto untried subject amid government and local opposition.

The increasingly autocratic Secretaries of the Scotch Education Department knew how to take advantage of just such a divided situation and when in the 1890s an expansion of the arts curriculum finally brought education into the Aberdeen and Glasgow programmes, they were no doubt happy to see those universities still refusing to establish chairs and taking the cheaper option of merely appointing local college staff as part-time lecturers in the subject at the university.

The plight of the two professors clearly remained hard, particularly as they had both accepted their posts in the hope of training teachers in the classroom. At various times they compared themselves to medical professors deprived of clinical wards and were both committed to the view that their subject could not simply be studied in abstraction. Yet not all was lost. Both were strong and colourful characters who were not easily put down. Indeed their treatment by government and their inadequate salaries seem to have been less a discouragement than a spur to activity in many useful directions.

Laurie, at the time of his appointment, was already a distinguished philosopher, an Inspector for the Dick Bequest and an advisor to some of the leading educational bodies in Scotland. He was also (somewhat ironically) Secretary of the Established Church's education committee and in one sense therefore an overseer of the Church's three teacher training colleges. He now continued to perform all these tasks and, with the added aura of his novel professorship, he was able to exert an influence, as a writer and lecturer elsewhere in the United Kingdom, out of all proportion to the actual work and academic status of his university appointment. As a leading member of the Teachers' Guild and as an inveterate witness at commissions and enquiries he helped to mould developments in England as much as in Scotland and has rightly been hailed as the father of the day training colleges which owed much to the non-residential models of college and university cooperation provided by Edinburgh and Glasgow.

Meiklejohn was more of a journalist, an ex-war correspondent and a veteran of the Prussian-Danish war, though also distinguished as a translator of philosophy. He was, moreover, a highly successful producer of best-selling school textbooks and of highly readable and influential articles for the educational press.

Neither man fitted our modern stereotype of the earnest Victorian educationist. Both were noted for their wit as after-dinner speakers and both were attacked by the highly serious student newspapers of the time for playing to the gallery. But their contribution to their subject in such highly unfavourable circumstances and the fact that they both remained in office for over a quarter of a century did much to give stability to the subject of education on the British university scene at a time when its position was still far from secure and the notion of such chairs was still far from generally accepted.

Throughout their careers both of the professors persisted in their attempts to embark on full teacher training. Laurie finally established a Schoolmaster's Diploma incorporating a limited amount of practical work in private schools, and aimed his course primarily at budding graduate teachers whose training still lay largely outside government supervision and, despite its title, this helped to swell the numbers of the female students who were increasingly occupying the front rows of his classes. Meiklejohn, on the other hand, persisted in his attempts to embark on general teacher training, attempting to turn to his advantage what had hitherto been considered a great drawback – the fact that St Andrews had no training college to provide him with students. He insisted that under his guidance the university itself could operate in college fashion and thus provide the basis for a local 'concurrent' scheme such as had long operated in Glasgow and Edinburgh. Reacting negatively to his proposals, the Scotch Education Department made it more than ever clear that they would never tolerate any threat to their control of elementary training. In fact, however, Meiklejohn's request sparked off a curious set of events which for a time suggested that teacher training might after all become primarily the responsibility of the universities.

The catalyst was the appearance of a quite new institution in the only major city still without a university, Dundee. There in 1883, largely on local initiative, there was founded a University College initially looking to the external degree system of London and very similar in many other ways to the new 'civic' institutions in England and Wales. The College found it difficult to establish itself, however, and eventually, under an Act of 1889 it entered into an 'association' with St Andrews, a dozen miles away across the Tay. Following the creation of day training colleges in the English university colleges, under the influence of Laurie and other Scots, it seemed to the authorities in St Andrews that the University College in Dundee might well be an appropriate place to establish a Scottish equivalent.

It was now difficult for Craik and the SED to argue that the provision of day training facilities in a large city with no church provision could be out of line with government policy and eventually in 1895 Craik had to announce a new structure that did at last bring the universities into the field of general teacher training alongside the churches. Hitherto all state financed teacher trainees had been college students, some of whom were allowed concurrently to attend university classes. Now a new category of trainees was established, called Queen's Students, who, granted they satisfied the universities' newly introduced entrance requirements, were to be primarily university students who would, where necessary, be allowed to attend concurrent college classes. These Queen's Students' studies, moreover, were to be organized by a university-dominated local committee on which the churches would be merely one element of many representing the community.

This, for Meiklejohn and the authorities in Dundee and Aberdeen, seemed to be a major step towards achieving all that the universities had hoped for in framing their expansionist plans following the Act of 1872 and they proceeded to set up broadly-based local committees which undertook the work with enthusiasm. At St Andrews the Principal himself chaired the Committee not as a mere figurehead but as a dedicated member. It really did seem that at last a national system of teacher training could emerge such as Laurie and Meiklejohn had envisaged in their inaugural lectures, a system firmly based within the universities in accordance with what they saw as the true national tradition and embracing teachers at all social and academic levels.

However, the full realization of any such vision, was that for the moment seriously thwarted by the fact that the two major universities chose to ignore the new scheme altogether for neither Glasgow nor Edinburgh rushed to establish a local committee. In many ways this was not surprising. They were already making an enormous profit out of the classes they provided for college students without the extra burden of maintaining a full-blown training system. Moreover, relations with the local college staffs, partly as a result of the concurrent scheme, had become increasingly close. There was no longer such an urgent feeling that students had to be 'saved' from the college atmosphere. Indeed Glasgow continued to appoint college staff to their own lectureship in education, not least John Adams, the later Head of the London Day Training College, and even Laurie felt that with the attendance of so many college people at his lectures he was able to exert an influence on the general body of teachers that had seemed impossible in the atmosphere of 1876.

It was not until the early years of the new century and the appearance of Laurie's successor, Darroch, in Edinburgh, that the two large universities finally considered the attractions of recruiting Queen's Students. But by then it was too late, for in 1904, when a Glasgow application finally went in, Craik, smarting perhaps from his earlier defeat, was already planning profound changes in the teacher training system, changes that were to sweep away once and for all not just the short-lived local committees but any real role for the universities in the professional training of either elementary or secondary teachers.

The ostensible reasons for the considerable changes that eventually occurred in 1905/06 had nothing to do with the universities at all but rather with the increasingly untenable position of the churches as the sole proprietors of the college system. There was considerable Parliamentary criticism of an arrangement that place teacher training for a secular school system in the hands of religious bodies that now made little or no financial contribution to its operation. To many members of a House of Commons more and more sensitive to questions of ecclesiastical intervention in education, the Scottish situation seemed particularly indefensible and there was a great relief when a quite unexpected circumstance now brought the matter to a head.

In 1900 the Free Church of Scotland had voted to join forces with the product of earlier secessions, the United Presbyterians, in a new United Free Church. However, a minority in the Free Church believed that this represented a doctrinal betrayal of its founders and those who had provided its endowments and, to the government's amazement, they succeeded in persuading the House of Lords that they, as the only true heirs of the Disruption, were entitled to retain control of all the Church's major assets including its teacher training establishments. Given that these included two of Scotland's largest colleges it was clearly impossible to allow such public institutions, almost totally financed by the state, to fall into such obscurantist hands. The SED had therefore to set about what many in the Commons had for long demanded — the nationalization of all the Presbyterian colleges.

At first Craik's own rhetoric suggested that the churches' natural successors as guardians of the colleges' spiritual qualities would not be the Civil Service or the Inspectorate but the long excluded universities and although he retired just before the plans were announced, the initial circulars augured well. Henceforth control of the college sector was to be based in four 'provinces' centred on the four ancient universities, each of which would have a provincial committee to organize teacher training within it. Darroch, Laurie's influential successor, assumed that such a system would naturally take the Queen's Student system on board and proceeded with plans for developing an Edinburgh scheme, it being generally assumed that under the new arrangements the universities would play a much greater part in teacher training and might well incorporate the colleges into their own structures. Many indeed anticipated the creation of four Scottish equivalents to Teachers' College, Columbia, an institution much admired in EIS and Scottish circles generally.

However, at the very first meeting of the first Provincial Committee to be convened, Craik's equally authoritarian successor, Struthers, made it clear that whatever plans the committees might suggest, it would be the SED that made the decisions and in the ensuing months there emerged a regime under which, as one newspaper put it, the provincial committees became 'mere phonographs for reproducing departmental records'. Struthers instructed the administrators of the new scheme that, far from gladly taking the opportunity to employ any university teachers who offered their services to teacher education, the Provincial Committee should always prefer to use 'their own staff' — that is, the staff of the colleges themselves — whenever that was practicable. Although he did not tamper with the existing system of concurrent college/university attendance he made it clear that actual professional training was now to be given in the colleges alone. The local committees were to be abolished and although henceforth all graduates were to receive a compulsory and far fuller training than hitherto, that training also was to be carried on in the colleges by college staff and recognition was henceforth to be withheld from the Edinburgh Schoolmasters' Diploma which had become so attractive to teachers in the burgeoning secondary sector.

In order to enforce his new rules Struthers was not above using moles in the provincial committees themselves, notoriously in Aberdeen where he felt that relations between university and college staffs, as a consequence of the highly successful local committee's work, were far too close for his liking. There, one lay member, a minor industrialist soon became Sturthers' confidant, seeking his advice, regularly reporting the confidential business of the key sub-committee that he chaired and even meeting him secretly in London.

The result was that the professors of education and the by now full-time lecturers in the subject at Glasgow and Aberdeen soon found their role once more limited to the teaching of those arts undergraduates who opted for education as a non-compulsory subject in their MA degree course — as always a never totally satisfying basis for their department's activities.

Educational Studies and the BEd

However, new opportunities soon began to present themselves that made their future more promising. One was a new burst of interest in educational studies on the part of the teachers themselves. Just as in the 1870s the EIS had campaigned vigorously for the creation of the education chairs, now they began to campaign for a professional degree that would be the distinctive mark of a teacher just like the professional degrees of doctors, ministers and lawyers. On the level and nature of that degree, there was as yet however, no agreement. Some felt, no doubt with status in mind, that it should model itself on the postgraduate LLB or BD. Others were more concerned with using the new degree to increase the profession's effectiveness and felt that it should take the form of a new first degree designed especially for teachers so that they could by such means be 'clinically' and not merely academically trained for their future duties.

At the same time leading members of the EIS were also drawing attention to international developments in educational thought and practice, many of them originating in Germany but as often as not arriving in Britain via North America. Certainly there was an ever increasing interest in the new scientific forms of psychology and in what was called 'experimental education', a term first introduced into Britain by R.R. Rusk, a Scottish lecturer in education who was eventually to play an influential role in the university study of the subject at both St Andrews and Glasgow.

In the end victory went to those backing the idea of a prestigious postgraduate degree and the analogy with the LLB was a particularly potent one in EIS debates before the First World War when considerable emphasis was placed on Scotland's need to catch up with the new scientific approaches to educational issues. As usual the first initiatives came from Edinburgh where the Provincial Committee had been particularly generous in its provision of a well-equipped educational laboratory to which university staff had access. Darroch himself was initially reluctant to plan much beyond a revised and more purely academic Schoolmaster's Diploma but he was pressed by Drever, the first professor of psychology, to go further and to plan a totally new kind of degree. Drever, like Darroch, was a pupil and protegé of Laurie and had begun his university career as a lecturer in comparative education. However, like Rusk, he had also completed a PhD in Jena and had returned full of enthusiasm for a more scientific approach to both psychology and education which were henceforth to appear as equal partners in the education degree pattern finally adopted by Edinburgh and followed by the other three universities.

The outcome was not an actual research degree on the common American model, later to become fashionable elsewhere in Britain, but an honours degree to be taken at postgraduate level, thus giving scope for the generalism of the Scottish departments all of which combined enthusiasm for the new experimental approaches, with a firm grounding in the older historical and philosophical materials and who were as willing to teach Plato and Rousseau as Wundt and Thorndike.

All four agreed on calling the degree Bachelor of Education with the successful completion of the first year of the course entitling the student to a separate academic diploma. This diploma could be conveniently taken by volunteer graduates currently undergoing their compulsory college training and thus a pool would be provided from which promising candidates for the full degree could more readily be drawn.

The only significant differences between the universities were to arise over the relatively trivial issue of the abbreviation of the title (Edinburgh opted for BEd and the others for EdB) and over whether it was possible to take the course on a part-time basis (only Edinburgh forbade it) though before the degree was launched Aberdeen fought a battle to call it an MEd in view of the plans of some English institutions to introduce a degree with that title. It was a mark of the importance then attached to the whole enterprise by the principals of the universities that a day-long meeting of all four was convened at the Station Hotel, Perth simply to thrash out the question of the Aberdeen proposal.

At the same time the considerable attention paid to the matter by the principals (the matter was discussed at no less than 160 meetings of official bodies in the four universities) did not mean that there was universal enthusiasm in university circles for such an innovation. Indeed, in Glasgow the by now traditional dragging of feet over all things educational extended on this occasion to a total refusal by the Senate to accept what was essentially Principal MacAlister's plan for the degree. Nevertheless, he proved willing to challenge the constitutional convention that in academic matters the Senate is supreme and quickly persuaded his Court to ignore the professors' opposition and to promulgate the Ordinance that he himself had framed, believing no doubt that it would be a real money-spinner in the years following demobilization.

However, he and his fellow optimists in the other universities were all proved wrong in their estimate of student numbers. Although all four Ordinances were in place by 1919, St Andrews was not to see its first graduate for another thirty years while the hordes of waiting candidates promised by the EIS in Aberdeen simply melted away. In Glasgow itself William Boyd, the first full-time lecturer, was at last able to persuade one young woman he had met at the university settlement to venture beyond the diploma stage but she soon dropped out and far from attracting young teachers to the new and exciting world of modern education, the Glasgow course found its first graduate in a man of over 50.

Boyd later confessed that at the time he would have preferred an undergraduate teachers' degree and his failure to recruit may simply have reflected this lack of enthusiasm. However, even in Edinburgh despite the enthusiasm of Darroch and Drever, only a handful of candidates presented themselves and it was not until the later demobilization of the 1940s that the Scottish education degree finally began to recruit students on the large scale envisaged by its founders.

They had seen it not merely as a way of increasing the teaching profession's status but also as the training ground for a more technically competent and well-informed professional elite, providing new and better leadership not merely in the staffroom but in the new county education authorities that replaced the school boards following the Scottish Education Act of 1918. In fact, however, only a few of the new authorities were large enough to employ any education staff, expert or otherwise. Some of them, with populations of 20,000 or less, could not even employ a full-time Director of Education and doubled the job with others posts such as County Clerk or Treasurer while in the schools the degree featured too rarely among the qualifications being considered by appointment committees for it ever to be a major influence on their decisions.

Even so the degree's very existence on however small a scale gave a new role and sense of purpose to the university departments. Despite the small number of candidates taking the full degree course, an increasing number of graduate and 'concurrent' undergraduate college students took the diploma and for professors and lecturers still barred from teaching training this encounter with a self-selected band of enthusiasts provided a closer and more substantial link than ever before between the university and the actual world of schooling. Moreover this growth in the diploma classes did in time produce a gradual increase in the number of those seeking the degree itself so that during the 1920s and '30s it began to build up its influence in new and sometimes unexpected directions.

If its importance in the schools themselves never became as great as had been expected, it certainly became significant in the world of the colleges. Given that most Scottish teacher trainees were graduates, it seemed highly desirable that those who were lecturing to them should have a higher degree and the BEd/EdB provided not merely a good generalist background for such lecturing but also a new technical expertise in areas such as testing and psychology. Also when Scottish education graduates turned their attention to posts in English colleges, which still employed many lecturers without even a first degree, their extra postgraduate qualification often took them swiftly into posts of considerable responsibility.

It was, however, in the psychological field that the Scottish degree achieved its greatest importance. When it was launched, and for a further thirty years, it was the only honours degree in psychology available in Scotland. It therefore attracted some able candidates who would not otherwise have thought of studying education at all, as well as tempting teachers into the new profession of educational psychologist. In Glasgow Boyd and his students established the first British clinic offering educational rather than psychiatric treatment to parents and children with problems and in Edinburgh also Drever's work among delinquents led to the growth of another, though quite different clinic.

Such was the interest of education staff such as Darroch, Boyd and Godfrey Thomson in mental testing and the interest of psychology staff such as Drever, Valentine and P.E. Vernon in schooling that it was often difficult to distinguish the work of one department from that of the other though not at all difficult to see why the British Psychological Society, then in its own pioneering days, could so readily accept the degree in the inter-war years as a full psychological qualification.

Godfrey Thomson, Bell Professor in Edinburgh from 1925 to 1951 was, of course, best known outside Scotland as a psychometrician and as a founding father of British secondary selection and it has often been too readily assumed that his BEd students provided a ready vehicle for that spread of standardized selection procedures which became the basis of the 11 + . In fact, however, although Scottish graduates were to be much preoccupied with selection in the 1940s and '50s, there is little evidence of any wide involvement in such tasks before the war. Sutherland (1984) has indicated how the use of such testing by English authorities at that time has been greatly exaggerated by Simon and Banks and in Scotland itself the available evidence suggests that four authorities at most made such testing a compulsory ingredient in their secondary school qualifying examinations even as late as the mid-'30s and none of them was an authority under the direct influence of Thomson. In fact much of his psychometric lecturing in Edinburgh took place in the medical faculty while his earliest and his latest lectures to education students were mainly concerned with the classic philosophical issues and with educational history rather than with testing. Technical issues he largely left to the competent test construction team that he had inherited from Darroch. He was in fact a pillar of the normal generalism that characterized all the Scottish departments, believing that any professor of education must be competent in many disciplines. He denied that his chair was a chair of psychometrics just as Laurie had denied that his chair was a chair of philosophy.

In Glasgow Boyd also combined many interests in the teaching of his EdB. Internationally known as a popularizer of Rousseau and Plato and as a pillar of the New Education Fellowship, he also defies modern categorization, being at once an enemy of examinations and an enthusiast for efficient secondary selection and for endless diagnostic testing. He lectured to mass teacher audiences on 'the latest developments' and, as a strong believer in research carried out by teachers themselves, he persuaded the EIS to establish its own research committee. Amateurish though his own methods were in many ways, it was his enthusiasm which eventually led, in 1928, to the Educational Institute joining forces with the local authorities in the foundation of the Scottish Council for Research in Education, a body pre-dating its English counterpart, the National Foundation for Educational Research, by some twenty years.

In Aberdeen also in the inter-war years the lecturer, Walker, working closely with the psychologist Rex Knight, adopted an equally non-specialist approach and though his number of graduates was small, they included some as nationally distinguished as their Glasgow and Edinburgh colleagues.

By 1939, over 200 students had taken the degree, mostly in Edinburgh and Glasgow, and the ban on university involvement in initial teacher training seemed no longer such a pressing issue. Quite separate functions for the university and college sectors seemed at last to have emerged. Yet this was curious because, since 1925, both the Bell professors had been operating at the very heart of the college system and an exploration of how this came about adds yet another paradoxical element to the story of educational studies in the Scottish universities, for at St Andrews at any rate the chair's increased influence was a direct consequence of an official university attempt to destroy it.

In 1921 a new university Principal, Irvine, had taken office at St Andrews. He was a research chemist in the new American mode and had little sympathy with his predecessors' love for school teachers or with their attempts to woo the EIS. Although he was himself a classic product of Scottish democratic institutions, having risen from lab. boy to principal in a remarkably short period of time, he shared his American friends' mistrust of education as an academic subject and set about ridding himself of a chair and a department that, admittedly, had not developed to the same extent as elsewhere. He began the process by proposing to appoint a lecturer instead of a professor as soon as the first vacancy occurred. When this happened, however, the EIS quickly took counsel's advice and effectively prevented him from doing so. Instead he sought a solution in Dundee where the Provincial Committee had built a magnificent new college that had failed to attract sufficient students. In order to cut their own losses and to help the Principal to rid himself of what he considered an expensive encumbrance, they agreed that the Bell chair and the headship of the college should be combined and when, a few months later, Darroch was drowned off the coast of Jura and the headship of Edinburgh's largest college, Moray House, also fell vacant, a similar proposal was made and accepted there by the University Court and the Provincial Committee.

Again there was much talk, from Drever in particular, of Columbia Teachers' College and of the renewed opportunity to create a Scottish equivalent in the capital city but as in 1906 such hopes soon faded. Although the new professor, Thomson, installed himself and his department in Moray House and remained there for over a quarter of a century, his two functions, as Head of the University Department and as Head of the College, largely failed to blend. Most of his College duties were handed over to a deputy who acted in much the same way as earlier college principals had acted, while the professor concentrated on quite different matters. Twenty years after his appointment he could still give evidence twice to the same official committees, wearing his two different hats, without ever imagining that the chair and the College headship had become a single entity. Indeed it was clear on at least one public occasion that Thomson saw himself primarily as Bell Professor and that he viewed the College and its affairs with some detachment even describing it, somewhat disparagingly, in his autobiography as 'over organized'. Certainly his celebrated series of standardized tests, although they took their name from Moray House, the home of their constructors, always remained firmly the property of the University Department.

Post-war History

In 1951 when it finally became time for Thomson to retire, many of his Senate colleagues saw it as an admirable opportunity to repatriate the Bell chair and to end the college connection. Such a view was hardly surprising. With the post-war expansion of the education system, the Ediburgh BEd degree and the diploma had been thriving while elsewhere in Britain educational studies had been acquiring a new high status as a field for respectable research. By the standards of the day Scottish research and Scottish training already had an enviable reputation. Only London had a comparable record as a producer of statistically competent education graduates while the products of the Glasgow and Edinburgh departments had played a key role in establishing the school psychological service not just in Scotland but also in England. No wonder, therefore, that a new goodwill was being shown to education by other departmental heads and that at last, amid this new buoyancy, Glasgow and Aberdeen at last felt able to establish their chairs.

The crucial factor in Edinburgh's final decision to end the joint university/college appointment was, however, of a quite different nature. Those who engineered the change were in fact no research-minded scientists but a group of arts professors led by their Dean, the philosopher John Macmurray, who despite their liking for Thomson as a person, nevertheless mistrusted his concern with statistics ('He seems more at home with 3.9999 children than with four'). They now appointed to the Bell Chair a committed humanist who saw his major mission as one to the teacher trainees in the diploma class and who deplored the growing alliance between education and the social sciences. Pilley came from a Bristol department where, in the English tradition, the main concern was to produce insightful teachers rather than a technically competent professional elite. The result of his appointment was to be a decade of acrimonious demarcation disputes between the College and the University Department and, following a doubling of the course length at the request of an increasingly demanding psychology professor, there was to be a rapid decline in the number of those taking the degree.

For many of his diploma students, Pilley's approach produced a welcome relief from the alternative college theory course that they regarded as arid and authoritarian but in a Scottish educational world increasingly dominated by the social sciences and their assumptions, Pilley's transformation of the department into a humanist haven eventually proved no more than a rearguard action, eventually as hopeless as the parallel, if less confrontational, attempt to reinstate such values at St Andrews where the system of joint appointments had also been abandoned and a former classics inspector, J.W.L. Adams, had been appointed to the chair in 1956.

The future seemed to lie rather with the occupants of the two new chairs, the Nisbet brothers, both students of Thomson, who were determined to adapt their already well-established departments to the new scientific climate without a total abandonment of the Scottish generalist tradition. In Edinburgh and St Andrews, however, once Pilley and Adams had left the scene, the universities decided on quite new orientations for their departments. In Edinburgh an English psychologist, Liam Hudson, set about 'picking winners' (to use his own phrase) and attempted to convert the department into a major home for PhD candidates, turning his back completely on the world of the diploma and Scottish teacher education, while the St Andrews chair, having been transferred in Adams' later years to the newly independent university of Dundee, was finally abolished and the department swallowed up in a new centre mainly related to the needs of general recurrent education.

Following the Robbins Report and the establishment of the new BEd as a teachers' first degree, the old BEd/EdB had to be renamed and in the years that followed, its nature also changed. As the MEd it became far more like its English equivalent. Everywhere it became more specialist in nature and further removed from the generalist (some would now say dilettante) world of Darroch, Boyd and Thomson. Meanwhile Glasgow and Aberdeen successfully sought to establish a Scottish presence in a new academic world dominated by the research councils with John Nisbet in particular occupying positions on United Kingdom funding bodies that ensured a continued awareness of Scotland's existence in London.

Meanwhile the once massive income from the proceeds of the Moray House tests gradually declined as more and more local authorities throughout Britain abandoned secondary selection and thus considerably reduced the size of what had been Edinburgh's main source of research funding since the war. Under Noel Entwistle, Hudson's successor, the department had gradually to rebuild its reputation as an organization of relevance to Scottish teachers though, significantly, the major centre of school-related research in Edinburgh now moved to the Department of Sociology whose Centre for Educational Sociology not only began to pick up the lion's share of grants in the educational field but, under McPherson, even managed to create its own forms of generalism, providing a welcome and a home for political and educational historians in a way that could never have been envisaged in the anti-social science atmosphere of Pilley's day.

A century after the foundation of the Scottish chairs, it is ironically only in Glasgow that a large moderately generalistic department under Nigel Grant, still thrives, and even there the hopes of the chairs' original founders still remain unfulfilled. Except at Stirling which in its own efficient but small scale way, continues the 'experiment' of training teachers, any attempt by the university departments to be involved in initial professional induction has largely been abandoned. Even the tenuous links with training provided by the diploma stage of the degree have largely been severed as the staffs of an increasingly strengthened college sector have, in a world dedicated to the tenets of comprehensive schooling, successfully protested against the creaming of their graduate classes by a seemingly irrelevant university sector. Any say that the departments at first had in the new undergraduate course for the post-Robbins BEd has also largely been eroded as the colleges administering the degree have asserted their independence and in many cases sought validation from the Council for National Academic Awards rather than from the local university.

It is all a strange and tangled story for a century that saw such progress in university educational studies elsewhere and for a country like Scotland with such strong university and educational traditions. Perhaps, indeed, it was the very strength of those traditons that produced the exceptionally powerful government department and the set of uniquely self-confident colleges that proved the undoing of the successors to Laurie and Meiklejohn. Certainly it is remarkable that a set of university departments which have housed so many distinguished leaders of educational thought and practice and have produced so many influential graduates, should end yet another century in such uncertainty about their academic role and their place in the Scottish educational community.

The Educational Institute which saw in the Bell chairs such great hope of renewed professional prestige and solidly defended their existence in the 1920s, has long since ceased to think of them, or their functions, as being of any great relevance to the profession's needs and with the gradual post-war abandonment of their distinctive generalism, the departments' previous work has become a natural prey for departments elsewhere in the university who, perhaps rightly, now feel that they can do their specialist work on educational topics far more efficiently than a department of dabblers. Perhaps Meiklejohn and Laurie's original dream of getting the whole university to accept schooling as a fit topic for academic treatment has, from the point of view of the Bell professors and their colleagues, been all too successful.

References

ANDERSON, R.D. (1983) *Education and Opportunity in Victorian Scotland*, Oxford, Oxford University Press.

BELFORD, A.J. (1946) *Centenary Handbook of the Educational Institute of Scotland*, Edinburgh, Educational Institute of Scotland.

BELL, R.E. (1983) 'The education departments in the Scottish universities' in HUMES, W. and PATERSON, H. (Eds) *Scottish Culture and Scottish Education 1800–1980*, Edinburgh, John Donald, pp. 151–74.

CANT, R.G. (1970) *The University of St Andrews: A Short History*, Edinburgh, Scottish Academic Press.

CRUICKSHANK, M. (1970) *A History of the Training of Teachers in Scotland*, London, University of London Press.

DARROCH, A. (1903) *Education as a University Subject*, Edinburgh, Edinburgh University Press.

DAVIE, G.E. (1961) *The Democratic Intellect*, Edinburgh, Edinburgh University Press.

DREVER, J. (1948) 'An autobiography', *Occupational Psychology*, January, pp. 20–30.

FINDLAY, I.R. (1979) '*Sir John Struthers*', unpublished PhD thesis, University of Dundee.

GRANT, A. (1884) *The Story of the University of Edinburgh*, London, Longmans Green.

HARTOG, P. (1937) *A Conspectus of Examinations in Great Britain and Northern Ireland*, London, Macmillan.

HEARNSHAW, L.S. (1964) *A Short History of British Psychology*, London, Methuen.

HUDSON, L. (1977) 'Picking winners', *New Universities Quarterly*, 32, 1, p. 89ff.

KNOX, H.M. (1950) 'The chair of education in the University of St Andrews', *Alumnus Chronicle*, 33, pp. 34–8.

LAURIE, S.S. (1901) *The Training of Teachers*, Cambridge, Cambridge University Press.

MACKIE, J.D. (1954) *The University of Glasgow 1451–1951*, Glasgow, Jackson.

MCPHERSON, A. (1973) 'Selections and survivals' in BROWN, R. (Ed) *Knowledge, Education and Culture Change*, London, Tavistock Press, pp. 163–201.

MCPHERSON, A. and ATHERTON, G. (1970) 'Graduate teachers in Scotland', *Scottish Educational Studies*, 2, 1, pp. 35–54.

MORGAN, A. (1929) *Makers of Scottish Education*, London, Longmans Green.

NISBET, S. (1967) 'The study of education in Scotland', *Scottish Educational Studies*, 1, 1, pp. 3–6.

ROBERTSON, J. (1964) *Godfrey Thomson*, Edinburgh, Moray House.

RUSK, R.R. (1919) *Experimental Education*, London, Longmans Green.

SCOTLAND, J. (1975) 'Battles long ago: Aberdeen University and the training of teachers 1907–08', *Scottish Educational Studies*, 7, 2, pp. 85–96.

SMITH, J. (1913) *Broken Links in Scottish Education*, London, Nisbet.

SMITH, J.V. and HAMILTON, D. (Eds) (1980) *The Meritocratic Intellect: Studies in the History of Educational Research*, Aberdeen, Aberdeen University Press.

STOCKS, J. (1986) 'Broken links in Scottish teacher training', *Scottish Educational Review*, 18, 2, pp. 110–20.

SUTHERLAND, G. (1984) *Ability, Merit and Measurement*, Oxford, Oxford University Press.

VERNON, P.E. (1962) 'The contribution to education of Sir Godfrey Thomson', *British Journal of Educational Studies*, 5, 10, pp. 123–37.

Chapter 7

Teacher Education in Northern Ireland

Margaret B. Sutherland

Two major aspirations are evident in the evolution of teacher education in Northern Ireland: they are the wish to make teacher education both liberal and practical, recognized as worthy of high academic status; and the wish to achieve, in the Northern Ireland situation, greater communication and understanding between the people of the two main religious denominations. Such aspirations are not peculiar to Northern Ireland: they are evident in the development of teacher education in other European countries. In educating secondary school teachers, many systems still struggle to reconcile academic and practical preparation: primary school teachers, in most countries, have only gradually been given good academic education and had their training recognized as part of higher education. Religious differences have certainly complicated and still do complicate not only teacher education but the provision of schools in many countries of the world. Thus a review of progress in Northern Ireland towards achieving — or incompletely achieving — high status for teacher education, and integration of those of different religions in one educational system, can serve to illuminate problems common to many countries.

The Education of Primary School Teachers Before 1922

Although the state of Northern Ireland did not come into being until 1920, that part of the country obviously shared in the nineteenth and early twentieth century developments of teacher education in Ireland as a whole. Initially, as in other countries, the education of teachers for primary schools was thought deserving of the most urgent attention. In nineteenth century Ireland, the aim of providing good teaching in primary schools was compounded by the hope that such schools would be attended by all children, irrespective of religious denomination. The Society for Promoting the Education of the Poor in Ireland (better known as the Kildare Place Society) provided in the first decades of the century schools to be attended by both Catholic and Protestant children, but the practice of Bible reading without commentary roused hostility. A similar policy of integrated education was adopted by the Board of Commissioners of National Education which from 1831 was responsible for education in Ireland. To ensure high standards in their national schools, the Commissioners set up some thirty model schools in different parts of the island which were to exemplify the best teaching and give training to pupil teachers and monitresses. This attempt at integration in national and model schools unhappily failed, because of a series of oppositions from different religious authorities, though the title of model school and the tradition of better-than-average teaching continued in some instances — indeed the title still survives in a few schools.[1]

The failure of these well-intentioned attempts at integration in the nineteenth century meant that a dual system of schools developed: so that today in Northern Ireland pupils in primary and secondary education are fairly evenly divided between local authority 'controlled' schools (in practice, mainly Protestant) and Roman Catholic 'voluntary maintained' schools: but the majority of grammar schools, for historical reasons, are mostly voluntary, some being Catholic, others non-denominational or Protestant. Only since 1978 has there been legislative provision for a category of 'controlled integrated' schools, deliberately bringing together pupils of different religious faiths: such schools are as yet extremely few in number. Teacher education in Ireland and Northern Ireland must be seen in this dual system context.[2]

The main development of teacher training in Ireland, as in other parts of the British Isles, was through the establishment of training colleges. The integrated policy was applied in the Marlborough Street Training College, while it was under the control of the Commissioners (the College was closed by the government of the Irish Free State in 1922): the Kildare Place College provided mainly, though not exclusively, for Church of Ireland students: Roman Catholic men and women were trained, separately, in four colleges provided by various teaching orders.[3] By 1902, some 55 per cent of primary teachers in Ireland had college training and this percentage had risen to over 80 by 1922. As it happened, all the training colleges were, with the exception of St. Mary's College for Roman Catholic women (founded in Belfast in 1900), situated in Dublin or other parts of the south so when the Northern Ireland state was created, there was an urgent need to make new provision for the education of elementary school teachers.

University Education of Teachers Before and After 1922

Yet another form of teacher education preceded the establishment of the

Northern Ireland state in 1920. In 1899 the University of Dublin, Trinity College, instituted examinations in the history and theory of education and in the practice of teaching: success in both would lead to the award of a Diploma in Education, though a year of teaching experience was required before candidates could proceed to the second examination. In 1905, a chair of education was established, the first Professor being Edward Parnall Culverwell: further provisions for qualifications in education, including the study of teaching methods in various subjects, and 'general knowledge of the hygienic principles bearing on schools and schoolwork', were made in subsequent years.[4]

A similar decision to incorporate teacher education in the university was made in the North, where Queen's University, Belfast, appointed in 1914 its first Professor of Education, C.W. Valentine.[5] Valentine offered courses leading to the University's Diploma in Education. The theoretical side of the diploma included principles of education, methods of teaching, the history of education, psychology and logic, school hygiene. Opportunities for teaching practice in schools were arranged, under the general supervision of the Professor. Provision was made for special study of methods of teaching 'one school subject or group of subjects, for example, classics, natural science, modern languages, geography and history, mathematics, and for 'weekly demonstrations, discussion classes, criticism lessons'. It was pointed out that lectures would be held at times which would suit practising teachers. The courses could be attended by non-graduates, or people not aspiring to the diploma itself: for these, certificates of attendance and due performance of the work of the class were available. Marks of distinction could be awarded for either side of the course but 'distinction in the theoretical part of the examination will not compensate for weakness in practical teaching'. It was also stated that success in thc examination in teaching would depend not only on performance in the lesson seen but on 'the records and reports of the student's teaching work during the session as made by the Professor of Education and the headmasters or headmistresses of the schools'. Soon an external examiner for practical teaching was introduced.

But a kind of academic discrimination was made a year later by a division into the Higher Diploma in Education and the Diploma in Education, the former to require wider reading and a higher standard in the examination, and to be open only to graduates, or those passing the training colleges' final examination in the first division and subsequently attending four courses in arts or science subjects in the University. Diploma candidates had to have passed the final training college examination or have had at least three years' teaching experience and passed the matriculation examination of the University or its equivalent. There was thus a continuing intention to include provision for teachers other than graduate secondary school teachers, even though two academic levels were recognized. This division survived until 1947 when new regulations established simply the Diploma in Education, open to (a) graduates; or (b) those who had passed the final training college examination. This diploma was to be taken by one year of full-time study, or three years of part-time study, one-third of the course being taught each year late in the day, so that practising teachers could attend. From 1949 the Northern Ireland Ministry awarded training scholarships to students taking the full-time diploma course.[6] The Diploma gave way in 1977 to the Graduate Certificate in Education, gained by a one-year, full-time course, by which time other developments in teacher education had made the University Diploma's part-time upgrading function unnecessary.

Unfortunately for education in Northern Ireland, C.W. Valentine left in 1919 to become Professor of Education in the University of Birmingham. In addition to initial training courses, he left in Belfast an Education Society for informal discussions among people of various kinds interested in education, and a stronger foundation, a higher degree in education, the degree of MA. For this higher qualification students who had taken Diploma courses in principles, practice and history of education, had to study educational psychology, the logical and ethical bases of education, principles of education, experimental pedagogy, practice of education (with reference to moral education, aesthetic education, special methods of teaching two subjects), and history of education. In experimental pedagogy, notably, candidates could[7] 'submit the records of any research of their own, and the examination paper will then have special reference to the topics dealt with in such research, or in the case of special merit, the candidate may be exempted from the paper'. This higher academic qualification (and training) for teachers also lasted for many years (experimental pedagogy being retitled experimental education), until in 1948 it was superseded as a taught course by the introduction of the BEd[8] on the Scottish universities' model, which in 1969 became the MEd[9], the new title being accorded also to holders of the old BEd, to avoid confusion with the new Robbins-type BEd. But the degree of MA (Education) continued to be available as a degree gained by thesis.

The foregoing developments meant that there was continuity, after the establishment of the state of Northern Ireland, at least in the provision of some non-sectarian (though alas, non-compulsory) teacher education for graduates and others. Queen's University has remained a provider of such education even though types of students and qualifications have changed since these earlier decades. The tradition of accepting a wide range of students meant in the immediate post-war decades some integration of primary and secondary, practising and 'new' teachers, in courses of professional studies. While full-time Diploma course students were almost invariably graduates intending to teach in secondary schools, part-time students included serving teachers at all levels. Admittedly, exchange of ideas between full-timers and part-timers was scarcely facilitated since they had only some lectures in common — tutorial discussions being held earlier in the day for full-timers. Yet the facilities offered to experienced non-graduate teachers, and to untrained graduates, to obtain a further qualification by part-time study, were of considerable importance (and widened the outlook at least of the University tutors) until the Robbins, or rather, in Northern Ireland, the Lockwood, era offered other facilities.

Developments in Elementary (Primary) School Teacher Education in the Inter-war Period

The Lynn Committee Proposals

Since partition of the country had left Northern Ireland largely unprovided with colleges for the training of elementary school teachers, the Final Report in 1923 of the Departmental Committee on the Educational Services in Northern Ireland (the Lynn Committee)[10] devoted much attention to teacher education, showing an admirable combination of realism and idealism. Pupil teachers and monitors were said to have been poorly prepared in knowledge of the ordinary school subjects, so 'apprentices to the teaching profession should secure during their course a good education of a secondary type'.[11] (In fact, the monitorial system was abolished in 1929 and the junior pupil-teacher studentships were gradually, by changes in 1931, 1939 and 1945, assimilated to ordinary secondary school scholarships. Entry to training colleges thus became determined by success in the normal upper secondary school examinations.[12] For the period of professional training, serious improvements in the quality of education offered to elementary school teachers were to be made. The Committee adopted the view of the 1922 Pollock Committee on the Training of Teachers in Northern Ireland[13] that prospective primary teachers could be divided into two classes: class A would be accepted by the University as competent to study university arts courses; class B would not. Class A was to take during the two training years four university BA courses. Other training college subjects were to be taught 'by university professors and teachers' and by technical college teachers and teachers appointed by the (government) Training Committee. Professional training of all students was to be given in the Education Department of the University, the staff there being increased by a master of method and two assistants. A demonstration school was to be used, and teaching practice to take place in a number of 'the best schools of the city'. A site at Stranmillis, Belfast, was to be developed for student hostels and other accommodation.

In putting forward such proposals, the Lynn Committee was concerned that class A students who wanted to complete a university degree would have difficulty in doing so because they would need to take another four courses after becoming qualified teachers. 'We do not think a university degree is essential, but we consider that facilities should exist for primary teachers of superior capacity to obtain degrees'.[14] Thus for the most able, two-year bursaries should be available to allow them to be full-time university students; and salary increments should be given for these years.

Further, although aware that many certificated primary school teachers aspired to obtain a degree in arts, the Committee held that arrangements could not be made to teach university arts courses in the evenings – and in any case, such part-time attendance would not give the participation in the life of the university which the Committee thought an essential component of study for a university degree. The Committee therefore made an alternative proposal that courses of lectures 'similar' to those of the arts degree be provided in Belfast and other centres: this should lead to an award which would qualify the teachers for the allowances given to those holding a Higher Certificate.

Recognizing that some graduates in arts or science might wish to become primary school teachers, the Committee proposed that a postgraduate course should be provided for them – and any deficiencies in their competence in English or mathematics should be made good. Training for teachers of technical subjects was also desirable and should be encouraged but the Committee acknowledged the practical difficulties of adding this to potential teachers' training and experience in technical subjects.

As for secondary schools, graduates intending to teach there should be required to undergo training 'in the history, methods and practice of teaching'. Teachers at upper levels should indeed have a university postgraduate Diploma in Education – but honours graduates could be exempt from this if they engaged in a year of approved postgraduate study or research. (In fact it was not until 1973 that training became compulsory for secondary school teachers in Northern Ireland though it had long been compulsory for those teaching in primary schools.)[15]

Less idealistic considerations did obtrude. The Committee urged that as the Ministry would incur much expense in both two-year courses of training and one-year postgraduate training. 'it should be made incumbent' on teachers, at the earliest possible time, 'to repay at least a part of the cost of their training'.[16] But the general intentions of the Committee in planning for better academic education for primary teachers and in developing professional preparation for all teachers, in association with the university, were remarkably liberal and far-sighted.

Short-lived Integration After 1922: The Stranmillis Problem

The Lynn Committee, whose authority was unfortunately weakened by the refusal of Roman Catholic Church representatives to serve on it[17], had envisaged the establishment of teacher training which would be non-denominational and closely linked to the University. Many students would attend University arts courses (the Queen's University was by origin and statute non-denominational). The professional part of teacher education was to be provided by University teachers as well as by teachers from the College of Technology and others specially appointed. In fact, the Professor of Education did have additional assistants appointed in the next few years and was joint Head of the University Department and of Stranmillis College until 1931 when a separate principal was appointed for the College.

Initially it seemed as if some degree of integration, both of University and College and of students of different religious denominations, would be achieved. St Mary's College received appropriate payments from the government training committee for courses taught to Roman Catholic women students within that College but Roman Catholic men students enrolled in the new, government-provided Stranmillis College. Yet the Roman Catholic authorities were not content that Roman Catholic students should mix with Protestant students during training, even though separate hostels would be provided. Since the Northern Ireland government argued that public funds could not be given to the endowment of a denominational institution, and that in any case the numbers of Roman Catholic male students were small, an arrangement was made for the payment of government scholarships to enable such students to be trained in St Mary's (Strawberry Hill) College, Middlesex, England. (This arrangement remained in force until war-time conditions made it difficult to implement: post-war, Roman Catholic men students first attended St Mary's College, Belfast, as a temporary measure, then were provided with their own separate premises in Trench House, Belfast, until in 1961 St Joseph's College for Catholic men students was established.)[18]

In this way, *de facto*, Stranmillis became a training college for Protestant students and the provisions for training primary school teachers were polarized by religious affiliations.[19] Any Roman Catholic students who trained in a non-approved college were aware that they would have difficulties in finding a teaching post in a Roman Catholic school in Northern Ireland – and rather few Catholics were likely to be employed in the officially non-denominational schools: but the emphasis of the Catholic hierarchy on separate training for Catholic students, as a means of safeguarding the distinctive ethos of Catholic schools, did maintain a barrier to integration at the teacher education stage. Even so, Stranmillis might have claimed to be non-denominational but for the determined campaign by Protestant Church authorities to be given the right to nominate their representatives to its committee of management. Resistance to this claim was considerable, and the teachers' unions – both the Ulster Teachers Union and the Irish National Teachers Organization – protested. But the government eventually compromised, or capitulated, in 1932, and such representatives were appointed, so that while remaining a College provided and controlled by the government, Stranmillis took on the character of a Protestant institution, the great majority of its students being Presbyterian or Church of Ireland, with smaller numbers of Methodists and 'others', a category which did not include Roman Catholics.[20]

The intended integration in university teaching of professional subjects similarly disappeared as the new Stranmillis College developed and Roman Catholic students were taught in St Mary's, Belfast, or Strawberry Hill. But provision was made from 1926/27 that during their two-year courses of training some Stranmillis students could gain credit for three university pass degree courses in arts: they could then, during an additional two years of training, complete their degree by taking the remaining five courses, studying at university though remaining enrolled in the College: or some could simply take the DipEd during a third year. St Mary's did not have the same formal arrangement with the University, though some St Mary's students took the courses necessary for a university degree during a four-year college course.[21] Not many students were affected by this provision and it also came to an end in war-time conditions.

Post-war Reforms: The Gibbon Report of 1947

In the euphoric times of legislation for secondary education for all (Northern Ireland Education Act, 1947), the Gibbon Committee on the Recruitment and Training of Teachers[22] made proposals in some ways parallel to those of the McNair Committee for England and Wales (1944)[23] and the Scottish Advisory Council Report for Scotland (1946)[24]. As they recognized, their recommendations had to be adapted to the special circumstances of Northern Ireland: thus they rejected the proposals for institutes of education or similar organizations as unnecessary in a state where there were only two general training colleges and one university. They were also unsure whether a university should properly be responsible for the training of teachers, in view of what this Committee (unlike the Lynn Committee) considered to be the academic and non-vocational nature of universities.

This Committee nevertheless favoured more mingling of students of different backgrounds and hoped this would be facilitated by increased future attendance of Stranmillis and St Mary's students at university undergraduate courses or in the university postgraduate training year, as well as in the specialist colleges for domestic economy and art and in colleges still to be developed for crafts, music and physical education. They did, however, note 'the decree of the Armagh Council of the Roman Catholic Church requiring that Roman Catholic teachers should be trained in Catholic training colleges'.[25]

The 1947 Act involved the creation of new kinds of secondary schools, the intermediate schools, as they were named then (subsequently, they have been designated 'secondary' schools which, oddly enough, differentiates them from the still-existing grammar schools). To provide for the new circumstances and improve teacher education, the Committee proposed — and the proposal was implemented in 1948[26], in advance of such reforms in England — that for primary teachers the training course be extended to three years and that a four-year course of training for secondary school teachers (mainly for the new Intermediate schools) be introduced in the colleges, with some degree of specialization in a secondary school subject and including English, history, geography or mathematics as a major subject of study. The total supply of teachers, depleted by war-time conditions, was increased by the Larkfield College Emergency Training Scheme from 1945/49.[27] A one-year postgraduate course of training was also to be provided in the colleges for intending intermediate school teachers — on the whole, the Committee expected the university postgraduate course to be taken by people intending to teach in grammar schools (though in practice such students entered either intermediate or grammar school teaching). In-service courses were further to be provided to enable teachers to meet the demands of the new intermediate schools.

Having set out and thoroughly considered the merits and demerits of consecutive and concurrent courses of teacher education[28], the Committee felt obliged to conclude that both forms must continue. But in addition to concurrent courses in the Colleges it proposed another kind of four-year concurrent course which would combine training college and university education for some intending secondary school teachers. These students, registered as college students, would spread attendance at the eight courses necessary for achieving a university degree through the first three years, the fourth year being wholly given to professional studies and training. Religious education and physical education were, however, to be provided in the training colleges throughout the four years. This proposal was implemented but this concurrent course naturally declined in popularity when, after 1961, university scholarships were more easily obtainable and many potential applicants for training college places were, as had been the case for some time, in possession of university entry qualifications.

Comments by the Committee on the merits of residential colleges for future teachers reveal some traditional attitudes towards this section of society. Though recommending some relaxation of regulations about compulsory study periods, compulsory church attendance, hours of returning to the college in the evenings, the Committee was not unanimous about the degree of liberty to be allowed to future teachers while they resided in training colleges. In fact, the Committee noted the argument[29] that 'a disciplined life is an essential part of training college life' and while welcoming the fact that church attendance was no longer compulsory for Stranmillis students, remained 'satisfied that students will attend church voluntarily'.

Reform in the 1960s

Education in the New University of Ulster

Education in Northern Ireland shared in the exuberant expansionism of the 1960s. It is especially remarkable that in proposing the foundation of a new university in Northern Ireland, the Lockwood Committee on Higher Education (1965)[30] gave major emphasis to the Education Centre to be established in this university. This Centre must be in the heart of the university campus. It was to provide a concurrent degree course for intending teachers, courses in education for other students, a three-year Certificate of Education course for students who did not satisfy matriculation requirements, and part-time and in-service professional training courses. The education of both secondary and primary school teachers was thus to be seen as clearly part of university education and the study of education was to be of major importance in the new university.

In practice, complications arose. The New University of Ulster was duly established in 1968 on a new site at Coleraine, County Antrim. But although the Lockwood Report had recommended the discontinuance of Magee University College, Londonderry, an establishment (under Presbyterian Church trustees) which had provided teaching in undergraduate courses recognized as equivalent to the first year of degree studies in Queen's or the first two years of degree studies in Trinity College, Dublin, arrangements were made to affiliate this College to the New University and so continue its existence. Its undergraduate students transferred to the Coleraine campus in 1971/72 and Magee College became a Centre for Continuing and Adult Education.[31] However some familiar difficulties of split-site administration were inevitable and, more importantly, the new arrangements did not really eliminate resentment in some quarters that the New University had not been located in Londonderry.

The New University worked hard to implement the Lockwood recommendations and initially seemed well on the way to doing so. Four schools of study were created (Biological and Environmental Studies, Social Sciences, Humanities, and Physical Sciences) and the Education Centre ranked as a fifth school of studies. The University was innovative in its use of the two-semester year and semester-long units of study. The Education Centre therefore provided a great variety of units, initially both for Certificate of Education students and for students taking honours degrees with various combinations of education and other subject units, as well as for students studying education without professional training in mind. But the three-year Certificate of Education was phased out in 1978/79, in response to a decision of the Northern Ireland Department of Education to make teacher qualifications equivalent to those to be offered in England and Wales in future. In fact, already 70 per cent of those enrolling for the Certificate of Education had been able to transfer into honours degree courses: for those unable to achieve that standard, a pass degree in education was made available.[32]

The work of the Education Centre became increasingly complex as further provisions for different kinds of student were made: by 1973 the Centre had already a total of over 500 full-time and part-time students. As an annual report pointed out, the rapid expansion of student numbers at a time when there was already a freeze on staff numbers, imposed heavy burdens. As the evolution proceeded, the Centre came to offer, for degree courses of three or four years duration, six types of programme which included varying numbers of units in education. Three of the programmes included professional teacher training and so required entry qualifications of 'O' levels, or equivalents, in English and mathematics. Students taking five of the six programmes were enrolled in the Education Centre but the Concurrent Subject Course was taken by students enrolled in one of the other main schools: this programme, spread over four or five years (for modern language students), gave fifteen units to the main subject and nine to education.[33] In addition to these undergraduate courses the Centre offered courses for a Diploma in Advanced Studies in Education, and as a kind of refresher for practising teachers, Diploma courses in physics, chemistry, mathematics and history, each with education. Higher degrees were also included and a Teachers' Centre was established from 1973.

But this original and enterprising development of teacher education was taking place in a university which was unfortunate in the timing of its birth. In the period which should have fostered its growth to a substantial and well-established institution, the 1970s recessions in higher education were already manifesting themselves. Moreover the 'troubles' of Northern Ireland, beginning practically simultaneously with the New University, meant that recruitment of students from 'across the water' became unlikely — though the disturbances may have encouraged some Northern Ireland students to remain at home rather than venture over to England, Scotland or Wales. Success by the New University in attracting students from the Republic of Ireland even aroused some local hostility among those who felt that outsiders were benefiting from the educational facilities provided by the British tax-payer. The percentages of postgraduate and of overseas students remained considerably lower than in other British universities.[34]

A further restriction for the Education Centre came in the mid-1970s with the announcement of the Minister with responsibility for Education in Northern Ireland that, in view of falling enrolments in schools and an expected surplus of teachers, the number of students to be admitted to teacher education was to be reduced: in succeeding years intakes were again reduced.[35] The Education Centre in the New University of Ulster, like the Belfast colleges and the Queen's University Department of Education, thus found its growth cut back.

Innovation and Change in Queen's University, Belfast

In Northern Ireland, as in England, a new degree, the BEd, was created and this meant the introduction of the kind of formal institutional links which the Gibbon Report had considered unnecessary. In 1967, Queen's University established a Faculty of Education and an Institute of Education.[36] The Faculty of Education included representatives of thirteen subject departments in the University, the Heads of the Colleges, members of the University Department of Education and the University's Extra-Mural Department, plus one recognized (college) teacher for each subject area, together with some other University representatives. The Faculty established boards of studies for each subject and had as its main function the work of coordinating and supervising the BEd degree for which teaching was to be given in the colleges. The Institute was to concern itself with the Certificate of Education, also attained through college training. It took responsibility for the Teachers' Centre (already established by the University in 1967) and other in-service provisions for teacher education.

There was some integration of the various providers of teacher education, under the aegis of the University. It should be noted that in the 1960s, integrative developments were being helped by changes in attitudes which enabled Roman Catholic students intending to be teachers at the secondary school level to take the DipEd or Graduate Certificate in Education courses of the Department of Education in Queen's University. (This integration in fact continues. There is even an optional methods course in religious education taught by tutors from the two main religious affiliations.) A valuable consequence of more relaxed attitudes was that teaching practice arrangements could be, (and are), made to enable students to undertake teaching practice in schools of a different religious denomination from their own.

Further reduction of barriers came through regulations in 1966 which meant that from then onwards the overwhelming majority of Roman Catholic primary and secondary intermediate schools accepted 'maintained' status which required one-third of their governing bodies to be representatives of public authorities and which gave them considerably greater financial support — 100 per cent of running costs and maintenance.[37] (Grammar schools had earlier found such representation acceptable and had benefited accordingly in financial provisons.)

The Ulster College

Provision for teachers of certain specialist subjects had been made in the Belfast College of Art, the Belfast College of Domestic Science, the Belfast College of Technology, the Londonderry Technical College (for commercial subjects) and the Ulster College of Physical Education: in such institutions, probably as a result of the impracticability of duplicating specialist training, students of different religious backgrounds had always studied together. The Lockwood Committee, while recognizing that a common site for all such institutions would be improbable, recommended that these existing provisions, together with a proposed new Regional College of Technology and colleges to be developed for commerce, catering, music and drama, should be brought together in one institution, the Ulster College.[38] This recommendation was implemented in 1971. Thus a new major teacher training agency came into being in Northern Ireland, providing education for teachers of the specialist subjects indicated. In the early years it described itself as the Ulster College, the Northern Ireland Polytechnic. It benefited from new building and some consolidation on one of its campuses at Jordanstown, near Belfast. It also showed initiative in developing a variety of courses not only for the subjects already listed but for communications and the teaching of the handicapped.

A Problem Situation of the 1970s: The Changes in 'Free Trade' in British Teacher Education

Some of the problems which overtook the reforming initiatives of the 1960s have already been indicated. Also noteworthy are changes in what have been described as the 'free trade' arrangements for payment of training grants to students in different parts of the United Kingdom, for such changes might be seen as offering some degree of protection or protectionism to the Northern Ireland teacher-training institutions. Since 1960 the English Ministry had agreed to pay training grants to students from England attending the Queen's University training course.[39] In 1963 free trade became general by the agreement of the Scottish Education Department and the Ministries of England and Northern Ireland to give grants to enable students normally resident in their territories to take either postgraduate or non-graduate training courses in any part of the United Kingdom. The value of such mixing of students from different areas was evident, though the tendency was clearly for more Northern Ireland students to 'emigrate' for their training than for others to come to Northern Ireland. The arrangements also increased the likelihood of coordination of teacher education requirements in different parts of the United Kingdom.

But by 1971 the Northern Ireland authority felt that the system could not be allowed to continue without reservations, so competition for a limited number of awards for entry to three or four-year teacher education courses in other parts of the UK was introduced, though at first entry to postgraduate courses was not affected.[40] As it seemed increasingly important to determine precisely the numbers of those training to be teachers in Northern Ireland, a situation in which about one-third of Northern Ireland students were going 'across the water' to train, and about 45 per cent subsequently returning to teach in Northern Ireland, became increasingly unacceptable. Gradually, the available number of awards to train outside Northern Ireland was reduced until, from 1978/79 the only awards available were for those admitted to courses, either concurrent or PGCE, which were of a type not available in Northern Ireland and which led to qualifications needed by teachers in Northern Ireland schools. This interruption of 'free trade' was viewed with great regret by the Northern Ireland authorities but it seemed necessary to continue the restrictions until 1988. In that year permission was again given for grants to students going to PGCE courses in Great Britain. As yet, it is too early to know whether this will lead to perceptible shortages of applications for entry to the Northern Ireland courses.

Integrations in the 1980s

Queen's University and the Colleges

The Chilver Committee was appointed in 1978 to make recommendations on the future structure of higher education in Northern Ireland. Since the reduced provision of teacher education places seemed to make decisions on this aspect particularly urgent, the Committee produced an interim report in 1980 on 'The Future Structure of Teacher Education in Northern Ireland'.[41] Concerned with the possible non-viability of small institutions, but recognizing the need to maintain flexibility and to maintain teacher education as a 'full partner' in higher education, it argued for an amalgamation in Belfast of the three colleges and the University Department of Education. These, the Committee proposed, should join together in a Belfast Centre for Teacher Education on the Stranmillis site, so that resources could be most effectively shared and the small colleges maintained as academically viable. It pointed out that 'to some extent, the three colleges and the Queen's University of Belfast can already be seen as a single academic entity' but it believed that the new amalgamation could be made so as to allow each component to retain 'a separate legal and administrative existence'.

Those familiar with the history of teacher education in Northern Ireland probably — and correctly — estimated the chances of implementation of this proposal as zero. In fact, objections were promptly raised. The Catholic authorities feared that in such a situation the characteristic ethos of their teacher education would be lost: and they pointed to the continuing existence of distinctively Catholic colleges in England and Scotland as support for their wish to maintain their own colleges in Northern Ireland. A massive number of signatures was obtained for a petition against the new proposal.[42] Protestant responses were also unfavourable and, on rather different grounds, the University found the new scheme unacceptable. The amalgamation did not happen.

Yet one of the Chilver recommendations about amalgamation was implemented. In spite of arguments that women applicants for entry to colleges tended to be more highly qualified than men applicants and that, consequently, joint entry would lead to acceptance of considerably more women than men, the Committee judged that St Mary's and St Joseph's Colleges should amalgamate. In fact, they did do so in 1985, the merged College taking the name of St Mary's.

Changes in the relationship between the colleges and the University were also taking place. Already in 1976, in response to the Lelievre Report of 1973[43], the University had altered what had been criticized as a cumbersome and duplicative structure of a separate Faculty and Institute of Education. The new Faculty of Education was to consist of five departments — the University's own Department of Education (now transferred from the Faculty of Arts), the Department of Further Professional Studies in Education (taking over the Institute functions), the Department of Educational Studies (supervising BEd arrangements and, while it continued to exist, the Certificate of Education), the University's Department of Physical Education and its Department of Extra-Mural Studies. The new professors were appointed to head the two new departments of the Faculty. Boards of studies, consisting of college and University departmental representatives, were to report to the Faculty on matters relating to the BEd and the Certificate of Education. An honours BEd degree was introduced.

But further attempts to simplify and make more effective the working together of the University and the colleges were made in the 1980s. In 1983, on the retirement of the Professor of Education, a decision was made to abolish the Department of Educational Studies and transfer its functions to the Department of Education. The Professor of Educational Studies became Professor and Head of the Department of Education. In 1986, further streamlining was attempted by the creation of a School of Education within the Faculty of Education. This School replaced the Departments of Education, Further Professional Studies in Education and Physical Education. It has four divisions – Educational Policy, Pre-service Education of Teachers (including the University's Graduate Certificate of Education and validation of college-based courses), In-service Education of Teachers, Physical and Health Education.[44] The proposals for this move towards greater unification noted the inconveniences caused by the existing variety of locations of various University education units and recommended integration on a common site in the University. (The need for additional resources was also recognized, though not all such recommendations have been implemented as yet.)

The University of Ulster

The main Chilver Report[45] made far-reaching and innovative proposals for change in the whole provision of higher education in Northern Ireland. Considering the precarious position of the New University of Ulster, it recommended the closure of that University or its merger with the Ulster Polytechnic. After considerable discussion, the decision to merge was in fact made.[46] Thus the brave experiment of the New University came to an end after only sixteen years of existence. Yet the creation of the University of Ulster by merging two institutions originally on different sides of the binary line was an interesting new departure in British higher education. It is as yet too early to know how effectively the dynamism of the Ulster Polytechnic's development will spread through the new organism. The problems of establishing unity of purpose and administration when sites are scattered, not only within Belfast, but at such widely separated locations as Coleraine, Belfast and Londonderry, must be considerable, even if they are not unknown in other parts of the United Kingdom where administrative, though not physical, mergers have taken place.

So far as teacher education is concerned, the merger must have consequences which were not necessarily a direct concern of the Chilver Committee. The University of Ulster now integrates the provision earlier made by its constituent bodies for the preparation of teachers, i.e. the education of teachers for various kinds of special education and specialist subjects like physical education and home economics, and the education of teachers, mainly by concurrent courses, for primary and secondary school work. Whether it will continue the Coleraine policy of concurrent courses or try to move rather to consecutive courses remains to be seen. This new University has, like Queen's

University, the advantage of being non-denominational, receiving students of all religious — or no religious — affiliations.

Teacher Education in Northern Ireland Today

The present teacher education situation is thus one in which provision is made by a newly-created University, with some policies still to be worked out, and by the long-established Queen's University of Belfast working in association with St Mary's College and Stranmillis College.

The logic of rationalization would suggest that a good development would be to have teacher education in the province provided entirely by its two universities. It could thus be claimed that one objective of the many educational reports of the past 100 years would be attained: giving the education of teachers its rightful place by making it a normal part of the activities of universities, future and serving teachers being educated in company with people preparing for, or engaging in, other professions. But some kind of logic of history would recognize the improbability of acceptance, by important parts of the community, of the abolition of the colleges. Changes have taken place in attitudes: many barriers have been eliminated or reduced: but loss of separate identity by the colleges, the abolition of formal links between churches and teacher education is still another matter.

Meanwhile it can be recognized that at least very many new teachers have had the opportunity to discuss with fellow students, during training courses, the distinctive characteristics of the dual system of education and their own experiences during learning and teaching practice within that system. The objective which the Lelievre Committee emphasized[47] — 'to encourage in teachers an understanding and a critical appreciation of the society within which they live' and 'to produce the kind of person who is prepared to analyze objectively and sympathetically the causes of harmful division and in the same spirit to seek to remove them' — is, as the Committee pointed out, an objective particularly important in the Northern Ireland context. Reaching this objective may become easier as student-teachers do meet and discuss — particularly, perhaps, as they consider the brave new attempts at creating 'controlled integrated' schools: but the objective still requires much conscious planning on the part of teacher educators in any kind of institution.

Student-teachers may also find worthy of discussion another feature of the Northern Ireland system in which many of them will serve — the continuing division into 'secondary' schools (with a minority of comprehensives) and selective grammar schools. This continuation of selection for secondary education — by procedures much modified over the years — is another Northern Ireland characteristic which has proved remarkably resistant to change and merits consideration by teachers.

In the evolution which has been outlined here, we can indeed trace some progress towards realizing the aims originally stated for teacher education.

The profession has become a graduate profession — even if it is not certain whether all degrees, University or University-validated or CNAA-validated, enjoy the same prestige, and qualitative judgments still have to be made as to the worth of the education offered to prospective teachers within or outside universities.

In integration of different religious groups in teacher education, again we have evidence of progress. It is especially to be noted that, while not all teachers are free from bigotry or deplorable prejudices, the majority of teachers have shown great goodwill in carrying out numerous projects[48] to promote community understanding, tolerance and cooperation: and great dedication to their work in continuing to serve under unusually difficult conditions of civic unrest. Teachers have exemplified good citizenship and proved determined to educate children towards a better future. Whether this is due to general education, to professional training or to living in a society which is in essence much more tolerant, friendly and cooperative than media reports would suggest, cannot be determined: but it does set standards for future teacher education in Northern Ireland.

Notes

1 For fuller accounts of these events see Barritt, D.P. and Carter, C.F. (1962) *The Northern Ireland Problem,* London, Oxford University Press: also Craig, A.R. and McNeilly, N. (1957) *Belfast Model Schools, 1857–1957,* Belfast, The Northern Publishing Office.

2 An outline of the dual system is provided in Sutherland, M.B. (1988) 'Religious dichotomy and schooling in Northern Ireland' in Tulasciewicz, W. and Brock, C. (Eds) *Christianity and Educational Provision in International Perspective,* London and New York, Routledge, pp 38–60.

3 The Lynn Committee Report — Ministry of Education for Northern Ireland (1923) *Final Report of the Departmental Committee on Educational Services in Northern Ireland,* Belfast, HMSO, p. 13.

4 See *Calendar,* University of Dublin, Trinity College, for the years in question.

5 See *Calendar,* Queen's University of Belfast for 1914/15 and 1915/16.

6 Government of Northern Ireland (1952) *Report of the Ministry of Education, 1949–50,* Belfast, HMSO, p. 20.

7 *Calendar,* Queen's University of Belfast, 1917/18.

8 *Calendar,* Queen's University of Belfast, 1948.

9 *Calendar*, Queen's University of Belfast, 1969.

10 The Lynn Committee Report (1923) *op. cit., supra.*

11 *ibid.,* p. 11.

12 The Gibbon Report — Government of Northern Ireland (1947) *Report of the Committee on the Recruitment and Training of Teachers*, Belfast, HMSO, Appendix I, p. 81.

13 Cited in the Lynn Committee Report, p. 14.

14 Lynn Report, p. 16.

15 Lelievre Report — Ministry of Education (1973) *The Education, Initial Training and*

Probation of Teachers in Northern Ireland Schools and Institutions of Further Education, Belfast, HMSO, p. 25.
16 Lynn Committee Report, p. 17.
17 Akenson, D.H. (1973) *Education and Enmity,* Newton Abbot, David & Charles, New York, Barnes & Noble Books, p. 52.
18 Government of Northern Ireland (1969) *Education in Northern Ireland in 1968*, Belfast HMSO, p. 31. This Report also contains a useful account of the training of teachers in Northern Ireland since 1921.
19 Akenson, D.H. (1973) *op. cit.*, provides a full account of events at this time.
20 For statistics of students' religious denominations see Reports of the Ministry of Education until the 1960s.
21 Gibbon Report, as cited above, reference 12, p. 13.
22 Gibbon Report.
23 McNair Report Board of Education (1944) *The Recruitment and Training of Teachers*, London, HMSO.
24 Advisory Council for Education (1946) *Report on the Training of Teachers*, Edinburgh, HMSO.
25 Gibbon Report, p. 35.
26 Government of Northern Ireland (1951) *Report of the Ministry of Education, 1948–49,* Belfast, HMSO, p. 31.
27 See Government of Northern Ireland (1948) *Report of the Ministry of Education, 1945–46,* p. 38 and (1951) *Report of the Ministry of Education, 1948–49,* p. 32.
28 Gibbon Report, pp. 34–7.
29 Gibbon Report, pp. 63–4.
30 The Lockwood Report – Government of Northern Ireland (1965) *Higher Education in Northern Ireland,* Belfast, HMSO, pp. 84–7.
31 New University of Ulster (1972/73) *Report to the University Court,* p. 21.
32 New University of Ulster (1978/79) *Report to the University Court.*
33 New University of Ulster (1982/83) *Calendar.*
34 New University of Ulster (1983/84) *Report to the University Court.*
35 The Chilver Interim Report – Department of Education for Northern Ireland (1980) *The Future Structure of Teacher Education in Northern Ireland,* Belfast: HMSO, pp. 5–6.
36 Queen's University of Belfast (1967) *Calendar.*
37 For fuller details, see Sutherland, M.B. (1988) *op. cit.*
38 The Lockwood Report, pp. 98–9.
39 Knox, H.M. (1977) 'Free trade in teacher education: A Historical Footnote', *The Northern Teacher,* pp. 24–5.
40 The Chilver Interim Report, Appendix, p. 69.
41 The Chilver Interim Report.
42 Lodge, B. (1982) 'Catholics voice protest over proposal to train with Protestants', *The Times Educational Supplement, Scotland,* 12 February.
43 The Lelievre Report.
44 Queen's University of Belfast (1987) *Calendar.*
45 The Chilver Report – Department of Education for Northern Ireland (1982) *Higher Education in Northern Ireland,* Belfast, HMSO.
46 New University of Ulster (1983/84) *Report to the University Court.*
47 The Lelievre Report, pp. 4–5.
48 As, for example, Education for Mutual Understanding, Community Relations in

Schools, participation in UNESCO and Council for World Citizenship projects: earlier work is referred to in Jenkins, D. *et al.*, (n.d.) *Chocolate, Cream, Soldiers,* New University of Ulster Education Centre Occasional Papers: recent contributions in Fisher, A. (1989) 'A window on the world that may mist up', *The Times Educational Supplement,* 7 April, p. A9.

Chapter 8

The Study of Education as a University Subject

Brian Simon

Background Considerations

First, it may be worth reflecting briefly on education as a university subject[1] — its evolution and character — as compared with other 'subjects', both 'pure' (history, physics) and 'applied' (engineering, medicine, law).

One thing is clear. Education as a specific focus of study did not enter universities in Britain until comparatively recently. It did so as a result of an external demand on the universities — to participate in the professional training of teachers. It was, therefore, a product of the rise of mass systems of education which were brought into being in most advanced industrialized countries as a result of industrialization and urbanization. The first university chairs in Britain, as is well known, were established in 1876 in Scotland, perhaps almost fortuitously[2]; but at that time there was no commonly accepted or organized body of knowledge illuminating the field — nothing, in any case, of a scientific nature. It was Alexander Bain, when Professor of Logic at Aberdeen, who published, in 1879, a seminal book entitled *Education as a Science*; but this could do little more than point the way in which the study of education might develop if such an approach became common (Humes, 1980). This book was certainly influential, but chiefly in the support it gave, both theoretically and practically, to practising school teachers.

The closing years of the nineteenth century saw a tempestuous development of educational institutions of various kinds. By this time elementary education had developed as a system, while secondary schooling was on the verge of a similar move. University involvement in the professional training of teachers began in the 1890s in relation to elementary schools as detailed earlier in this book. Only after the 1902 Act did attention begin to focus on teachers required by the new system of secondary schools.

So a specialist staff began to be recruited, responsible for training teachers. New institutions and university departments were brought into being; after a struggle, chairs were established and professors appointed.[3] The 'subject' was now gradually embodied in universities, if in a somewhat peripheral manner. (It is worth noting that the departments were crucial to the emergence and strengthening of the modern universities in the first two decades of the century, since their subsidized students swelled the somewhat exiguous student totals.) With this development university norms began to apply, relating to publication and 'research', and, in this manner, a body of knowledge and norms of procedure began to be created.

Evidently, then, education, as a subject of university study, being a 'practical activity', relates more closely, for instance, to engineering and medicine than to other university subjects. The practice of education, even if defined (as Bain did) to exclude anything other than schooling, involves hundreds of thousands of teachers and millions of students. Evidently the scope and focus of study of this process cannot be easily defined nor rigorously enclosed within strict or distinct limits. On the contrary, knowledge from a variety of disciplines is relevant, and has been seen to be relevant from the start. The study of education requires not only a multidisciplinary approach, as, for instance, is also the case with subjects like politics and geography; but also poses problems of particular sharpness concerning the relation of theory to practice. What, for instance, are the specific features of a strictly educational theory? And from what disciplines and in what manner can theoretical knowledge be advanced? These are the sorts of questions that are relevant to this issue.

Although the purpose of this chapter is to focus on the last thirty years, during which a massive expansion of education as a university subject took place, a few words should be said about the early period since this set the pattern for later developments. In a lecture delivered in South Africa in 1918, Fred Clarke, later Director of the London University Institute of Education, and throughout his life a seminal thinker on this topic, bemoaned the fact that those concerned with the study of education at universities had failed to advance the subject as it deserved (Clarke, 1923). The reason for this, he claimed, was that originally their main function was seen as the preparation of elementary school teachers; official regulations (from the state) being designed to prevent the development of any kind of critical awareness on the part of these students. The professor's job at that time was seen as largely administrative. Even when, from the early twentieth century, attention shifted to the preparation of teachers for secondary schools, similar conditions persisted, if not for the same reason. Time spent travelling round the country watching students teach, with the focus on induction specifically into subject teaching, has left little time or energy either for serious research, or for study and reading. As a result, to extend Clarke's analysis, the actual conditions in which the bulk of staff of education departments operated functioned to restrict the vision of their members, and did not allow the proper development of educational studies as a university subject. It was, no doubt, partly as a reaction to this situation that some of the new universities found in the late 1950s and early 1960s deliberately established education departments without this responsibility

– an example being the Department of Educational Research at Lancaster.[4]

One important exception to this rule may, however, be noted. In Scotland the training colleges, which play an important role in national consciousness, successfully fought for a monopoly of teacher training so that (with the exception recently of the University of Stirling) all graduates receive their professional training in such colleges. University education departments in Scotland (at Edinburgh, Glasgow, Aberdeen and Dundee) do not themselves undertake the initial training of teachers in the same way as the bulk of their English (and Welsh) counterparts. These have, as a result, tended to remain small (in comparison with English departments) but, since they have concentrated, and still do, on advanced studies (higher degrees and diplomas), these departments enjoy the conditions that Clarke regarded as essential for the advance of educational knowledge.

One further introductory point may be made. The bulk of university study and teaching in England and Wales has (historically) been directed at graduate students undertaking the one-year course for what is now known as the postgraduate certificate of education (PGCE). This course functions within severe constraints. Since graduate students have to be inducted into the actual job of teaching (and this involves the equivalent of one full term's teaching practice in the schools), there is time only for an elementary introduction to the study of education; little study of an 'advanced' character has been possible. These conditions operated from the start of university departments in the 1890s until comparatively recently – certainly up to the end of World War 2.

This situation began to change from the 1950s. There were, perhaps, two main reasons for this. One was the expansion of university departments which related closely to the concomitant, and massive, growth of the school system in terms of sheer numbers of pupils and teachers. Another was the establishment, following the McNair Report (1944) of institutes of education in all the main universities in England and Wales (except Oxford and Cambridge). These had primarily an in-service function, but also brought the training colleges (as they were then known) into a much closer relation with the universities than had previously been the case – further they were initially directly funded by the Ministry of Education, and had a research function built in. Here then was a new source of staff concerned with the study of education (and freed from initial teacher training). Following the Robbins Report (1963), most universities fused their departments and institutes to develop 'schools of education'. This allowed an infusion of staff who were not 'method' lecturers (subject specialists), many of whom had been engaged in research, and a new and much greater flexibility in the deployment of staff than had been the case earlier. Concentration on specific sub-specialisms in research and teaching now became possible. Related to this, the new and massive expansion of the teaching profession in the '60s created a sudden demand for college of education staff who required some form of induction into their new jobs, now being defined anew (see below). This concatenation of circumstances, together with the establishment of many new universities, led to a big increase in the provision of advanced courses by university education departments — both diploma and higher degree.[5] Such courses, covering relevant specialisms, meant that now, for the first time, serious study and teaching on a university level was taking place across the field of education as a whole. The content and character of such teaching will be discussed below. What is worth noting at this stage is the comparative recency of such developments — now, of course, threatened, like other university studies, by the radical measures of the present government to contract universities (and education departments).[6]

Content of Study and Teaching: 1890s to 1914

If, so far, I have focused on background considerations, the way is now clear for a closer look at the content of study and teaching at universities. This can best be refined into four periods; first, the early phase, from the 1890s to 1914 or thereabouts, when the prevailing theory can best be defined as an eclectic version of Herbartianism. Second, the inter-war phase, dominated by Percy Nunn with the emphasis on individualism and resort to biological explanations of human development compatible with the rise of psychometry (mental measurement) as a 'science'. This phase projected into the 1950s but was superseded by a sociological tendency manifested in the work of Karl Mannheim and Fred Clarke in particular which may be described as a third phase. Radically new developments took place from the early 1960s with the redefinition of what was involved in educational studies by the 'new' philosophers (those involved in the so-called 'revolution in philosophy' based on linguistic analysis) — a trend to which we shall devote considerable attention. This phase was marked by the partial supersession of what had come to be regarded as traditional studies relating to the psychology and history of education by the new disciplines of philosophy and sociology which, as is well known, recorded a remarkable advance from the early 1960s. It may be that a fifth phase is now apparent, the contemporary concern with classroom studies marking a new interest in what may be called 'pedagogy' — an important aspect of teacher education which seems to have suffered a remarkable neglect historically in Britain.[7]

Before the universities entered the field, publications relating to teacher education (and related studies in training colleges) had tended to focus very specifically on the craft of teaching. The many student manuals produced in the 1880s and '90s, for instance, were concerned with the practical application of a general theory of learning, usually derived from Bain's influential book referred to earlier, and in turn based on Locke's philosophical position and, in particular, its application to education through the elaboration, by David Hartley and others, of associationist psychology. This outlook was generally optimistic — Locke held, it will be remembered, that nine parts in ten of what a man became was due to his education and upbringing. There is no space here to discuss this interesting phase further, except to note that, since this time, what may be called strictly 'pedagogical' studies have not flourished. It was at this time that the universities entered the field, and a broader and perhaps more 'scholarly' perception of what was involved in the study of education gradually made headway. The concern with theory, however, which this perception involved, carried with it the danger of losing touch with practice.

However, it was with the now rapidly developing system of secondary education that the universities were mostly concerned. These new schools required a theoretical underpinning for the teaching process. The main source for this theory was found in the teachings of the German philosopher-educationist Johann Friedrich Herbart, whose main works had been published early in the nineteenth century, but whose ideas had been taken up and adapted to the problems of mass schooling in Prussia by a series of distinguished university educationists of whom Rein of Jena, was the latest and perhaps the best known. The Herbartian system, as developed by his followers, was highly systematic in terms of teaching (with its five 'steps' for each lesson), was based on a modified theory of associationism, and was, therefore, basically optimistic in terms of its assessment of the power of education to influence not only intellectual development but also character and moral outlook. Many of the leading early professors of education in Britain declared themselves to be Herbartians, wrote books popularizing Herbart's outlook, and applied his ideas to the practice of teaching individual subjects.[8] It can hardly be claimed, however, that Herbart's English proponents developed his ideas in any significant way, as perhaps John Dewey may be said to have done in the United States.

Although Herbartianism provided the overall thrust of this early development, other tendencies were also apparent. First, among the early professoriat was a number of distinguished historians of education who made a substantial contribution to knowledge. Among these were such men as Foster Watson, at Aberystwyth, who had studied history under A.W. Ward at Manchester, and whose contribution to the scholarly study of educational history was strikingly original and broad in its scope (Armytage, 1961). Others were J.W. Adamson, of King's College, London, where the Chair of Education was later designated specifically for history (Barnard, 1961); and W.H. Woodward of Liverpool who masterminded the first systematic series of studies on this topic published by the Cambridge University Press. Indeed studies in the history of education, if in the sense largely of the history of ideas, characterized the approach of the Scottish universities, S.S. Laurie, the first holder of the chair at Edinburgh being one of the pioneers. Laurie held the view that 'the study of the history of education in the writings of the most distinguished representatives of various schools of thought is an important part of the general preparation of those who adopt the profession of schoolmaster' (Laurie, 1903). This view of the role of history had already been adumbrated by R.H. Quick in his pioneering book on the subject (Quick, 1868), and was to remain a main ingredient of education courses up to the

1950s and 1960s, when a new wave of historians tended to reject this approach, their main thrust then being to interpret changes in educational ideas and practice in terms of changes in economic and social conditions. By that time the 'great educators' approach had been relegated to the past (Simon, 1966 and 1973).

Together with history, psychology came into prominence in teacher education courses from the later 1890s – primarily at first (and for a long time after) in the form of 'child study', an adaptation of the developmental approach stemming from the widespread child study movement in the United States. The leading figure here was James Sully, whose *Teachers' Handbook of Psychology* had been published in 1886. It was Sully who, according to Burt, was 'the first to introduce systematic instruction on child psychology into courses for teachers and students preparing to enter the teaching profession' (Tibble, 1966). If, in his first edition, Sully dealt with mental development mainly in terms of growth of the faculties of the mind, later editions (the fifth was published in 1909) stressed the role of the child's activity in self-development, so linking more closely with the ideology of the 'new education' which now began to make its mark.

This first phase, then, which saw the inception of university studies in education, sees the emergence of psychology and history as the main underlying 'disciplines' applying to education. As regards the study of the process of education, the dominant ideology (Herbartianism) was still associationist and so positive (or optimistic) in its outlook. However, this dominance was soon to be challenged by the proponents of the new so-called 'experimental pedagogy' – an odd expression relating largely to the growth of mental testing, of related statistical procedures, and their application to education.[9]

Study and Teaching: The Inter-war Years

The second phase covers the inter-war years which were, in many respects, a period of stagnation (as in the case of the economy as a whole). Nevertheless it can also be seen as one of consolidation in that now university education departments came to a certain maturity after their initial establishment earlier. By then most universities in Britain had such departments, while the London Day Training College, as it used to be known, was transformed in 1932 into the premier university centre in the country in terms of size, quality of staff and professoriat and prestige; it was now a full school of the University known as the Institute of Education. There were at this period some 700 students annually studying for the postgraduate certificate (or diploma, as it used to be called), while advanced courses at London and elsewhere (particularly Leeds, Manchester, Birmingham and Liverpool) were being mounted in specialist areas.[10] In Scotland, also, this was a period of development particularly at Edinburgh and Glasgow, where the BEd (a specialist degree for practising teachers, usually studied part-time) had a continuous supply of students, a high proportion of whom later went on to administrative or teaching posts in higher education (Wiseman, 1953; Bell, 1982). Both departments became known for the rigorous study of education, if in particular of psychometric techniques.[11] It is worth noting in addition that the Scottish Council for Research in Education was founded in 1927, some twenty years earlier than the National Foundation for Educational Research was established in England.

In terms of the content of studies (or student programmes), however, this period saw little change. The overall transition to the philosophic idealist, biologically orientated, individualist approach has already been referred to. Percy Nunn's *Education: Its Data and First Principles*, first published in 1920, set the tone. This textbook, which ran through some twenty reprintings and two new editions by 1945, was the bible on which the inter-war generation of students was nurtured; though this is perhaps hardly the appropriate word, since Nunn put the major emphasis on nature, being himself a strong proponent of intelligence testing and its application to education.[12] Indeed if any specific ideology or thrust characterized the inter-war period, it is the growing emphasis on precise measurement, together with a strong belief (or better, faith) in the primacy of inborn mental powers. This theoretical emphasis paralleled developments in the schools, where a rationalization process involving concentration and classification of children was under way. It was this approach which now came to establish its hegemony in psychological and educational studies generally — at the London Institute, for instance, where Nunn was seconded in this field by Burt and later Hamley, at Manchester under Oliver and elsewhere. At the same time one may note the fact that the inter-war period also saw the triumph of the ideology of 'progressivism', at least so far as the primary schools were concerned. The three main Hadow reports of the period, *The Education of the Adolescent* (1926), *Infant and Nursery Schools* (1931) and *The Primary School* (1933), produced by the Consultative Committee to the Board of Education, which were required reading for many students, all reflected the prevailing 'child-centred' ideology which received support from Nunn's biologically-based theories as well as from psychometry which was based on similar assumptions concerning the determining power of innate characteristics.[13]

If, then, there were certain definite and specific developments in psychology (and the emergence of 'educational psychology' as an accepted sub-discipline), so far as teacher education as a whole was concerned, few other developments took place. Although Adamson published his major historical work in 1930 (*English Education 1789–1902*), little was done in this field to build on the work of the pioneers referred to earlier. History of education, however, continued as a main staple of lecture courses for intending teachers (at the London Institute and King's College, by A.C.F. Beales, for instance). Susan Isaacs, on her advanced diploma course again at the London Institute, introduced Freudian theories and this initiative was reflected in other departments (Gardner, 1969). Basically the one-year course remained an amalgam of lectures on the 'Principles of Education', normally given by the holder of the chair and very much subject to his/her personal predilections, usually some history (though often still largely of the 'great man' variety), somee psychology, now beginning to include an introduction to mental measurement, together with 'method' courses — that is, courses for graduates in specialist subjects on how to teach those subjects. Indeed, as indicated earlier, it was this activity that involved the great majority of staff of university departments, such lecturers normally being appointed after success as a school teacher. The base for serious study of education was, therefore, still attenuated. Indeed failure to come to terms with and engage on such study on the scale insistently required by social developments was the core of Fred Clarke's charge, and challenge, in his short but pungent *The Study of Education in England*, published in 1943 when he was still Director of the London Institute of Education.

Study and Teaching: 1945 to mid-1960s

Following World War 2, when popular concern for educational advance was enshrined in the Education Act of 1944, we reach the first post-war period of development marked by increasing numbers of students (and therefore staff), and the establishment of institutes of education already referred to. Nevertheless, for some time, the scope of studies remained much as it had been in the inter-war years. In the school system, psychometry, now widely regarded as strictly scientific in its methods and procedures, and closely embodied in the system through its use for selection both within and between schools, now gained a dominant position, one reflected in educational studies in the great predominance of psychological studies for higher degrees, a high proportion of which were psychometric in character (Wiseman, 1953). The English university centre of this movement (outside London) was Manchester whose higher degree courses were dominated by the study of the theory and practice of mental testing with much attention given to related statistical procedures. Indeed Wiseman argued that, given the predominance of psychological studies, now was the time for a large increase in appointment to professorships of psychologically, and particularly psychometrically qualified personnel.

The main change of emphasis in the later 1940s and '50s has already been mentioned. It was symbolized in the succession of Fred Clarke to Percy Nunn's Directorship of the Institute of Education (London University), though this had taken place some years earlier (in 1936). This marked the beginning of a transition to concern with the social function, or, better perhaps, the sociological role of education. In a seminal book, *Education and Social Change*, published in 1940, Clarke had achieved the first serious sociohistorical analysis of the topic in his title. Although in a sense only a sketch, Clarke's insights, and his proposals for future studies, foreshadowed many of the developments in the sociology and history of education that in fact took place from the 1960s on. Noting that writers on education 'show little explicit awareness of the social presuppositions of their thought', and criticizing the 'highly generalized principles' of education that figured largely in textbooks as the supposed *determinants* of educational practice, he insisted that thought and practice 'are much more closely conditioned by social realities which are themselves the result of social and economic forces'. Clarke mounted a sustained attack on the way English educationists 'take for granted' traditional structures and procedures. This led him not only to point the need for a new function for educational historians, but also the way to a new approach to the sociology of education which, at this time, was in its infancy. Both had the function of unravelling the real relations, and conflicts of interest underlying the rhetoric of contemporary discourse. Further, with Clarke's work, inspired partly by Karl Mannheim (whom Clarke involved in educational studies at the Institute during the war), emerged the first clear articulation of the social engineering function of education — an aspect that was to be energetically pursued in the 1960s by a Labour government with the assistance of a new breed of sociologists some of whom (for example, Jean Floud) had studied under Mannheim at the London School of Economics, and who began to publish their early works in the mid-1950s.[14]

Study and Learning: Coming of Age

The period of decisive change, however, is that which followed in the early-mid-1960s — the fourth phase of my earlier schema. Some reference to the changed context may be desirable. In sharp contrast to present concerns, this was a period when education was beginning to be seen as central to economic advance (with wide acceptance, by policy-makers, of the new, US based, human capital theory). At the same time the move to comprehensive secondary education was getting under way. The fatalistic theories of psychometry were now under sharp and increasing criticism, and were themselves often radically modified by psychologists themselves (Vernon, 1957); in place of these there was now a national concern with the so-called 'wastage' of human abilities. In 1963 the Robbins Committee reported proposing a massive increase in higher education with a twenty-year plan of advance — a report immediately accepted by the Conservative government of the day. A year later Labour won the election for the first time for thirteen years — pledged to carry through the white hot technological revolution.

The Robbins Committee proposed advance towards a graduate teaching profession recommending the establishment of the BEd as a means by which college of education students might graduate through a four-year course of study of which education was to be a major component. This implied a much closer university involvement with studies in the colleges than had been the case before, specifically since the degree was to be awarded by the validating universities themselves. In this situation, educational studies, not yet underpinned by any generally accepted theoretical position, required some form of legitimization (as the sociologists put it). Indeed, generally speaking, the nature and scope of educational studies needed clarification.

The main thrust for this rethinking came, interestingly enough, from the field of philosophy of education, which had first acquired a named chair — at the London Institute — in 1947. Richard Peters, who had taught philosophy at Birkbeck College, and who succeeded Louis Arnaud Reid in 1962, launched the main attack. Educational studies, he argued, in particular the main general courses offered both at universities and colleges under the heading 'principles of education' were an 'undifferentiated mush'. It was necessary to define as precisely as possible the nature of education as a process, to sort out and redefine the contribution of philosophers to its study, and to clarify the main disciplines on which the study of education was based. 'Such conceptual clarification', said Peters, 'is preeminently the task of the philosopher of education' (Peters, 1963; see also Peters, 1966 and 1977). Further, it was argued, education was not itself a 'subject' with its own language, forms of thought and concepts. It was best seen as an area of practical activity, one to which various disciplines contributed in the formulation of general principles of action (Hirst, 1966). At a seminal conference at Hull early in 1964, organized jointly by the predecessors of the Universities Council for the Education of Teachers (that is, professors of education) and the Department of Education and Science (for which the initiative came, interestingly enough, from the Department). R.S. Peters took the offensive, supported by Wiseman (psychology), Bernstein (sociology) and others — the keynote lecture being delivered by the Chief Inspector responsible for teacher training (Gill). What was necessary was the rigorous study of those disciplines which underlay, or contributed to, educational knowledge. Those studying education, particularly at advanced level (and such courses were now proliferating) needed to be inducted into the thinking relevant to the philosophy of education (which should concern itself primarily with conceptual clarification), the sociology of education, now rapidly developing in its own right, the psychology and history of education (though history was the only one of these disciplines unrepresented among the Hull conference lecturers). Thus the model known to educationists as 'the four disciplines' was born.

This model quickly became institutionalized — in a sense it simply crystallized contemporary developments in the field. It was acceptable to universities since, to put it no higher, it seemed to lend academic respectability to the study of education. MA courses in the philosophy, psychology, sociology and history of education now mounted at several universities quite rapidly produced a new brand of college lecturers who, having teaching experience, were seconded to universities for advanced study. In the massively expansionist character of the 1960s, when colleges of education expanded three-fold in ten years, these often found employment at colleges teaching one or other of these specialist sub-subjects now embodied in BEd syllabuses and examinations.[15] At the same time university departments, with their enlarged staff, several of whom were now (with the fusion with institutes of education) freed from 'method' work, also reflected this new conceptual model in their organization – these specialist lecturers having the dual function of teaching their subject to postgraduates, higher degree and diploma students, and of monitoring the teaching of these new academic disciplines in the colleges.

This period, from the mid-1960s, now saw a proliferation of educational theory – and of educational studies. This is surely partly attributable to the great increase in the number of those professionally involved, at the training level in colleges and universities, in the study and teaching of education. One enterprising publisher, Routledge & Kegan Paul, now started a 'Students Library of Education' which again reflected the philosophers' model. The Editorial Board originally comprised a philosopher of education (Peters), a sociologist (Taylor), a psychologist (Morris) and an historian (Simon), the Board being chaired by Tibble whose interests were catholic; it was later joined by Paul Hirst, a philosopher of education and a leading theoretician of the new model. It may be worth noting that there was no clear place in the original schema for books on the actual practice of teaching (or 'pedagogy') which eighty or more years ago had formed the main staple of publications for students in education. In the outcome an extra section was added, but it was difficult to determine who should be responsible. This is, perhaps, symptomatic of this whole tendency; its implications will be discussed briefly later.

The new conceptual model, as already indicated, called for special attention, in advanced studies in particular, to the four 'basic disciplines' held to underlie or contribute to the study of education. Two of these, psychology and history, had from the 1890s featured centrally in educational studies, even if their content had changed. By the mid-1960s, for instance, psychological studies no longer paid the same attention to psychometry as in the past; indeed this sub-discipline was already coming under severe criticism, while the decline of the actual practice of selection and streaming in the school system meant that it no longer played the dominant role it had earlier. Instead interest now shifted to studies of child development (which had featured earlier) while a new concern with cognitive development focused attention on the work of the Swiss researcher, Jean Piaget, and, if perhaps to a lesser extent, on the Soviet psychologist, Lev Vygotski, whose seminal book *Thought and Language* was translated in the early 1960s. For psychological underpinning in the field of curriculum development, interest turned specifically to the work of Jerome Bruner in the United States, whose studies and research tied in with the curriculum reform movement which took off with considerable force in the early 1960s. Indeed, freed from the straitjacket of mental testing, psychological courses now related more closely to actual developments on the ground in what was essentially an expansionist era (for a recent survey, see Clarke, 1982). At the same time this period saw a renewal and strengthening of historical studies, the new wave of historians taking to heart Fred Clarke's precepts in line with the trend in historical scholarship generally towards a new emphasis on social history and sociological determinants (Simon, 1982). A History of

Education Society, reflecting this vigorous development, was established in 1967.

It was the two relatively new disciplines, however, which made the greatest impact: philosophy and sociology. It was not only that the philosophers, for instance, displayed considerable energy, with an impressive output of books and textbooks for students; it was also the case that the definition of the philosopher's role, while restricting this largely to the task of clarification of concepts relevant to educational discourse and action, also outlined a precise but limited field which bore directly on important issues facing teachers and educators generally. The importation of this form of critical analysis, while sometimes appearing somewhat arid and 'academic' nevertheless certainly provided a stimulating addition to courses of educational study. Dearden (1982) charts this initial impact, referring to the 'burst of activity' in the 1960s, the 'publications explosion' of that period, and the formation of the Philosophy of Education Society in 1966. However, the main impact on educational studies of the 1960s was probably that made by sociology.

The sudden emergence of sociology as a legitimate field of university study which took place with astonishing rapidity in the early 1960s (in 1963 there were only two chairs in sociology in the country; two years later there were twenty-three) presaged the emergence of the sociology of education as a very important sub-discipline; one which rapidly became established in university education departments through the mid-late 1960s and later (the Open University, in particular, developed as a centre of such study). Since the work of several leading sociologists lay specifically in the field of education (for instance, Jean Floud and A.H. Halsey), and since, in the social democratic consensus of those years there developed a close link between sociology and policy-making at government level, sociology very quickly achieved an important, if not dominating, position in educational studies generally — while empirical (and official government) studies of the late 1950s and 1960s provided a mass of data particularly on the relations between social class and educational opportunity which became an important issue at this time. The 1960s also saw widespread interest in the application to education of sociolinguistic studies carried through, in particular, by Basil Bernstein. If the latest review of sociological studies in education reports a certain disarray over the last decade, internal conflicts within the field, as now apparent, have not detracted from the stimulation that studies in this area have provided for educationists generally.[16]

Within this brief review, mention should certainly be made of two further areas of study that have developed over the last two decades, both reaching a certain maturity. Interest in, and study of, the economics of education grew with extreme rapidity in the 1960s closely related (as mentioned earlier) to governmental concern with the implications of human capital theory, and involving contributions by many distinguished economists. This study is now institutionalized at certain universities, as is also the study of administration, proposed long ago by Fred Clarke as an area needing development.[17] At the

London Institute there are chairs in both these specialisms, as there are also in two other fields, each involving interdisciplinary study — comparative education and curriculum studies.

Enough has been said to indicate that the concept of educational studies both broadened and deepened very considerably in the 1960s and early 1970s. There was now a closer relation with what might be called 'main-line' studies in universities as a whole. Further these studies were now a great deal more penetrating than in the past — particularly advanced studies of various kinds, which expanded throughout this period. Another stimulating factor was the formation of the Educational Research Board of the Social Science Research Council (1965) prepared to fund fundamental research into education in a consistent way for the first time. Education departments were now becoming more closely linked with systematic research activities — another aspect of university studies which had only marginally been provided for in earlier dispensations. The consequent expansion of qualified research personnel was reflected in the foundation of the British Educational Research Association (BERA) in 1973. In general, then, it can be said that, in the 1960s, university studies in education came of age.

All this was not achieved, without some loss. As educational studies became more rigorous and inevitably academic, the historic neglect of pedagogy was accentuated. By 'pedagogy' is meant the theory and practice of teaching. As we saw earlier, in the old school board days of the 1880s and 1890s, strictly pedagogical study formed the central focus of teacher training programmes, taught, in most cases, by the 'master of method'. Later this function was relegated, in universities, to the so-called 'method' tutors, who concentrated on this alone. In the new dispensation, method tutors continued this function, but, apart from occasional involvement in curriculum reform issues in their subjects, played no part, generally speaking, in the reconstructed courses in the basic disciplines. The result was a certain separation between theory and practice on PGCE courses at least, in that, with the possible exception of psychology, none of these disciplines was seen to have a direct effect on the practice of teaching. (The counter-argument was strongly put, however, that they had an important *indirect* effect.)

Dissatisfaction arising from this source eventually spurred the Universities Council for the Education of Teachers to mount a thorough enquiry into the PGCE year (in 1974). The outcome, briefly, was that the course for students preparing for secondary teaching should focus very specifically on the skills and abilities intending teachers require for effective teaching in their first job (UCET, 1979).[18] This marked an important move away from concentration on the 'basic disciplines' as a main focus for this particular course. At the same time the new interest in classroom observational studies, whether those using anthropological techniques or systematic observation using pre-coded schedules, fuelled this movement.[19] The result has been that, over the last four or five years, PGCE courses have tended to shift towards a strictly professional training — a focus on pedagogical issues previously neglected.

This trend has also had its effect on advanced studies, with a move towards school based courses in which students are encouraged to investigate and evaluate inner school problems of various kinds — a tendency institutionalized in particular at the Centre for Applied Research in Education (CARE) at the University of East Anglia and to some extent at the Cambridge Institute of Education.

If the 1960s (and early 1970s) can be regarded as a success story, so far as educational studies are concerned, these developments may be put at risk through the reduction of staff in universities and within education departments resulting from present government policy. The health of these departments has depended, to a large extent, on recruiting a wide range of members with a variety of expertise appropriate to an interdisciplinary field like education. Philosophers, sociologists, psychologists, historians, anthropologists, economists, as well as specialists in pedagogy are required to carry through the many responsibilities that have now accrued historically. These range from undergraduate teaching in some universities, the postgraduate education course which provides the bulk of students, involvement in publicly-funded research projects, in-service courses for practising teachers in the vicinity, as well as diploma and higher degree courses (both part and full-time) with some doctoral students. Outside the London Institute of Education, with its staff of over 200 (160 academic, fifty research), most of the modern universities in England (for example, Leeds, Manchester, Birmingham) maintain relatively large departments to carry out these functions. The Bristol department, one of the most prestigious in historical terms, was first threatened with total closure, then by reduction by half, but seems now to have emerged relatively unscathed. Other departments, while not yet so sharply threatened, are having to shed staff. Though quality, of course, cannot be equated with quantity, such measures inevitably imply a contraction in the scope of studies outlined in this chapter. Exactly how this will affect developments and in particular the paradigm outlined above, only the future will show.[20]

Notes

1 An earlier essay on this topic is 'The development of the study of education' by Tibble (Ed) (1966). A survey of recent developments across the whole field is provided in the thirtieth anniversary issue of the *British Journal of Educational Studies*, Vol. XXX, No. 1. This contains articles covering developments in the period 1952–1982 in the sociology, philosophy, psychology and history of education, as well as in educational administration and the economics of education. Reference may also be made to the recent publication of selected inaugural lectures in education in Gordon (1980).

2 The finance derived from Dr Andrew Bell's will from moneys left for elementary schools. Following the 1872 (Scotland) Act, the trustees granted sufficient sums from this endowment to create chairs at Edinburgh and St Andrews (Gordon, 1980).

Professor J.M.D. Meiklejohn's inaugural address (St Andrews) is reprinted in this volume.

3 For an example of opposition to this, see 'A proposed chair of education in Mason College, Birmingham', in Storr (1899), 373 ff. In this case the opposition came from secondary schoolmasters in Birmingham.

4 As many as thirteen of the new universities established from the late 1950s offer education as an undergraduate study, usually in combination with other subjects. Very few of the 'modern' universities do, though the University of Wales is an exception.

5 In 1981, a total of 7188 part- and full-time students were studying for higher degrees in England and Wales (DES *Annual Report*, 1981).

6 See other chapters by Turner, Ross, Gosden and Edwards in the present volume for a full account of the events described in this paragraph.

7 The argument in my essay, 'Why no pedagogy in England?' (Simon and Taylor, 1981) is relevant to this discussion but will not be repeated here.

8 For instance, John Adams (later Sir John and first Director of the London Day Training College) whose book *The Herbartian Psychology Applied to Education* was published in 1987 (see Rusk, 1961). Other leading Herbartians included J.J. Findlay and J.W. Adamson.

9 *The Journal of Experimental Pedagogy* was established in 1909 as the organ of this movement. For a contemporary assessment, see Adamson (1912) pp. 106–29. Early numbers included articles by Cyril Burt and other proponents of mental testing.

10 In 1937/38 there were a total of fifty-two full-time and 191 part-time 'advanced' students studying for higher degrees, diplomas, or undertaking research (University Grants Committee, 1937/38).

11 Paterson (1975) contains a fascinating account and interpretation of this development at Edinburgh: see also Bell (1975), and especially Bell (1982) which includes material on Glasgow and much interesting discussion on the specific problems facing educational studies in Scotland in the 1920s and later. See also Bell in the present volume.

12 For Nunn, see Tibble (1961). For an acute analysis of Nunn's biologism, see Gordon and White (1979), pp. 207–13.

13 The best studies are Sellcck (1968 and 1972).

14 Clarke's indebtedness to Mannheim was generously expressed in his note 'Karl Mannheim at the Institute of Education' in Mitchell (1967, Appendix B). Clarke persuaded Mannheim, who held a teaching post at the London School of Economics, to teach Institute students during the war. He was appointed to a chair in the sociology of education at the Institute in 1946, dying in 1947. His work and influence is assessed in Stewart (1953) and more generally in Floud (1969).

15 Academic staff at colleges of education increased from 3334 in 1960 to 11,937 in 1970. The number of students rose from 33,993 in 1961 to 107,386 in 1970. It should be remembered that the traditional two-year course was increased to three years from 1960. Referring to the changed content of study at the colleges, Joan Browne writes: 'Such books as M.V. Daniels: *Activity in the Junior School* and Susan Isaacs: *The Children We Teach*, were replaced or supplemented by *The Study of Education*, edited by Professor Tibble and its many offshoots, and by specialist texts on the psychology, sociology and history of education' (Browne, 1980).

16 Banks (1982) surveys recent developments, including the thrust of the 'new' sociology, of neo-Marxism, and their relations to the 'old' (or mainstream) sociology.

The extreme divisions of the 1970s, she claims, are being overcome, while the subject itself, which displayed 'great vitality' in the 1970s, 'is still very much alive'.

17 Williams (1982) surveys studies in the economics of education. The author argues that economic and political circumstances are likely to enhance the importance of this subject in the future. For university studies in administration, see Bone (1982). A British Educational Administration and Management Society was established in 1971.

18 For the leading papers presented to this working party, by Paul Hirst, Colin Lacey, Brian Simon and others, see *British Journal of Teacher Education* (1976), 2, 1. For specific references by Hirst, Lacey and Simon see below.

19 Jackson (1968) was the pioneering study using anthropological techniques. This was accompanied by Hargreaves (1967) and Lacey (1970), both products of the Department of Anthropology and Sociology of the University of Manchester. Systematic observational studies include the ORACLE publications, for example, Galton, Simon and Croll (1980) and subsequent volumes.

20 Editorial note: This paper has been reprinted as originally published and only subsection titles and notes and references have been changed to conform to the style of the present volume.

References

ADAMSON, J.W. (1912) *The Practice of Instruction* (2nd edn) revised, London, National Society Depository.

ARMYTAGE, W.H.G. (1961) 'Foster Watson: 1860–1929', *British Journal of Educational Studies*, 10, 1, pp. 5–18.

BANKS, O. (1982) 'The sociology of education, 1952–1982', *British Journal of Educational Studies*, 30, 1, pp. 18–31.

BARNARD, H.C. (1961) 'John William Adamson: 1857–1947', *British Journal of Educational Studies*, 10, 1, pp. 19–32.

BELL, R.E. (1975) 'Godfrey Thomson and Scottish education', summary in *Research Intelligence*, 1, 2, pp. 65–8.

BELL, R.E. (1982) 'The education departments in the Scottish universities' in HUMES, W. and PATERSON, H. (Eds), *Scottish Culture and Scottish Education, 1800–1980*, Edinburgh, John Donald.

BONE, T.R. (1982) 'Educational administration', *British Journal of Educational Studies*, 30, 1, pp. 32–42.

BROWNE, J. (1980) 'The transformation of the education of teachers in the nineteen sixties' in FEARN, E. and SIMON, B. (Eds) *Education in the Sixties*, London, History of Education Society.

CLARKE, A.M. (1982) 'Psychology and education', *British Journal of Educational Studies*, 30, 1, pp. 43–56.

CLARKE, F. (1923) 'The university and the study of education' in CLARKE, F. (Ed) *Essays in the Politics of Education*, Oxford, Oxford University Press.

DEARDEN, R.F. (1982) 'Philosophy of education, 1952–1982', *British Journal of Educational Studies*, 30, 1, pp. 57–71.

FLOUD, J. (1969) 'Karl Mannheim' in RAISON, T. (Ed) *The Founding Fathers of Social Science*, Harmondsworth, Penguin.

GARDNER, D.E.M. (1969) *Susan Isaacs*, London, Methuen.

GALTON, M., SIMON, B. and CROLL, P. (1980) *Inside the Primary Classroom*, London, Routledge & Kegan Paul.

GORDON, P. (Ed) (1980) *The Study of Education, Vol. I, Early and Modern, Vol. II, The Last Decade*, London, Woburn Press.

GORDON, P. and WHITE, J. (1979) *Philosophers as Educational Reformers*, London, Routledge & Kegan Paul.

HARGREAVES, D. (1967) *Social Relations in a Secondary School*, London, Routledge & Kegan Paul.

HIRST, P. (1966) 'Educational theory' in TIBBLE, J.W. (Ed) *The Study of Education*, London, Routledge & Kegan Paul, pp. 29–58.

HIRST, P. (1976) 'The PGCE course: Its objectives and their nature', *British Journal of Teacher Education*, 2, 1, pp. 7–21.

HUMES, W.M. (1980) 'Alexander Bain and the development of educational theory' in SMITH, J.V. and HAMILTON, D. (Eds), *The Meritocratic Intellect*, Aberdeen, Aberdeen University Press.

JACKSON, P. (1968) *Life in Classrooms*, New York, Holt, Rinehart.

LACEY, C. (1970) *Hightown Grammar*, Manchester, Manchester University Press.

LACEY, C. and LAMONT, W. (1976) 'Partnership with schools', *British Journal of Teacher Education*, 2, 1, pp. 39–52.

LAURIE, S.S. (1903) *Studies in the History of Educational Opinion from the Renaissance*, p.v.

MITCHELL, F.W. (1967) *Sir Fred Clarke, Master-Teacher, 1880–1952*, London, Longman.

PATERSON, H.M. (1975) 'Godfrey Thomson and the development of psychometrics in Scotland, 1925–1950', (available in mimeograph; for summary, *Research Intelligence*, 1, 2, pp. 63–65).

PETERS, R.S. (1963) 'Education as initiation' (inaugural lecture), in GORDON, P. (Ed) *The Study of Education*, 1, London, Woburn Press.

PETERS, R.S. (1966) 'The philosophy of education' in TIBBLE, J.W. (Ed) *The Study of Education*, London, Routledge & Kegan Paul, pp. 50–90.

PETERS, R.S. (1977) 'The role and responsibility of the university in teacher education' in PETERS, R.S. *Education and the Education of Teachers*, London, Routledge & Kegan Paul.

QUICK, R.H. (1868) *Essays on Educational Reformers*, London, Longman Green.

RUSK, R.R. (1961) 'Sir John Adams: 1857–1934', *British Journal of Educational Studies*, 10, 1, pp. 49–57.

SELLECK, R.J.W. (1968) *The New Education, the English Background, 1870–1914*, London, Pitman.

SELLECK, R.J.W. (1972) *English Primary Education and the Progressives 1914 1939*, London, Routledge & Kegan Paul.

SIMON, B. (1966) 'The History of Education' in TIBBLE, J.W. (Ed) *The Study of Education*, London, Routledge & Kegan Paul, pp. 91–132.

SIMON, B. (1973) 'Research in the history of education' in TAYLOR, W. (Ed) *Research Perspectives in Education*, London, Routledge & Kegan Paul.

SIMON, B. (1976) 'Theoretical aspects of the PGCE course', *British Journal of Teacher Education*, 2, 1, pp. 23–38.

SIMON, B. (1982) 'The history of education in the 1980s', *British Journal of Educational Studies*, 30, 1, pp. 85–96.

SIMON, B. and TAYLOR, W. (Eds) (1981) *Education in the Eighties*, London, Batsford.

STEWART, W.A.C. (1953) 'Karl Mannheim and the sociology of education', *British*

Journal of Educational Studies, 1, 2, pp. 99–113.

STORR, F. (Ed) (1899) *Life and Remains of the Rev R.H. Quick*, Cambridge, Cambridge University Press.

TIBBLE, J.W. (1961) 'Sir Percy Nunn: 1870–1944', *British Journal of Educational Studies*, 10, 1, pp. 58–75.

TIBBLE, J.W. (Ed) (1966) *The Study of Education*, London, Routledge & Kegan Paul.

UNIVERSITY COUNCIL FOR THE EDUCATION OF TEACHERS (1979) *The PGCE Course and the Training of Specialist Teachers for Secondary Schools*, London, UCET.

UNIVERSITY GRANTS COMMITTEE (1937/38) *Returns*, London, HMSO.

VERNON, P.E. (Ed) (1957) *Secondary School Selection*, London, Methuen.

WILLIAMS, G. (1982) 'The economics of education: current debates and prospects', *British Journal of Educational Studies*, 30, 1, pp. 97–107.

WISEMAN, S. (1953) 'Higher degrees in education in British universities', *British Journal of Educational Studies*, 2, 1, pp. 54–66.

Chapter 9

Teacher Education in Multicultural Britain

Maurice Craft

Context

During the 1980s a series of massive changes in British education have been introduced by the government, affecting all areas of provision and practice, and significant among them are changes in the initial and in-service training of teachers. The advent of the Council for the Accreditation of Teacher Education (CATE) in 1984 established new and detailed procedures for the approval of courses of initial teacher training; and the introduction of Grant-Related In-Service Training (GRIST) in 1986 decisively influenced the provision of long, award-bearing in-service courses in favour of those which are shorter and of more immediate, practical relevance. Even greater changes will follow with the implementation of the 1988 Education Reform Act, as teachers are prepared for the introduction of a new National Curriculum and its assessment; and as heads and senior teachers are equipped to cope with the Act's requirements in respect of local financial management, open enrolment and opting out, as well as staff appraisal and curriculum planning.

The Swann Report (DES, 1985), a major review of education in a multicultural society appeared in 1985 after a six-year sifting of evidence, and it too included a substantial section on teacher education. This sought to convey the central, strategic significance of equipping all new and practising teachers — 'the key figures in the education process' — with an informed awareness of what teaching in a multicultural society involves, something which the Rampton Report (DES, 1981) had attempted to do much more briefly a little earlier in the decade. The need for all teachers to take this particular responsibility seriously had been regularly highlighted for some twenty years, and there has been hardly a government report or other major enquiry into immigration, race relations or ethnic minority children which has not made reference to teacher education. The Scarman Report on the Brixton Disorders, for example, asserted:

> There is a clear need for improved training of teachers in the particular

> needs, the cultural background, and the expectations of minority group children and parents (Home Office, 1981, para. 6.20)

But as long ago as 1969, the Select Committee of Race Relations and Immigration observed:

> We would like to see every college of education in the country teaching its students something about race relations, and the problems of immigrants. To say that there is no need to educate all students about such matters because, as one college has said, 'very few of our students go into schools where they are likely to meet mixed classes', is to miss the point. Teachers should be equipped to prepare all their children for life in a multicultural society (para. 214)

This was an important statement because it pointed up the two broad objectives of a multicultural approach in teacher education to be found in most writing on the subject: first, preparing students to cope effectively with the particular needs of minority group children; and second, to help student teachers to acquaint *all* the children in their future classes with the realities of a culturally plural society. This second, broader objective was apparently overlooked by Lord Scarman's Report, but it was fundamental to Swann whose Report was called *Education For All.*

These two quotations will suffice, for a fuller documentation can be found elsewhere, (Craft, 1981; Watson, 1984). But perhaps two points might be emphasized. First, that this concern of the 1980s was not a new enthusiasm, the need had been recognized for quite some time. Second, that the intention was more than simply seeking to equip teachers to cope more effectively with the particular needs of minority children. It was also — and more importantly — to consider ways of enabling teachers to convey to *all* children a more intelligent appreciation of the diversity of our society. We are not alone in this in the UK. On the continent, the foreign migrant worker population is now in the region of fifteen millions, comprising some 14 per cent of the Swiss labour force, 9 per cent of the French and 7 per cent of the German (Banks and Lynch, 1986; Castles *et al.*, 1984). Linguistic and cultural diversity is a reality in most countries, and whether we regard this as an enrichment to be maximized (as we should) or as a potential source of conflict or even violence (and it sometimes is), we can hardly ignore the heavy responsibility which lies with teacher education. In the United States, teacher educators have similarly become more sensitive to this responsibility. In 1980, the American Association of Colleges for Teacher Education published detailed strategies for implementing a multicultural perspective, and in Australia a national review of such strategies has been carried out (Lynch, 1985; Hicks and Monroe, 1984; Suzuki, 1984; Washburn, 1982).

As the Swann Report indicates, a number of initial teacher training (ITT) institutions have for some years offered a multicultural element by means of special *options* in the BEd or PGCE; some specialized Diploma and MEd courses exist; and there has been a growing number of relevant in-service (INSET) short courses offered by LEAs and ITT institutions over the years. But these have reached mainly the committed. A second approach is to include an element in the ITT *core course*, which ensures that all students gain some exposure to the issues. But this can only be of limited duration, and some have argued that it risks trivialization and that it is preferable to train specialists in greater depth (Latham, 1982). Thirdly, there is '*permeation*' where everything which is taught in ITT and INSET reflects the multicultural context of the world outside schools. This does not necessarily require additional time, but rather a modified perspective, 'another screen or lens through which to operationalize [or] interpret . . . generic and theoretical concepts and principles of pedagogy' (Gay, 1983). It may simply involve a wider range of exemplification: in making reference, say to age or gender or social class variations in learning, one might also indicate *ethnic* variations. Permeated syllabuses have been developed in a number of institutions, and this is returned to in more detail later. Meanwhile, the advantage of options and core studies is that a single lecturer or LEA adviser can make a beginning, and this itself can provide the basis of some staff development as other colleagues are drawn in.

Since the publication at the beginning of the decade of four major reports on multicultural education (DES, 1981; Eggleston, 1981; House of Commons, 1981; Schools Council, 1981), several of them including particularly pointed references to the tardy response of ITT and INSET to the needs of a culturally plural society, and particularly since the Swann Report in 1985, there have been numerous developments affecting teacher educators. A large number of LEAs, for example, published policy statements on multicultural education; many made specialist appointments to their in-service advisory staffs, as has HM Inspectorate which came to include more than twenty members with specialist concerns in this field. All ITT courses submitted to the CNAA for validation or renewal are now expected to demonstrate some awareness of the multicultural dimension, in accordance with the Council's national guidelines on this matter which were published in 1984. The Universities Council for the Education of Teachers published similar guidelines in 1985, and a 'training the trainers' initiative was convened at Nottingham University from 1982/87 (Atkins and Craft, 1988). All initial teacher-training courses on *both* sides of the binary line are, as indicated earlier, submitted to the national Council for the Accreditation of Teacher Education, whose stated criteria include the requirement that:

> Students should be prepared . . . to teach the full range of pupils whom they are likely to encounter in an ordinary school, with their diversity of ability, behaviour, social background and ethnic and cultural origins. They will need to learn how to respond flexibly to such diversity and to guard against preconceptions based on the race or sex of pupils. (DES, 1984b, Annex para. 11).

In the United States, such a requirement was enacted by the National

Council for the Accreditation of Teacher Education in 1977, in order 'to help institutions and individuals become more responsive to the human condition, cultural integrity, and cultural pluralism in society', and it stated that 'multicultural education should receive attention in courses, seminars, directed readings, laboratory and clinical experiences, practicum and other types of field experiences' (NCATE, 1977). As to in-service teacher training in Britain in the 1980s, education for a multiethnic society was included in the list of national priorities for several years until the advent of the Education Reform Act.

There have also been significant changes in the public examination system during the decade. The GCSE general criteria include a section entitled 'Recognition of cultural diversity', which states:

> In devising syllabuses and setting question papers, examining groups should bear in mind the linguistic and cultural diversity of society. The value to all candidates of incorporating material which reflects this diversity should be recognized.

The School Examinations and Assessment Council and the examinations boards have the responsibility of ensuring that the new GCSE syllabuses and examinations meet this multicultural criterion. It is therefore essential that all secondary teachers are adequately prepared by teacher educators for this task.

Strategies

So much for context. What then should teacher educators be expected to do, given the now much greater recognition of cultural diversity in our national life? This section will look briefly at three major aspects of strategy: first, those involved in preparing students to meet the particular needs of minority children; secondly, strategies concerned with the needs of all children in a plural society; and thirdly, those focused upon intercultural relations.

The Particular Needs of Ethnic Minority Children

What are these particular needs, now that there are far fewer immigrants and that the great majority of minority children have been born here? English as a second language is far less important, but large numbers of children are still entering school having spoken little English at home (even though born here), and are growing up with varied degrees of bilingualism. The capacity for code-switching within two or three languages with parents, peers and teachers, is a considerable source of national strength. As a former Secretary of State observed, 'Linguistic minorities need not be seen as having a problem

— lack of practice in English — but as having an asset, a skill in language' (DES, 1984a). At the same time, there are many pupils who require English language support across the curriculum at both primary and secondary levels in order to ensure full equality of opportunity, for standard English is the language of school and the world of work. In 1982, a national survey in teacher education found that some three-quarters of ITT institutions in England and Wales sought to convey to all students, through core courses, an awareness of dialect and language differences, and a 'repertoire' approach to language learning in schools. However, only half included any work on the existence and main characteristics of minority community languages in Britain or included reference to current professional discussion of mother tongue teaching, bilingualism etc.; and less than one-third claimed to convey a minimal competence to offer language support across the curriculum in linguistically diverse schools (Craft and Atkins, 1983). There were evidently many opportunities here for ITT specialists in language development and linguistics, but there is little more recent data on the matter (Arora, 1988).

Going a little further, providing some teaching through the mother tongue at infant and junior levels, and offering community languages in the modern languages curriculum of the secondary school are now encouraged in a number of LEAs. But preparation for all these roles in ITT and INSET is probably still limited. As indicated above, in 1982, a number of institutions claimed to convey an awareness of the existence and main characteristics of ethnic minority community languages in Britain, and to consider the issues of mother tongue teaching, bilingualism etc., with their students. But far fewer said they offered any specific techniques for teaching in multilingual classrooms (the acquisition of some basic vocabulary, for example); and no more than one or two ITT institutions said they offered any preparation for student teachers who wished to teach Asian languages or Italian to 'O' and 'A' level (Craft and Atkins, 1983). At that time, there was *no* provision in modern Greek, Turkish or in any Asian language and only a little in Spanish or Italian, compared with the far more widespread provision in French or German. The situation in ITT-based in-service work appeared to be little better, although the EEC-funded Linguistic Diversity Project (for primary teachers) at Nottingham University is one of a number of subsequent INSET initiatives.

And yet the 1987 Language Census identified 172 spoken languages in London schools, with 23 per cent of the school population (i.e. 64,987 children) using a language other than, or in addition to, English at home (ILEA, 1987a). A 1983 survey by the Brent LEA had reported in the same vein: of 35,051 pupils surveyed in 103 of the Authority's 104 schools, 35 per cent spoke a language other than English, and while Gujarati and Urdu predominated, more than twenty different languages were in existence at that time (Brent LEA, 1983a). The London University Linguistic Minorities Project similarly identified nine languages in Coventry, ten in Peterborough, and eleven in Bradford (LMP, 1983). In fact, 'the majority of LEAs now have a multilingual school population', according to a national survey by the former Schools

Council, carried out in 1983, and at least one-half of all LEAs in England and Wales then had a *minimum* of one primary school with over 10 per cent of pupils who were bilingual (Tansley and Craft, 1984). This survey also reported the growing provison by LEAs for community languages teaching in mainstream primary schools, which seemed to signal a need for suitably qualified teachers.

As to the particular language needs of children of West Indian origin, it is possible that rather more ITT institutions offer relevant language work, for as indicated above issues relating to accent, dialect, and language repertoire are very widely claimed to be part of the normal, core language work in ITT. But we do not actually know how many BEd or PGCE students consider bi-dialecticism, and the classroom discussion (and classroom use) of Creole dialects. This is probably unlikely to be widespread. (See also Houlton (1986) on all these issues.)

A further element of the strategy of preparing ITT students to meet the particular needs of ethnic minority students are those less tangible aspects of professional skill which are associated with problems of *identity*, the intergenerational stress experienced by minority children growing up in the two often contrasting cultures of home and school. As Wilce (1984) reported:

> The majority of teenage Asian girls are the British-born offspring of first generation immigrants. As such they can walk a tightrope existence — the normal tensions of adolescence stretched to breaking point by the differing expectations of home, school and themselves . . . Most girls adapt to their two worlds with admirable skill — often by keeping home and school as separate as possible . . . Changing from school uniform to Shalwar Kamiz (the traditional dress of the Punjab), from English to Punjabi, and noisy self-expression to a more subdued form of behaviour, are all part of the daily routine.

This is a culture clash which may be experienced by some Asian children, and especially girls, born in British industrial cities into families from more rural, hierarchical, and sexist environments; a culture clash additionally involving the interface of religious and secular perspectives, and which ought not to be underestimated.

Clearly, it is important to avoid sweeping generalizations. Culture clash may also occur in many other ethnic minority groups, and is far from unknown among working-class children of the majority culture. Furthermore, the Asian community is heterogeneous in the extreme, and it includes many highly Westernized families. But the often quite sharp differences in perspective between adolescents and their parents which is such a well-recognized feature of all rapidly-changing societies will obviously be heightened for those children whose parents are from overseas — whether from Cyprus, Italy, the West Indies, the Indian sub-continent, or elsewhere. This is a particular need so far little recognized in ITT or INSET; and it has implications for classroom teaching skills, for pastoral care and counselling, and for home-school relations, all of which one would expect to be reflected in core courses in educational theory and professional studies.

A third area of particular need must be the continuing under-achievement of children of Bangladeshi, Turkish and West Indian origin, the latter being a special concern of the Rampton Committee (DES, 1981), and which has attracted further attention in the Swann Report and in more recent studies (ILEA, 1987b; Kelly, 1987). By no means all children of Caribbean origin are under-achievers; but even those who do well may sometimes prefer to move into further education and the labour market, rather than take the sixth form route into higher education (Craft and Craft, 1983). It would seem that a fuller understanding by their teachers of school values, ethos and teacher expectation effects (Figueroa, 1984), of research into family values and self-esteem, of dialect issues and the questions of identity touched on above, should all be engendered in initial and in-service teacher education. On none of these variables, however, is there anything like a clear indication of cause and effect, and students should be sensitized to the range of possible factors. There are no simple answers. Tomlinson (1986) is a valuable study of ethnic minority achievement and equality of opportunity.

The Needs of all Children

A second aspect of strategy for initial and in-service teacher education highlighted by the Swann Report related to the needs of *all* children growing up in a culturally plural society. It may, of course, be argued that our minority population only amounts to around 5–6 per cent in all, including the Irish (about 700,000), Asians, West Indians, Jews, Germans, Italians, Poles, Cypriots and Spanish, and smaller groups from elsewhere in the Mediterranean, Africa and the Far East. The total may stabilize at around 10 per cent by the end of the century (Coleman, 1982: Runnymede Trust, 1980), a far smaller proportion than, say, that of Australia where some 25 per cent of the population were born abroad. On the other hand, our ethnic minority citizens are likely to be encountered everywhere in Britain, and particularly in the conurbations where their proportions are often much higher (perhaps 50 per cent of the total population in some electoral wards in Greater London, for example). And as the ethnic minorities are a young population, their children form more than 5–6 per cent of the total *child* population.

It therefore follows that if schoolchildren from the majority culture are to be made aware of the nature and extent of ethnic minority groups in modern Britain (many of whose members were born here), their *teachers* need to be adequately informed. Then again, demographic information is one thing. But some understanding of the concept of culture, of the intrinsic value of all cultures, and of the diverse origins of most cultures — an attitudinal dimension — is also involved here. Few have expressed this concern more effectively than Ralph Linton in his classic, *The Study of Man*, published some fifty years ago. The following well-known passage is a commentary upon what we take to be our own distinctive, unique, homogeneous national culture:

> Our solid American citizen awakens in a bed built on a pattern which originated in the Near East but which was modified in Northern Europe before it was transmitted to America. He throws back covers made from cotton, domesticated in India, or linen, domesticated in the Near East, . . . or silk, the use of which was discovered in China. All of these materials have been spun and woven by processes invented in the Near East. He slips into his moccasins, invented by the Indians of the Eastern woodlands, and goes to the bathroom, whose fixtures are a mixture of European and American inventions, both of recent date. He takes off his pajamas, a garment invented in India, and washes with soap invented by the ancient Gauls. He then shaves, a masochistic rite which seems to have been derived from either Sumer or ancient Egypt.

Linton continues in this vein, describing the diverse orgins of each garment donned. He goes on,

> On his way to breakfast he stops to buy a paper, paying for it with coins, an ancient Lydian invention. At the restaurant a whole new series of borrowed elements confronts him. His plate is made of a form of pottery invented in China. His knife is of steel, an alloy first made in southern India, his fork a medieval Italian invention, and his spoon a derivative of a Roman original.

Linton then describes the varied origins of each part of the American's breakfast, and he concludes as follows:

> When our friend has finished eating he settles back to smoke, an American Indian habit, consuming a plant domesticated in Brazil in either a pipe, derived from the Indians of Virginia, or a cigarette, derived from Mexico. If he is hardy enough he may even attempt a cigar, transmitted to us from the Antilles by way of Spain. While smoking he reads the news of the day, imprinted in characters invented by the ancient Semites upon a material invented in China by a process invented in Germany. As he absorbs the accounts of foreign troubles he will, if he is a good conservative citizen, thank a Hebrew deity in an Indo-European language that he is 100 per cent American. (Linton, 1936)

This passage is all about the *diffusion* of cultural elements from one society to another; and it would seem to be painfully self-evident that if schools are to make a real contribution to social harmony and to equality of opportunity in society at large, *all* children — and therefore teachers — need a far more sophisticated grasp of the diverse origins of the majority culture, and of the regional, religious, social class and other variations within it. The aim should be the achievement of a less judgmental and less ethnocentric approach among teachers. As Fisher and Hicks (1985) indicate, for example, everyday words such as pyjamas or shampoo are of Indian origin; telephone or cycle are Greek; piano or corridor Italian; and boss or hiccup, Dutch. The English language itself is, of course, drawn from other European languages, just as the grand public architecture of London, Liverpool or Leeds is based on that of ancient Rome and Athens.

In ITT, as indicated earlier, this may mean the insertion of special *options*, or of multicultural elements in the educational theory or professional studies *core*. It is difficult to see how material of this kind could be avoided in a core strand in the sociology of education, if such exists; and it is there, in language work, in any discussion of what is 'deficient' or 'different'. But as the Swann Report indicated, it should also mean the *permeation*, through all that is taught, of a multicultural sensitivity, both in ITT and INSET, including both pedagogy and main subject content. In BEd science and mathematics main courses, one might expect the diverse origins of scientific and mathematical discovery to be made more explicit. Our numerals themselves originated in India, and comprise only one of many systems of computation. Biology, in particular, in considering diverse dietary patterns and diet-linked diseases, race and genetics, differential fertility and mortality, or childbirth and child care, readily lends itself. In history, the varied origins of the British people, their language and culture, and their continuous economic and political interactions with overseas territories as a trading and imperial nation present many opportunities for broader comment and interpretation. A Eurocentric view appears to imply that North America, Africa or Australia were empty continents awaiting 'discovery' and settlement. In literature and the arts, some appreciation of the huge variety of these forms of experience may be conveyed through the inclusion of examples of minority group literature, drama, art and music; and they may, of course, be used as a powerful means of extending knowledge of other peoples, their perceptions and preoccupations. The visual arts have always provided a means of considering the social and cultural context — in religious art, for example. Music and dance may have a similar value, apart from naturally extending aural skills, and competence in performing and composing. Naturally, we are not here considering matters of content alone, but also of *process*. Collaborative learning techniques whereby children work in small groups using selected research materials have always complemented more formal classroom methods, and they may have a particular potential in multi-ethnic schools where pupils' intercultural experience may thus be more effectively disseminated.

Some school curriculum areas lend themselves to permeation more readily than others: home economics, for example, offers ample opportunity for the recognition, discussion and inclusion of cultural differences in diet, food preparation, family roles, and childrearing, and much scope for building bridges between minority and majority cultures. Modern language teaching is inextricably bound up with the study of other cultures; in some areas it can include some of the overseas languages widely spoken in pupils' homes, and it can very often draw upon the bilingual experience of many pupils. Geography has long ceased to be about 'capes and bays', and cannot escape consideration of social life, and of world trading relationships. In both ITT and INSET, permeation is a responsibility for each subject specialist, assisted perhaps by the lecturer/adviser more knowledgeable in multicultural education.

In this way and using the resource materials currently available (for example, Craft and Klein, 1986; Craft and Bardell, 1984; Klein, 1984; Lynch, 1981), it is possible for ITT and INSET to modify curricula in the interests, first, of the minority pupil whose heritage will no longer appear to be undervalued; second, of the majority culture pupil whose schooling will now be less ethnocentric and more educative; and third, of working towards less prejudiced (or 'racist') attitudes and values, a matter which is taken up in the next section. Nor, as suggested at the outset, should all this be seen as new-fangled and revolutionary. More than three decades ago a UNESCO study of history textbooks and international understanding declared that, 'this is no time for maintaining ancient hatreds which cloud the understanding and befog the judgment' (Lauwerys, 1953).

But permeation is a sizeable, long term enterprise, and it is easy to oversimplify the matter (Bliss, 1987). To teach students to teach children in a non-ethnocentric way, requires non-ethnocentric teacher educators, which brings us back to the central question of staffing and to the staff development policies of ITT institutions and of LEAs (in respect of INSET Advisers). Secondly, syllabuses and teaching methods are operationalized by the use of appropriate textbooks and other materials. Some of these teaching resources may include racist language or imagery and be quite unsuitable; but other resources which embody ethnocentric approaches may provide an excellent *stimulus* to classroom discussion. Students will nonetheless require careful guidance on how best to select and use teaching materials, for educating *all* children in a multicultural society (Klein, 1984).

Intercultural Relations

This third aspect of pedagogic strategy for multicultural teacher education is labelled 'intercultural relations' in preference to the narrower and more restricted term 'race relations'. Given the kind of world we inhabit, some awareness of the nature and origins of intercultural prejudice and discrimination ought to find a central place in the curriculum of ITT and INSET. It should not be forgotten that at the beginning of the decade, a British Home Secretary declared that,

> . . . the anxieties expressed about racial attacks are justified. Racially motivated attacks, particularly on Asians, are more common than we

> had supposed; and there are indications that they may be on the increase. (Whitelaw, 1981)

More recent studies have substantiated this fear (CRE, 1987). Clearly, teacher education carries a major responsibility here.

Work on prejudice and discrimination might include, for example, the examination of stereotyping on ethnic, racial, religious and regional lines, and immediately raises the question of where this can be best located in the ITT curriculum. It used often to be found in core studies in the sociology of education or the psychology of perception. But it could also be raised in every part of the ITT curriculum when ethnocentric or racist texts and other classroom materials are discussed with students (Klein, 1985). Secondly, students need to be introduced to techniques for managing classroom discussion on issues relating to race and racism which can often be highly emotive (Stradling 1984), a further task for the professional studies area. But *how* an element of intercultural relations should be included in initial or in-service training is also important. In all the foregoing, there has been the assumption that *information* is decisive, conveyed either through ITT options, core courses or permeation, or through INSET workshops or named awards. This cannot be lightly dismissed. Reports of an important cohort study of student teachers' awareness of cultural diversity in the UK appear to reveal a large degree of sheer ignorance (Hodgkinson, 1984). On the other hand, 'intercultural relations' is much more firmly in the area of *attitudes*: is the development or change of students' attitudes best achieved through lecture courses, through the more active involvement of participants in seminars and discussions, through practical work with children in schools (or with parents in minority communities), or through workshops? (Burtonwood, 1986).

Work on intercultural relations sometimes uses workshop introspection (or 'race awareness' sessions) as a means of getting below the surface into the deeper assumptions which motivate behaviour. Opinions vary about the efficacy of such an approach (Banton, 1985), and some prefer the more oblique and less confrontational mode embodied in techniques such as the Nottingham University 'Lifestyles' pack, developed for the former Schools Council and used by teachers' centres and police training courses in many parts of the country. As regards ITT and INSET coursework, active and prolonged *discussion* (perhaps including simulations) should be an essential supplement to reading, essay writing and lectures; and sustained *practical work* may be an even better supplement to the formal acquisition of information. The practice of attaching students from rural colleges of education to inner city study centres for teaching practice, for example, certainly appears to be beneficial. There may also be distinctive needs according to whether ITT students are training for work in primary or secondary schools (Carrington, *et al.*, 1986). It may be that further systematic study of the appraisal of attitudes towards cultural diversity among practising and student teachers needs to be undertaken, as is being attempted in the United States (Giles and Sherman, 1982).

It will by now be clear that this third category, 'intercultural relations', is really an aspect of the education of all children; it is, after all, an extension of what was suggested earlier in respect of combating ethnocentrism. But intercultural relations has been treated separately in order to give it a special emphasis, for prejudice and discrimination on grounds of ethnicity, race, and religion are undoubtedly realities in most, if not all, contemporary societies, and teacher educators must take account of this. A tough-minded approach to prejudice and discrimination must surely be part of the professional awareness of all teachers in a plural society, requiring teacher educators to prepare their students for participation in whole-school appraisal schemes, and for self-evaluation in the classroom, as a central element of professional practice. Every student in initial or in-service training should be adequately equipped to examine the organization of his/her school, the structure of its curriculum and the nature of his/her classroom practice to ensure that minority children are not being disadvantaged, however unwittingly, by discriminatory cultural assumptions or other practices. All teachers must be sensitive to discrimination, for example, in the provision of school meals, or in the insistence upon school uniform in the case, say, of Muslim girls or Sikh boys. Minority mores in respect of diet or modesty may be involved. The 'tracking' of certain pupils into maths/science streams, into PE and sports activities, or into early leavers' classes may result from an unintended labelling of aptitudes and abilities, (for example, Carrington, 1986). Racist remarks should not be tolerated, either in the staffroom or the classroom, and offensive graffiti should be removed immediately. In all schools, multiethnic or not, teachers need to call attention — across the curriculum — to derogatory interethnic and interracial perceptions and disadvantage, both historically and in the present. Staff appointments — in all schools, not just those in multiethnic localities — should aim to reflect the nation's cultural diversity, while maintaining equal standards of professional qualification and ability (Berkshire LEA, 1983; Brent LEA, 1983b; ILEA, 1983b), and to this end ethnic monitoring is now being introduced nationally.

This 'anti-racist' perspective is sometimes contrasted with 'multicultural' education (for example, NAME, 1984) and this is unhelpful, for activities such as the above are clearly an essential part of any multicultural programme. But some commentators would go much further and would attribute *all* ethnic minority disadvantage in education to 'racism'. Parekh (1983) however, has argued persuasively against 'the fallacy of the single factor' in the analysis of what are obviously highly complex phenomena; and in any case, 'race' and 'racism' are vague and less than meaningful terms (Patterson, 1985). For some enthusiasts, 'anti-racism' is fundamentally concerned with structural inequality (Hannan, 1983), and can involve putting a particular gloss on all history teaching, an explicitly anti-capitalist gloss (Institute of Race Relations, 1982). For Mullard (1984), 'anti-racist' education is part of a vast process of 'liberation from social bondage (oppression, exploitation and discrimination) of Black and other similarly situated groups'. These more extreme viewpoints on the left thus seem to redefine 'education' as traditionally understood, and in oversimplifying very complex questions perhaps have more in common with comparable views on the extreme right (for example, Pearce, 1985) than they might care to recognize.

Cohesion and Diversity

Underlying many of the debates about multicultural education is the question as to how we should resolve the competing pressures for social cohesion and for social diversity. At what point does the acculturation necessary for full participation in society become a repressive assimilation? At what point does the celebration of diversity cease to enrich and become a source of social instability? (Craft, 1984).

As we know, the prevailing social and political climate has moved towards pluralism in values of all kinds in the past twenty-five years. As was indicated above, perhaps only 5–6 per cent of the British population are members of ethnic minority groups, a very small proportion, and one which might reach 10 per cent by the end of the century. But *our view* of minorities of all kinds has altered. At the time of the New Commonwealth immigration of the 1950s and 1960s, the prevailing ethic was one of *assimilation*, immigrants were to be absorbed into the population as quickly as possible — linguistically and culturally. *Integration* was a term which then came into use, and this also implied assimilation but allowing for some linguistic and cultural residues. Roy Jenkins' celebrated statement in 1966 referred to 'not a flattening process of assimilation, but . . . equal opportunity accompanied by cultural diversity in an atmosphere of mutual tolerance'. In the 1970s and 1980s, we have come to talk of *cultural pluralism,* a term which places greater emphasis on diversity and the intrinsic validity of different cultures. And then there is *segregation,* which is a *de facto* reality in some inner urban districts and in a handful of urban schools; but which is also an objective for some minority communities who seek their own schools on grounds of religion.

The trend is clear. It is now increasingly acceptable to recognize linguistic and cultural pluralism. In 1980, the DES Curriculum Document, it will be recalled, stated:

> What is taught in schools, and the way it is taught, must appropriately reflect fundamental values in our society.

and it continued:

> Our society has become multicultural; and there is now among pupils and parents a greater diversity of personal values.

This was a significant statement for our society has not 'become multicultural'. It has always been multicultural, in terms of ethnicity, social class, religion and region (to say nothing of age and sex); it is simply more acceptable nowadays to recognize the fact. Furthermore, not only is the trend towards the celebration of diversity very evident here, it is also found in many other societies. There is now a sizeable literature, with titles such as *The Ethnic Revival* (Smith, 1981), *The Re-discovery of Ethnicity* (TeSelle, 1973), and *The Rise of the Unmeltable Ethnics* (Novak, 1973). But it is important to be quite clear about the line of argument. There can be little doubt that a basic acculturation for all children is the essential key to full participation in society. It greatly increases equality of life-chance, it provides access to the opportunity structure. But beyond that basic acculturation the celebration of diversity enriches us all; and for the individual, it may be a very necessary source of identity in the alienated conditions of a complex, industrial society. It is a delicate balance: acculturation up to a point, pluralism beyond that point.

For teacher educators, this balance lies at the heart of language policy, for example. All children will need a sound basic grounding in written and spoken English; and it may be that teaching some young children through the mother tongue will facilitate this — a transitional bilingualism. On the other hand, the pursuit of culture maintenance would argue that opportunities for sustaining mother tongue teaching into secondary education to public examination level should be available for those children who wish it, and teacher education should be making provision for this. Equally, all children in British schools need to acquire a detailed knowledge and appreciation of British social institutions and the British cultural heritage; to neglect this on ideological or other grounds would simply perpetuate educational and social disadvantage, as many argued some years ago in respect of proposals for a 'relevant' curriculum for working-class children (for example, Shipman, 1973). But to fail to widen the curriculum, by means of permeation, in order to reduce ethnocentrism or to highlight the contributions of all peoples to world culture — nor to prepare teachers for this role — is surely to miss valuable opportunities. As Gay has put it, 'ethnic and national loyalties' and affiliations are not necessarily contradictory or mutually exclusive' (*op. cit.*)

The Changing Scene

As the decade draws to a close teacher education in multicultural Britain has begun to move in different directions. The 1988 Green Paper (DES, 1988a) proposing the introduction of 'licensed teachers' widens the door for teachers with overseas qualifications, but it will also open it to unqualified teachers in inner city — including multiethnic-schools where staff shortages are greatest. Of equal concern, the increase in school-focused and school-based INSET during the 1980s will have reduced the likelihood of any training in multicultural education in 'all white' areas. This 'school-based identification of need' has been fostered by GRIST (the LEA training grants scheme), and the consequent major shift towards shorter courses of immediate relevance at the expense of longer, higher education based courses will have seriously weakened those advanced diplomas and degrees offering specialization in multicultural issues.

These have been the courses which hitherto offered an in-depth preparation for LEA advisers, inspectors, senior teachers and lecturers — a pivotal cadre of trainers. As indicated earlier, the DES national priorities for INSET were substantially switched in the summer of 1988 — understandably — towards the new National Curriculum, assessment and educational management; but developing the curriculum for a multiethnic society was cut, except for some provision in further education. The Education Support Grants have similarly given emphasis to these new priorities.

Multicultural education has certainly lost the salience of recent years as the wide-ranging changes engendered by the 1988 Education Reform Act have begun to emerge, but the needs will remain. Some minority group children will continue to require special help, and *all* the nation's children will still need informed teachers who can effectively counter inter-ethnic ignorance and prejudice. The pursuit of equal opportunity has not been disavowed, and with continuing skill shortages the talents of all our young people will certainly be in demand. The Swann Committee's advocacy in 1985 of an appropriate *Education For All* can hardly be regarded as out of date.

Under the 1988 Act itself the prospects seem rather mixed, but the greatest concern undoubtedly lies with *open enrolment* and how it will operate. Will there be a migration of children and of teachers towards schools with a reputation for high achievement? In five years' time, will there be a new drive to train specialist teachers with the skills to cope in schools caught in a spiral of decline, schools with above-average proportions of lower working class and of black children? The local management of schools, on the other hand, may be helpful in giving minority parents a more effective voice. But will the Act's provision for 'opting out' to grant maintained status lead to more all-black schools for religious and other reasons, and will this *de facto* segregation help produce a more harmonious society? As for the new National Curriculum, it contains no explicit provision for cross-curricular permeation in respect of a pluralist perspective, but the legislation is permissive. The detailed organization of the school curriculum is explicitly left to the headteacher: the amount of time to be devoted to each component, the way in which it is provided in the school timetable, teaching methods, books and materials, all will remain professional concerns. Minimum course requirements will be stated, but 'What is taught may go much wider; the teaching of other subjects and of cross curricular issues is not precluded' (DES, 1988b, para 24).

So the responsibility falls very clearly to teachers and to initial and in-service teacher education. So, too, does the responsibility for interpreting each of the approved programmes of study. The Secretary of State's proposals for Science (5–16) (DES, 1988e) take full account of recent thinking in respect of both the particular needs of ethnic minority pupils and the needs of *all* pupils. The latter could hardly be stated more clearly:

> the science curriculum must provide opportunities to help all recognise that no one culture has a monopoly of scientific achievement . . . It is important, therefore, that science books and other learning materials

> should include examples of people from ethnic minority groups working alongside others and achieving success in scientific work. (para. 7.16).

The Mathematics Report (5–16) (DES, 1988f) similarly recommends that all children should be made aware '... that mathematics is the product of a diversity of cultures' (para. 10.20), but its other comments indicate a more limited grasp of the issues than that of either the Science or the English (5–11) Working Groups. The English Report (DES, 1988g) demonstrates very considerable sensitivity in respect of dialect, bilingualism and the range of literature to be employed. Both the Secretary of State's remit letter to the new National Curriculum Council, and the Draft Circular on the school curriculum and assessment express clear commitments to equal opportunity in a plural society, something which should equally form part of the brief for future teacher educators. As the Draft Circular puts it, 'It is intended that the curriculum should reflect the culturally diverse society to which pupils belong and of which they will become adult members' (para. 13).

The Report of the Task Group on Assessment and Testing (DES, 1988c) which sets out the new assessment procedures at ages 7, 11, 14 and 16 also demonstrates some sensitivity to the multicultural dimension which needs to be noted by teacher educators, advocating that the assessment tasks '... be reviewed regularly for evidence of bias, particularly in respect of gender and race' (para. 52). The Report recommends that pupils whose first language is not English may need to be exempted from tests in English; but, as it goes on:

> This should be taken as an indication that the child requires help in acquiring English, and should not lead to damaging assumptions about his or her levels of competence in other aspects of learning. (DES, 1988d, para. 16).

Provision for religious education has been formally included in the Education Reform Act, and with worship in schools is likely to be '... wholly or mainly of a broadly Christian character', in the words of the DES *Circular* on religious education and collective worship, (DES, 1989, page 3). But the parental right of withdrawal remains, and the head and governors of any school may seek approval from the local Standing Advisory Council on RE for non-Christian acts of worship if they feel that numbers justify it. As the Circular puts it, 'The Secretary of State believes that governing bodies and headteachers should seek to respond positively to such requests from parents' (para. 42).

So while the Education Reform Act has given no particularly priority to the educational concerns of a culturally plural society, it has conveyed a number of signals and the responsibility now passes to the profession. This once again places teacher education in a significant and influential position, for unless initial and in-service trainers grasp the opportunities presented — and they do exist — the advances in widening educational opportunity for ethnic minority children and for sensitizing all children to diversity during the 1980s could be lost.

References

ARORA, R. (1988) 'Developments in teacher training' in MERCHANT, G. (Ed) *Training for Linguistic Diversity: Proceedings of a Seminar for Teacher Trainers,* Nottingham, University of Nottingham Press.

ATKINS, M.J. and CRAFT, M. (1988) 'Training the trainers in multicultural education: The evaluation of a national programme', *British Journal of In-Service Education*, 14, 2, pp. 81–91.

BANKS, J.A. and LYNCH, J. (Eds) (1986) *Multicultural Education in Western Societies,* London, Holt, Rinehart and Winston.

BANTON, M. (1985) 'Race awareness training: Back to the drawing board', *New Community,* 12, 2, pp. 295–7.

BERKSHIRE LEA (1983) *Education for Racial Equality,* Reading, Berkshire Education Committee.

BLISS, I. (1987) *Multicultural Permeation: A Case-study in Initial Teacher Training,* Nottingham, University of Nottingham Press.

BRENT LEA (1983a) *Mother Tongue Teaching* (Report No. 47/83 from the Director of Education, presented to Brent Education Committee on 4 July 1983).

BRENT LEA (1983b) *Education for a Multicultural Democracy,* Brent LEA.

BURTONWOOD, N. (1986) 'INSET and multicultural/anti-racist education', *British Journal of In-Service Education,* 13, 1, pp. 30–5.

CARRINGTON, B. (1986) 'Social mobility, ethnicity and sport', *British Journal of Sociology of Education*, 7, 1, pp. 1–18.

CARRINGTON, B. *et al.* (1986) 'Schools in a multiracial society: Contrasting perspectives of primary and secondary teachers in training', *Educational Studies,* 12, 1, pp. 17–35.

CASTLES, S. *et al.* (1984) *Here for Good: Western Europe's New Ethnic Minorities*, London, Pluto Press.

COLEMAN, D.A. (Ed) (1982) *Demography of Immigrants and Minority Groups in the United Kingdom,* London, Academic Press.

COMMISSION FOR RACIAL EQUALITY (1987) *Living in Terror: A Report on Racial Violence and Harassment in Housing*, London, CRE.

CRAFT, A.Z. and BARDELL, G. (1984) *Curriculum Opportunities in a Multicultural Society*, London, Harper & Row.

CRAFT, A.Z. and KLEIN, G. (1986) *Agenda for Multicultural Teaching,* London, School Curriculum Development Committee.

CRAFT, M. (1981) 'Recognition of need' in CRAFT, M. (Ed) *Teaching in a Multicultural Society: The Task for Teacher Education,* Lewes, Falmer Press.

CRAFT, M. (1984) 'Education for diversity' in CRAFT, M. (Ed) *Education and Cultural Pluralism,* Lewes, Falmer Press.

CRAFT, M. and ATKINS, M.J. (1983) *Training Teachers of Ethnic Minority Community Languages,* Nottingham, University of Nottingham Press.

CRAFT, M. and CRAFT, A.Z. (1983) 'The participation of ethnic minority pupils in further and higher education', *Educational Research,* 25, 1, pp. 10–19.

DEPARTMENT OF EDUCATION AND SCIENCE (1981), *West Indian Children in Our Schools,* (The Rampton Report), London, HMSO.

DEPARTMENT OF EDUCATION AND SCIENCE (1984a) Text of Sir Keith Joseph's speech to the EEC Mother Tongue Colloquium in London, 26 March 1984.

DEPARTMENT OF EDUCATION AND SCIENCE (1984b) *Initial Teacher Training: Approval*

of Courses, (Circular 3/84), London, HMSO.
DEPARTMENT OF EDUCATION AND SCIENCE (1985) *Education For All* (The Swann Report), London, HMSO.
DEPARTMENT OF EDUCATION AND SCIENCE (1988a) *Qualified Teacher Status: Consultation Document,* London, HMSO.
DEPARTMENT OF EDUCATION AND SCIENCE (1988b) *Draft Circular: The Education Reform Act 1988: The School Curriculum and Assessment,* London, HMSO.
DEPARTMENT OF EDUCATION AND SCIENCE (1988c) *National Curriculum: Task Group on Assessment and Testing: A Report,* London, HMSO.
DEPARTMENT OF EDUCATION AND SCIENCE (1988d) *National Curriculum: TGAT Report – A Digest for Schools,* London, HMSO.
DEPARTMENT OF EDUCATION AND SCIENCE (1988e) *Science for Ages 5–16,* London, HMSO.
DEPARTMENT OF EDUCATION AND SCIENCE (1988f) *Mathematics for Ages 5–16,* London, HMSO.
DEPARTMENT OF EDUCATION AND SCIENCE (1988g) *English for Ages 5–11,* London, HMSO.
DEPARTMENT OF EDUCATION AND SCIENCE (1989) *The Education Reform Act 1988: Religious Education and Collective Worship,* Circular 3/89, London, HMSO.
EGGLESTON, S.J. *et al.* (1981) *In-Service Teacher Education in a Multicultural Society,* Keele, University of Keele Press.
FIGUEROA, P. (1984) 'Minority pupil progress' in CRAFT, M. (Ed) *Education and Cultural Pluralism,* Lewes, Falmer Press.
FISHER, S. and HICKS, D. (1985) *World Studies 8–13: A Teacher's Handbook,* London, Oliver & Boyd.
GAY, G. (1983) 'Why multicultural education in teacher education programs?', *Contemporary Education,* 54, 2, pp. 79–85.
GILES, M.B. and SHERMAN, T.M. (1982) 'Measurement of multicultural attitudes of teacher trainers', *Journal of Educational Research,* 75, 4, pp. 204–9.
HANNAN, A.W. (1983) 'Multicultural education and teacher education', *European Journal of Teacher Education,* 6, 1, pp. 79–86.
HICKS, R.D. and MONROE, E.E. (1984) 'The infusion of multicultural education in teacher education programmes', *Journal of Multilingual and Multicultural Development,* 5, 2, pp. 147–58.
HODGKINSON, K. (1984) reported in *The Times Educational Supplement*, 27 July, page 1.
HOME OFFICE (1981) *The Brixton Disorders,* (The Scarman Report), London, HMSO.
HOULTON, D. (1986) *Teacher Education in a Multilingual Context,* Nottingham, University of Nottingham Press.
HOUSE OF COMMONS (1981) *Racial disadvantage,* 5th Report from the Home Affairs Committee, Vol. 1, London, HMSO.
INNER LONDON EDUCATION AUTHORITY (1981) *Education in a Multi-ethnic Society: An Aide Memoire for the Inspectorate,* London, ILEA.
INNER LONDON EDUCATION AUTHORITY (1983) *Multi-ethnic Education in Schools,* London, ILEA.
INNER LONDON EDUCATION AUTHORITY (1987a) *1987 Language Census,* London, ILEA.
INNER LONDON EDUCATION AUTHORITY (1987b) *Ethnic Background and Examination Results, 1985 and 1986,* London, ILEA.
INSTITUTE OF RACE RELATIONS (1982) *Roots of Racism,* London, Institute of Race Relations.

JENKINS, R. (1966) address to the National Committee for Commonwealth Immigrants, 23 May.

KELLY, A. (1987) 'Ethnic differences in science choice, attitudes and achievement in Britain', unpublished paper presented to the annual meeting of the British Educational Research Association, Manchester, September.

KLEIN, G. (1984) *Resources for Multicultural Education,* (2nd ed), London, Schools Council.

KLEIN, G. (1985) *Reading into Racism: bias in children's literature and learning materials,* London, Routledge & Kegan Paul.

LATHAM, J. (1982) 'Exceptional children and exceptional teachers? An alternative policy for teacher education in a multiracial society', *Journal of Further and Higher Education,* 6, 2, pp. 40–7.

LAUWERYS, J.A. (1953) *History Textbooks and International Understanding,* Paris, UNESCO.

LINGUISTICS MINORITIES PROJECT (1983) *Linguistic Minorities in England,* London, University of London Institute of Education.

LINTON, R. (1936) *The Study of Man,* New York, Appleton, pp. 326–7.

LYNCH, J. (1981) *Teaching in the Multicultural School,* London, Ward Lock Educational.

LYNCH, J. (1985) 'An initial typology of perspectives on staff development for multicultural teacher education' in MODGIL, S. *et al.* (Eds) *Multicultural Education: The Interminable Debate,* Lewes, Falmer Press.

MULLARD, C. (1984) *Anti-Racist Education: The three O's,* London, National Association for Multi-Racial Education.

NATIONAL ASSOCIATION FOR MULTI-RACIAL EDUCATION (1984) *Teacher Education,* London, NAME.

NCATE (1977) *Standards for Accreditation of Teacher Education,* Washington DC, NCATE.

NOVAK, N. (1973) *The Rise of the Unmeltable Ethnics,* New York, Macmillan.

PAREKH, B. (1983) 'Educational opportunity in multiethnic Britain' in GLAZER, N. and YOUNG, K. (Eds) *Ethnic Pluralism and Public Policy,* London, Lexington Books/Heinemann.

PATTERSON, S. (1985) 'Random samplings from Swann', *New Community,* 12, 2, pp. 239–48.

PEARCE S. (1985) *Educational and the Multiracial Society,* Monday Club Policy Paper.

RUNNYMEDE TRUST (1980) *Britain's Black Population,* London, Heinemann.

SCHOOLS COUNCIL (1981) *Multi-ethnic Education: The Way Forward,* London, Schools Council.

SELECT COMMITTEE ON RACE RELATIONS AND IMMIGRATION (1969) *The Problems of Coloured School Leavers*, London, HMSO.

SHIPMAN, M.D. (1973) 'Curriculum for inequality?' in HOOPER, R. (Ed) *The Curriculum: Context, Design and Development,* London, Oliver & Boyd, pp. 101–6. (See also the proposals by Bantock and Midwinter in the same volume.)

SMITH, A.D. (1981) *The Ethnic Revival,* Cambridge, Cambridge University Press.

STRADLING, R. *et al.* (1984) (Eds) *Teaching Controversial Issues,* London, Arnold.

SUZUKI, B.H. (1984) 'Curriculum transformation for multicultural education', *Education and Urban Society*, 16, 3, pp. 294–322.

TANSLEY, P. and CRAFT, A.Z. (1984) 'Mother tongue teaching and support: A Schools Council enquiry', *Journal of Multilingual and Multicultural Development,* 5, 5, pp. 367–84.

TE SELLE, S. (1973) *The Re-Discovery of Ethnicity,* New York, Harper Colophon.

TOMLINSON, S. (1986) *Ethnic Minority Achievement and Equality of Opportunity,*

Nottingham, University of Nottingham Press.
WASHBURN, D.E. (1982) 'Curriculum pluralism: Are teachers prepared?', *Phi Delta Kappan,* 63, 7, pp. 493–5.
WATSON, K. (1984) 'Training teachers in the UK for a multicultural society', *Journal of Multilingual and Multicultural Development,* 5, 5, pp. 385–400.
WHITELAW, W. (1981) Foreword to *Racial Attacks,* London, Home Office.
WILCE, H. (1984) 'Walking the tight-rope between two cultures', *The Times Educational Supplement,* 10 February.

Chapter 10

The University Professor of Education

Peter Gordon

Early Professorships

At a session of the Health Education Conference on the Training of Teachers, held in London in 1884, Professor J.M.D. Meiklejohn devoted his paper to a study of professors and lectureships in education. He began:

> There is, in the three kingdoms, no one man who gives the whole of his time to observing and to thinking about the educational processes which are going on in our schools every day. There are hundreds of professors of Medicine [but] there is, in no University in England, a single person whose duty it is to give a teacher his daily practice. So far as the English Universities are concerned, education is still in its amoebic and empiric stage. Hence, much friction, great waste of mental power, great waste of time, and disappointing results.[1]

Meiklejohn was speaking from personal experience. His own chair at St Andrews, founded in 1876 from the funds of Dr Andrew Bell, together with that of S.S. Laurie at Edinburgh in the same year, was for the teaching of the theory, history and practice of education. Of these first two professors of education, Meiklejohn was the more colourful character having been a schoolmaster, lecturer and a journalist, and was arrested as a spy when acting as war correspondent in the Danish-German War of 1864. Laurie, as Secretary and Visitor of Schools for the Education Committee to the Church of Scotland from 1855, became interested in raising the professional status of teachers. Both men served on the Scottish Endowed Schools Commission, Laurie as Secretary from 1872 and Meiklejohn as Assistant Commmissioner (1874) until his appointment to St Andrews.

There was a difference of emphasis between them in deciding how best to promote the connection between the teaching profession and the university. Meiklejohn recommended a thoroughgoing revision of teaching methods appropriate for children and an examination of contents 'instead of being left to the thoughtless mercies of a traditional curriculum'. Meiklejohn's own contribution was to produce a large number of school textbooks, particularly in English and geography.[2] Laurie, on the other hand, urged the university to take a great interest in the training of teachers.

> Those better trained intellects, those more ambitious natures, ought to have the University open to them not only as at present for instruction but for professional training . . . It is true that certain picked students are now sent from the training colleges to certain universities to attend two of the classes there, and thus sniff the academic air; but this device can never supply the place of a university curriculum and of university life.[3]

The practice of education, however, was only the last of three parts of the title of these Scottish chairs.

In England, a plea for university involvement in education was made at a meeting of the Headmaster's Conference in 1873, where it was agreed that opportunities for teachers to reflect on the nature of their profession were necessary: chairs of education at Oxford and Cambridge were suggested. Two years later a Society for the Development of a Knowledge of the Science of Education was formed in 1875. Psychology was seen as the basis for this new science and Alexander Bain's book *Education As A Science,* published in 1879, was influential in promoting this view. One member of the Society was Joseph Payne of the College of Preceptors, who promoted the training of secondary teachers. A former elementary school teacher himself, Payne had given evidence in 1865 to the Taunton Commission on teaching methods and curriculum and was a member of the National Association for the Promotion of Social Science. He was given the post of Professor of Education by the College in 1872, the first non-university post of its kind in England. Unlike his Scottish counterparts, Payne devoted his energies to a number of practical causes, particularly the teachers' registration movement, the enhancement of teachers' status and the education of women, being Chairman of the Women's Education Union.

If progress was to be made in developing education as a university subject, then the lead would have to be taken by Oxford and Cambridge in establishing chairs. Neither did so: the first Cambridge professor of education was appointed only in 1938 and Oxford waited until 1989 before it followed suit. Cambridge had made a beginning in 1879 by setting up a Teachers' Training Syndicate which provided lectures in the history, practice and theory of education, with a certificate for candidates who were successful at the examinations. The staff included such luminaries as the Reverend R.H. Quick, who taught the history of education, and J.G. Fitch, formerly Chief Inspector for Training Colleges, who dealt with the practice of education.

The newer civic universities began to forge closer links with their communities in offering educational facilities. For example, as early as 1853, Owens College, Manchester was providing classes for teachers in mathematics and classics and in 1885 Nottingham held evening classes on the science of teaching and school management: two years later the college approached the Education Department with a view to training teachers. This offer was refused.[4]

As was shown in early chapters in this book, the Cross Commission recommended the establishment of day training colleges and that local university colleges should take part in the experiment. In some instances, such as Birmingham, where the School Board had aspirations to start its own day training colleges, the prospect was not altogether a welcome one. On the other hand, more formal participation in the field was growing; the University of London had held its first examination in the art, theory and history of education in 1883 and teachers, formerly confined to training colleges for their training, were studying for degrees. A system of day training for teachers involving local university colleges was approved by the Education Department in 1890 by awarding grants for this purpose. Starting with six university training departments in that year, nine more were added by 1894. Only a further eight were to be added during the next forty years. Confined in the first instance to the training of elementary school teachers, a number of universities were reluctant to establish chairs in education. Instead heads of teacher training departments were appointed who in some cases later were granted the title of professor.

For the first professors to be created under the new dispensation we have to look to Wales. The University College of Aberystwyth housed the earliest Welsh Day Training Department from 1892 and consisted of ten men and twenty women. Henry Holman, a Cambridge graduate with first class honours in the moral science tripos, was the Head of Department, Master of Method and Lecturer when the Department opened. In the following year, he became Professor of Theory of Education, with a great interest in the teachings of Seguin. After only one year in the post, he left in 1894 to become one of Her Majesty's Inspectors of Schools. His distinguished successor, Foster Watson, similarly began as a lecturer and head of department, becoming professor after one year in 1895. Watson remained at Aberystwyth until 1913. His work as a historian of education is well-known, especially his books on *The English Grammar Schools to 1660. Their Curriculum and Practices* (1908) and *The Beginnings of the Teaching of Modern Subjects in England* (1909). Watson was also eager to advance the status of the study of education equally with that of other university subjects. He was responsible for establishing education as part of the degree course in 1905 and at honours level in 1911. Watson introduced a three-year undergraduate course which was followed by a one-year teaching course, setting a pattern which is still universally followed.

Opinions differed as to the role of a professor in a day training department. At Bangor, which opened a department in 1894, J.A. Green was appointed because of his wide teaching experience: as a pupil teacher, later a certificated one, and Master of the Hackney Pupil Teachers School. Green, who was called Head of Department and Master of Method, was preferred to Foster Watson, who was much better qualified academically but had little background of elementary school teaching.[5] Green became Professor of Education six years later.

This uncertainty as to the role of the professor was reflected in the nomenclature given, and duties stipulated by, the various universities. As was stated earlier, the first two holders of chairs, in Scotland, professed theory, history and practice. The first English chair, that of Mark Robinson Wright at Durham College of Science in 1895, was initially entitled Professor of Normal Education, though it was changed later to Professor of Education as an indication of the lesser emphasis on the training aspects.[6] Nevertheless a number of professors combined the roles of master of method and the advancement of the academic study of education until well into the present century.

There is little doubt that the public debate on the need for the training of the secondary school teacher, which reached its climax in the last decade of the nineteenth century, played a significant part in the establishment of chairs in education after 1900. A Conference on Secondary Education was convened by the Vice-Chancellor of Oxford University in October 1893 as the Bryce Commission on Secondary Education was taking evidence. Whilst there were university representatives who were only too willing to act as devil's advocate, it was agreed that 'the universities can and ought . . . to train their teachers, the masters at these schools'.[7] The role of theory and the usefulness of the disciplines of education for the intending teacher were recognized. The Bryce Report followed the suggestion of witnesses that at least a year should be spent after graduation in the study of the theory and practice of education, either in a university or elsewhere.[8] A resolution at a Conference on Secondary Education held at Cambridge University in April 1896 stating that 'nobody who is taking up work of this kind can afford to neglect the history of education and of the great educators nor the study of the methods that have proved successful in the past' was passed by 107 votes to seven.[9]

An opportunity to implement some of these schemes was afforded after the turn of the century. In May 1901, the Chairman of the London Technical Education Board, Sidney Webb, reported to the Board on the need for an institution to provide for teachers wishing to make 'any special study of the theory, history and practice of education', to fulfil the requirements of the Board of Education for a day training college and to enable students to take the London University's degrees of BA and BSc and the Teachers Diploma. Webb recommended that there should be a principal, who would receive a salary of £800 a year, and who would hold the rank of professor of the University.[10] The London Day Training College, thirty years later retitled the University of London Institute of Education, opened in 1902. John Adams was appointed its first Principal and Professor of Education, a post which he held for twenty years.

Adams' pedigree was an impressive one. Born and educated in Glasgow, he had attended St David's School, Jordanhill Training College and Glasgow

University, where he gained first class honours in mental and moral science. This was followed by schoolmastering, first as Head of Jean Street School, Glasgow, and then Rector of Campbell town Grammar School. Adams became Principal of Aberdeen Free Church Training College in 1890, moving to the sister college at Glasgow in 1898, where he also held a lectureship in education at his old university. A month after taking up his London post, Adams spoke out vigorously at a Cambridge Conference on the Training of Teachers in Secondary Schools for Boys in a debate on the merits of giving schools responsibility for training teachers rather than the university. He expressed the need to develop the theory of education alongside the practical: 'from the university point of view, it is surely important so to work at this study and to present it to the university as to shew that it is worthy of high academic rank side by side with other university pursuits'.[11] He ended his address with a sharp rebuke 'I suggest that you are not giving Mr Keatinge [Head of the Oxford Training Department] a fair chance when you compel him to spend all his energy in running about Oxford from school to school in the way he has described to us today'.[12]

So far, most professors of education had been concerned with historical aspects of the subject. Adams had already demonstrated in his writings, particularly *The Herbartian Psychology Applied to Education* (1897), that he wished to see the teacher as a mediator between theory and practice. The notion of training colleges often implied that the student followed a rigid programme of the 'right' way to teach. 'The trainer must stoop to conquer. Only by obeying the laws according to which the creature to be trained naturally develops can the trainer exercise the influence he desires'.[13] Adams continued to pursue his research into the nature of theory, which culminated in his impressive work *The Evolution of Educational Theory* (1912).

During the period between the beginning of the century and the Great War, many professors addressed themselves to the deficiencies of teacher training. J.W. Adamson, who had been a distinguished evening student at King's College, London and second master at a London boarding school, was appointed Normal Master when the Day Training College was established at King's College in 1890.[14] He became a Professor there in 1903, and, as Head of the Training Department, addressed himself to the problems facing many of his students, who were concurrently studying for a degree whilst undertaking teacher training. His inaugural address was a plea for the separation of the technical training of the future teacher from general education with the latter being postponed until the former was completed.[15] (It was not until 1926 that the three-year concurrent course was discontinued.) E.T. Campagnac, a former HMI, appointed to the Chair in Education at Liverpool University in 1909, shared this concern with Adamson. He attempted to alleviate the situation by amending the constitution of the Department's Training Board in order to bring the work under closer scrutiny by the Arts and Science faculties.[16]

For the purposes of credibility, appointments to chairs continued to be made from the ranks of successful teachers. One of the original six day training departments had been granted to Manchester University. This was for men only but in 1892, a women's department was also set up. H.L. Withers, previously Principal of Borough Road College, and an Oxford graduate who had also taught at the City of London School, Manchester Grammar School and Clifton College, became its first professor in 1898. The chair had been endowed by Sarah Fielden of Todmorden, who had conducted her own school there on methods which she devised. It is not surprising therefore that holders of the chair were expected to be concerned with the practical aspects of teaching. Withers fully fitted this requirement. Besides becoming Chairman of the Teachers' Registration Council in 1902, Withers involved himself in the day to day running of the department and advising the London School Board on his own speciality, the teaching of history. After only three years incumbency, he died in 1902.[17]

In the subsequent reorganization of the department, an opportunity presented itself to provide more specialization, represented by the appointment of two professors, the first example of its kind in a British university, in 1903. The first, J.J. Findlay, continued the practical classroom-based tradition. After gaining firsts in mathematics and history at Wadham College, Oxford, and studying at Jena and Leipzig, where he was awarded a doctorate, Findlay taught at Bath College and Rugby and was head of two Wesleyan proprietary schools, in Taunton and Sheffield, before moving to a similar post at Cardiff High School for Boys. At Manchester, Findlay, an admirer of the German education system, helped to make the University an important centre for the diffusion of Herbartian ideas and stressed the centrality of humanities in the curriculum.[18] Findlay's views were later modified by the writings of Dewey, and his own publications, particularly *Principles of Class Teaching*, were influential.

In his inaugural lecture, inevitably entitled 'The training of teachers', Findlay remarked on 'the universal satisfaction that the University has seen fit to create a Chair of the History and Administration of Education, and that this responsible office is to be discharged by the one man in Great Britain who is master of the subject.'[19] This reference was to Michael Sadler who since 1895 had been Director of the Office of Special Inquiries at the Department of Education, producing a series of valuable volumes on many aspects of education in different parts of the world. Sadler's resignation from the Office had followed a bitter exchange of correspondence with his former Assistant, Morant, now Permanent Secretary to the Board. He was now able to take up this part-time appointment, which he held until 1911. Sadler, with his vast knowledge of the workings of the administrative and political machinery responsible for the provision of education, established a history of education course dealing with the period 1800 to 1902. He was the first English historian of education to acknowledge the value of sociology in his writings[20] and there were no immediate successors. His inspiring annual course of twenty-four lectures was apparently well received. One of his ex-students later wrote, 'At the end of several lectures the whole body of 100 or more students rose to show their appreciation by prolonged applause.'[21]

Up to the end of the first decade of this century, all appointments to chairs of education were men. A number of women were masters of method, including the redoubtable Catherine I. Dodd at Manchester and Mrs L.D. Hendry at Sheffield. Opportunities for advancement within departments were limited. Miss Dodd, after fifteen years at Manchester, became headmistress of a secondary school and later, Principal of Cherwell Hall, Oxford, a training college for secondary school teachers, from 1917 to 1921. Mrs Hendry moved after eight years at Sheffield to become, in 1905, Vice-Principal of the City's Training College.[22] The first and only woman professor to be appointed before the First World War was H. Millicent Hughes, afterwards Mrs Mackenzie, who had been Head of the Women's department at Cardiff Day Training College from 1891 to 1904 and an Associate Professor for the next six years. Miss Hughes, a Bristol graduate with good teaching experience, had published on a variety of topics, including the educational ideas of Hegel, education in the USA and freedom in education. She became Professor at Cardiff in 1910, occupying the post until 1915.[23] It was Cardiff, too, which had two further women as professors, Barbara Foxley, from 1915 to 1925, and her successor, Olive Wheeler, in the latter year, when the men and women's Departments at the College were amalgamated.[24] The first professor at Bristol in 1920 was Dr Helen Wodehouse then Principal of Bingley Training College and formerly a Lecturer in Philosophy at Birmingham University.

How far the holders of posts were able to make advances in the study of education was limited by the immediate task in hand, the initial training of teachers. Findlay had complained in 1902 that the majority of writers on the subject 'have hitherto adopted methods of exposition which are frankly empirical. They have recognized that the time has not arrived to offer the profession a scientific exposition of education . . . and have taught education as a practical art'.[25] And as late as 1916, M.W. Keatinge, still the Head of the Oxford Department, could write, 'Of the many eminent schoolmasters whom it has been my privilege to know, but few can be suspected of ever having opened a book on educational theory'.[26]

Those pessimistic views did not take account of changes which were already under way. In 1908, Morant had promoted Regulations for the Training of Teachers in Secondary Schools which required the establishment of separate secondary departments for graduate students only, who would study a single curriculum subject and undertake sixty days' teaching practice. As Morant stated in the Prefatory Memorandum, 'however good the lectures given on the theory and history of education may be, they [the Board] will attach the first importance to arrangements which will enable every student to see good teaching at close quarters'.[27] Three years later, in 1911, the Board introduced the four-year course, with the final year taken up with professional studies. Both these administrative changes allowed for a more extended view of the educational disciplines.

Educational Psychology and a Science of Education

One of the early beneficiaries was educational psychology. Chairs in education had already been established whose occupants were working in this field, such as James Welton at Leeds in 1904 and J.A. Green, who had moved to Sheffield in 1906. Green was the first Editor of the *Journal of Experimental Pedagogy* in 1911, and published his *Introduction to Psychology* in the following year. Green held the chair at Sheffield for sixteen years. The importance of psychological understanding was demonstrated by Henry Bompas Smith, Sadler's successor at Manchester in 1912 and Director of the Department until 1932. His inaugural lecture was entitled 'Education as the training of personality' which was delivered in 1913; in it, he welcomed the light that a study of psychology might throw on teaching methods.[28] Inspiration was drawn from James Sully the father of child psychology in this country, who held the chair in Psychology at University College, London: among his successors were C.E. Spearman and Cyril Burt. The London Day Training College provided a string of notable personalities who advanced the discipline. The work of John Adams has already been discussed. His successor in 1922 as Director, Percy Nunn, had been Vice-Principal in 1903 and Professor of Education from 1913. From his interests in science, mathematics and psychology, he drew his views on the full development of the pupil's individuality: Nunn's writings were influential in the progressive movement in primary education.[29] Birmingham was prominent in the psychological field with the appointment of C.W. Valentine in 1919 who remained there as Professor of Education until 1946. Like others, he had previously done research in experimental psychology before transferring to education. Valentine's interests included the transfer of training, the reliability of examinations, the educational value of Latin and Greek, the normal child and mental testing.[30] He was the editor of the *British Journal of Educational Psychology*, established in 1931, and which helped to promote new ideas in the discipline.

The search for a true science of education proved elusive and mental testing was seen as at least a technique which could be applied to educational problems in a scientific manner.[31] Cyril Burt, the first psychologist appointed by the London County Council, was part-time professor at the London Day Training College, 1924–32. A more direct link with mental testing was the appointment of Godfrey Thomson, who had been professor at Newcastle since 1920, to the chair at Edinburgh five years later, which carried with it the post of Director of Studies at Moray House.[32] For the next twenty-six years Thomson, whose interest was in the factorial analyses of human ability, developed large scale tests which were intended to provide for equality of opportunities for children of all classes. These became, together with the work of other psychologists, the basis of the '11 + ' tests for entrance to grammar schools.[33] A different but equally important activity where expert academic advice was sought arose out of the deliberations of Consultative Committees of the Board of Education. For instance, the Hadow Reports on *The Education of the Adolescent* (1926) and

The Primary School (1931) both contain in the Prefaces an appreciation of Nunn, who, it was stated, placed at their disposal 'his wide knowledge and sound judgment, and who has rendered invaluable help in the preparation of the Report(s)'.[34]

It is difficult to generalize about the pattern of professorial appointments before the Second World War, apart from the emphasis on psychology; Frank Smith, (Newcastle, 1925) was a distinguished historian of education and so too was H.C. Barnard (Reading, 1939); John Dover Wilson (King's College, London, 1925) a former HMI was a Shakespearean scholar whilst G.R. Owst (Cambridge, 1939) was a medieval historian. Four more university departments were set up during this period – Swansea (1921), Durham (1922), Leicester (1929), and Hull (1930), though in some cases not without difficulties.[35] Only the first two university colleges were granted chairs before the outbreak of war, F.A. Cavenagh at Swansea in 1921 and Arthur Robinson at Durham in 1922. By the third decade of the century, all universities had education departments, the majority with professorships and in a number of cases two chairs.

Institutes of Education

The number of chairs in education was increased after the Second World War with the implementation of the McNair Report of 1944. It had recommended the establishment of area training organizations (ATOs) serviced by institutes of education, which, among other duties, provided an education centre for students in training and serving teachers, and promoted facilities for further study and research. These institutes were housed in universities: by 1948, fourteen of them had been constituted. Their directors usually were of professorial rank and seven of the universities appointed from the professor who was in charge of the university training department, or university department of education (UDE) as many were now called. At Birmingham when the University set up its Institute, it appointed two professors to replace C.W. Valentine, who had recently retired, M.V.C. Jeffreys as Director and Fred Schonell, as Head of the UDE. A joint Department of Research was formed with staff of both the Institute and UDE.[36]

It is clear that the new institutes of education offered an opportunity for the expansion of specialisms within educational studies and this was reflected in the appointments to chairs which followed. The first Professor of Educational Psychology was appointed at Durham in 1948.[37] The already strong psychological emphasis at Birmingham was seen in the appointment of E.A. Peel there in 1951. At Sheffield, there was a distinct leaning towards historians. George Henry Turnbull, an authority on Fichte and seventeenth century scientific history, held the chair for thirty-two years, from 1922 to 1954. His successor was W.H.G. Armytage, an eminent historian of education, who was at Sheffield from 1954 to 1982. Between them, they covered a span of sixty years.

The post-war period witnessed the entry of subject experts from university departments other than education. For instance, Louis Arnaud Reid, who had been Professor of Philosophy at Armstrong College (now University of Newcastle-upon-Tyne) from 1932 to 1947, became the first holder of a Chair in Philosophy of Education, at the University of London Institute of Education. Karl Mannheim, a former Professor of Sociology at Frankfurt-am-Main University (1930–33) developed the sociology of education at the London University Institute of Education, from 1946 until shortly before his early death, in 1947. At the same university, A.V. Judges, who had been Reader in Economic History at the London School of Economics from 1939, was appointed to the Chair of History of Education at King's College, London in 1949 continuing until his retirement in 1965.

As the largest institution concerned with teacher education in the United Kingdom, the London University Institute of Education was to the forefront in appointing six new chairs, such as those of J.A. Lauwerys (comparative education), P.E. Vernon (educational psychology) and W.O. Lester Smith (sociology of education).[38] The latter had as a background, experience in education and administration in Warwickshire and Essex.[39] Lionel Elvin, a former Principal of Ruskin College, Oxford and Director of the Education Department at UNESCO, became Professor of Education in tropical areas in 1956. He was appointed Director of the Institute in 1958 following the death of G.B. Jeffery, an able administrator and former Professor of Mathematics at King's College, London.[40] Jeffery's predecessor was Sir Fred Clarke, who had jointly held the posts of Professor and Director at the Institute from 1936 to 1945. Where these two roles were combined in most Institutes of Education (the London Institute was never a constituent member of the wider Institute) the incumbent needed to have a range of political as well as academic skills not required by his predecessors.

Post-1960s

Changes in the structure of higher education during the 1960s led to further changes in the scope of the activities of the Professor of Education. By 1963, the number of university students was more than double the pre-war figure. Between 1961 and 1965, seven universities were established — Canterbury, Essex, Lancaster, Norwich, Sussex, Warwick and York. Further, the Robbins Committee on Higher Education, which reported in October 1963, recommended that nine English colleges of advanced technology should be awarded full university status — Aston, Bath, Bradford, Brunel, Chelsea, City (London), Loughborough, Salford and Surrey. Unlike pre-war universities, not all of the sixteen new universities chose to establish education departments. Thus there were no professors of education at City, Essex and Salford. The notion of schools within universities, drawing on allied disciplines, became popular. At Sussex the unusual title of School of Education and Social Work was adopted in order, as Boris Ford, its first Professor, stated, 'to give such studies a distinct identity and prestige from the first'.[41] Professor Ford, editor of the *Journal of Education* and the *Universities Quarterly*, had held the Chair of Education at Sheffield 1960–62, moving to Sussex in 1963. Professor Alec Ross of Lancaster recounted in his inaugural lecture, 'When I first came to Lancaster the Vice-Chancellor told me that the University wanted to do something *useful* in the field of education'.[42] The Lancaster title Department of Educational Research, as it was called, indicates its purpose. Frank Musgrove at Bradford similarly held the title of Professor of Educational Research and during his tenure there between 1965 and 1970 set out an ambitious agenda for investigations at micro and macroscopic levels.[43]

The Robbins Report also favoured the raising of the status of training colleges, which since 1960 had extended their courses to three years. The Report recommended that the newly-named colleges of education should form a part of higher education, a suggestion which the government at the time rejected. However, it did agree to the introduction of a four-year degree course, the Bachelor of Education (BEd), for appropriately qualified students: the degree was to be validated by universities. In 1968, the year of the first graduates of this degree, five universities were involved: by 1972, there were twenty-three.[44] This validating function was greeted by the universities with varying degrees of enthusiasm. Professors of education were involved in persuading colleagues on boards of studies to participate in the negotiations.[45] In London, Doris Lee, a mathematician by training, was appointed to a Chair in Education with special reference to Education in the Colleges of Education.[46]

Until 1951, university departments of education had been fairly narrowly confined by the Ministry in the nature of courses which were offered. More specialized research and new educational disciplines were subsequently introduced. The social aspects of education, as revealed, for example in official publications such as *Early Leaving* (1954), the Crowther Report *15 to 18* (1959) and the Newsom Report *Half Our Future* (1963), were seen as important features of educational study. Sociological enquiries into educational waste and 'equal opportunity of acquiring intelligence' raised important issues on selection procedures. Many sociologists were appointed to chairs in education, though only Basil Bernstein, at the London Institute of Education, had, from 1967, the title Professor of the Sociology of Education.[47] The first Chair of Child Development in this country was occupied by Jack Tizard from 1964 at the London Institute, an honour denied to a distinguished predecessor, Susan Isaacs, who was Head of the Department between 1933 and 1939. It is of interest that Professor Tizard's inaugural address was entitled 'Survey and experiment in special education', anticipating the later interest in this area.[48] Another two firsts, also at the Institute, were the establishment of a Chair in Higher Education, to which W.R. Niblett was appointed in 1967, and a Chair in the Economics of Education, filled by Mark Blaug from 1971. The teaching of the disciplines of education increased in the 1960s with the huge expansion of numbers in colleges in education. The philosophy of education received a powerful boost through the writings of Richard Peters, who succeeded Louis Arnaud Reid at the London Institute in 1962 and the appointment of Paul Hirst, at King's College, London three years later. Brian Simon, appointed in 1966 to the Chair in Education at Leicester, provided a stimulus to the study of the history of education. The training of educational administrators as a sound theoretical base for management in education was promoted by William Taylor, Professor of Education at Bristol from 1966 and George Baron, later Professor of Educational Administration at the London Institute of Education.[49] Altogether between 1960 and 1967, the number of chairs in education almost doubled, from forty-one to seventy-six.

The changing scope of the work of professors of education can be seen in their increasing involvement in the affairs of public bodies. Professor C.E. Gittins, who was appointed to the Chair at University College, Swansea, in 1957, became Chairman of the Central Advisory Council for Education (Wales) which was responsible for the reorganization of primary education in Wales at the same time that the Plowden Committee was at work in England. The Report, *Primary Education in Wales*, published in 1970 and known as the Gittins Report, recommended changes ranging from the training of teachers to the content of the curriculum. The growing interest in curriculum renewal had earlier, in 1961, led to the Nuffield Foundation awarding grants in mathematics and science for this purpose. In the following year, the Ministry of Education established a Curriculum Study Group to give a more positive direction to the school curriculum. Apart from civil servants and HMI, the Group was advised by Dr Jack Wrigley, then at the London Institute of Education. When the Group was superseded in 1964 by the Schools Council, Wrigley, who had been appointed to a Chair at Southampton in 1963, was its first Director of Studies. Philip Taylor, who became the first English Professor of Curriculum and Method at Birmingham in 1966, was Director of Research at the Council between 1964 and 1966.

After the heady optimism arising from demographic and administrative forces which had led to expansion in university professorships in the middle 1960s, the mood changed. New needs were discerned for students in training with the coming of comprehensive education and the move towards the abolition of selection: the effectiveness of conventional teaching methods, the appropriateness of curricula and methods of organizing teaching groups were all questioned. The Plowden Report's 1967 recommendations for positive discrimination in educational provision through designated educational priority areas and the growth of community schools became realities, and highlighted the need to match these changes within university departments. Since the White Paper *Education: A Framework for Expansion* was published in 1972 following the James Report on teacher education, alternative paths to training were made available to institutions on the other side of the binary line through the development of the Council for National Academic Awards. Many colleges of education were closed or merged with polytechnics or became institutes of higher education and in 1975, university supervision of teacher training through area training organizations ceased. The economic recession of the early 1970s had consequences for university departments in their funding and size.[50]

It may be argued that the terms of reference of new appointments to chairs in education can be seen as a response to many of these events and in some cases anticipated them. Robin Pedley, who was Professor at Exeter from 1969, promoted the notion of a comprehensive university, responsible for all post-school education, bringing all the main providing agencies together in each of the fifty-eight new unitary authorities then being proposed by the Maud Commission on Local Government.[51] The politics and economics of changes in higher education were explored by two new professors appointed to Lancaster, N.J. Entwistle and Gareth Williams.[52]

From the time of the 'Great Debate', started by the Prime Minister James Callaghan, at Ruskin College, Oxford, the school curriculum became the subject of much discussion. We have already seen that the Schools Council in the previous decade had been involved in promoting curriculum development. Denis Lawton, who, at the London Institute was Director of the *Social Studies 8–13* project and an active member of the Council, was given a Chair in Curriculum Studies at the Institute in 1974. Lawrence Stenhouse, Director of the Nuffield/Schools Council Humanities Curriculum Project, which promoted teacher autonomy based on teacher research and self-monitoring, was an influential figure in curriculum innovation and evaluation after moving to the University of East Anglia.[53] Stenhouse was professor there from 1978 until his death in 1982: several of his fellow researchers now hold chairs in various universities. The practical skills required by new secondary school teachers were explored by Ted Wragg at Nottingham through the Teacher Education Project. Further work was continued at Exeter University, where he has been Director of the School of Education since 1979.[54] A number of schools of education have appointed professors who specialize in individual curriculum subjects. Science education was, until recently, rather poorly represented, though Chelsea College, London University (now Kings/Chelsea) established chairs in biology, science and mathematics education.

The growing interest of successive Secretaries of State and the DES in courses of teacher training was made manifest by the disbanding in 1985 of the Advisory Committee for the Supply and Education of Teachers (ACSET). It was replaced by the Council for the Accreditation of Teacher Education (CATE) which carried out visits to all training institutions in the higher education sector and laid down centralized criteria for courses. One of the results has been diminution in the contributions of the educational disciplines — history, philosophy, psychology and sociology — to these courses and a consequent retreat from theory. R.F. Dearden, a philosopher of education, appointed to a Chair of Education in Birmingham in 1978, very interestingly explored the relationship between theory and practice in his inaugural lecture.[55] Few new chairs in the 'disciplines' have been made in the last decade.

Societal issues which affected teacher training and schooling have been investigated by holders of chairs in recent years. Alan Little, Lewisham Professor of Social Administration at Goldsmiths' College, London, in his 1978 inaugural lecture discussed the expertise and resources which need to be provided for heightening the awareness of the educational implications of a multicultural society.[56] The Report of the Warnock Committee of Enquiry into the Education of Handicapped Children and Young People (1978) led to the 1981 Education Act, which introduced the new concept of special educational needs. The first Department of Special Education had been established at Birmingham some years previously and under its Head of Department, Professor Ronald Gulliford, had anticipated many of the Warnock Committee's findings.[57]

From the late 1970s the character of university schools of education was changing because of the need to cater for the rise in primary school population at a time of falling rolls in secondary schools. Neville Bennett, appointed as Professor of Educational Research at Lancaster in 1978, drew attention to the primary classroom and teacher-learning processes as areas for investigation. At Leicester, the large-scale ORACLE project (Observational Research and Classroom Learning Evaluation), developed by Professor Maurice Galton and his team, was also in the primary field.[58] Appointments to chairs in primary education have recently been made in a number of universities.

These interests do not exhaust the list of professorial activities which are under the umbrella of education. Information technology, vocationalism and schooling, in-service training and educational policy-making and management studies in education are further examples. The advent of the National Curriculum following the Education Reform Act of 1988 and its implications for schools of education will present a new challenge for those responsible for the direction of their departments. Nevertheless, despite the changing functions of these holders of chairs over the last century, the basic aims, as stated by the very first professor, J.M.D. Meiklejohn, remain unaltered

> The thoroughgoing examination of the development of the growing mind: the engineering of studies for school purposes: and the best means of preserving the vigour and freshness of the teacher's mind — these are the three tasks at which a Professor of Education has to work.[59]

Notes

1 Meiklejohn, J.M.D. (1884) 'Professorships and lectureships in education', *International Health Exhibition Literature*, 16, London, W. Clowes, p. 97.

2 Reproduced in Gordin, P. (Ed) (1980) *The Study of Education. A Collection of Inaugural Lectures*, 1, London, Woburn Press, pp. 8–9.

3 Laurie, S.S. (1882) 'The teaching profession and chairs of education', *The Training of Teachers and other Educational Papers*, London, Kegan and Paul, Trench pp. 8–9.
4 Gordon, P. (1986) 'Teaching as a graduate professor 1890–1970' in Wilkes, J. (Ed) *The Professional Teacher*, London, History of Education Society, p. 80. See also Jones, D.R. (1988) *The Origin of Civic Universities: Manchester, Leeds and Liverpool*, London, Routledge, p. 79.
5 Thomas, J.B. (1983) 'The beginnings of teacher training at University College, Bangor', *Transactions of the Caernarvonshire Historical Society*, 44, pp. 129–30.
6 Whiting, C.E. (1932) *The University of Durham*, London, Sheldon Press, p. 204.
7 Oxford University (1893) *Report of a Conference on Secondary Education, 10–11 October*, Oxford, Clarendon Press, p. 80.
8 Bryce Commission (1895) *Report*, 1, pp. 203 and 208.
9 Cambridge University (1896) *Report of a Conference on Secondary Education, 21–22 April*, Cambridge, Cambridge University Press, p. 105.
10 London Technical Education Board (1901) *Minutes of Proceedings*, 9, 6 May, p. 214.
11 Cambridge University (1902) *Report of a Conference on the Training of Teachers in Secondary Schools for Boys, 14–15 November*, Cambridge, Cambridge University Press, p. 30.
12 *ibid.*, p. 31.
13 Adams, J. (1902) *The Training of Teachers*, reproduced in Gordon, P. (Ed) (1980) *op. cit.*, p. 44.
14 Hearnshaw, F.J.C. (1929) *The Centenary History of King's College London 1828–1928*, London, Harrap, p. 369.
15 Adamson, J.W. (1904) *Our Defective System of Training Teachers*, London, Ginn, p. 44.
16 Kelly, T. and Whelan, R.T. (1981) *For Advancement of Learning. The University of Liverpool 1881–1981*, Liverpool, Liverpool University Press, p. 161.
17 Fiddes, E. (1957) *Chapters in the History of Owens College of Manchester University 1851–1914*, Manchester, Manchester University Press, p. 174.
18 Connell, W.F. (1980) *A History of Education in the Twentieth Century*, Canberra, Curriculum Development Centre, p. 63.
19 Findlay, J.J. (1903) *The Training of Teachers*, London, Sherratt & Hughes, p. 20.
20 Gordon, P. and Szreter, R. (1989) *History of Education: The Making of a Discipline*, London, Woburn Press, p. 5.
21 Quoted in Higginson, J.H. (1980) 'Establishing a history of education course: The work of Professor Michael Sadler, 1903–1911', *History of Education*, 9, 3, p. 251.
22 Chapman, A.W. (1955) *The Story of a Modern University. A History of the University of Sheffield*, Oxford, Oxford University Press, p. 163.
23 Thomas, J.B. (1984) 'The origins of teacher training at University College, Cardiff', *Journal of Educational Administration and History*, 16, 1, p. 14.
24 Tuck, J.P. (1973) 'From training college to University Department of Education', in Lomax, D.E. (Ed) *The Education of Teachers in Britain*, London, Wiley, p. 89.
25 Findlay, J.J. (1902) *Principles of Class Teaching*, London, Macmillan, p. xii.
26 Keatinge, M.W. (1916) *Studies in Education*, London, A. & C. Black, p. vii.
27 Board of Education (1908) *Regulations for the Training of Teachers for Secondary Schools*, Cmnd. 4184, p. iv.
28 Bompas Smith, H. (1913) *Education as the Training of Personality*, Manchester, Manchester University Press, p. 1.
29 Tibble, J.W. (1961) 'Sir Percy Nunn, 1870–1944', *British Journal of Educational Studies*, 10, 1, pp. 68–70.

30 Aldrich, R. and Gordon, P. (1989) *Dictionary of British Educationists,* London, Woburn Press, p. 250.
31 See, for example, Professor William McClelland's inaugural addrress at St Andrews on his appointment to the Bell chair, reported in *St Andrews Citizen*, 14 November 1925, p. 8.
32 Sutherland, J. (1955) 'Sir Godfrey Thomson', *British Journal of Educational Psychology,* 25, 2, p. 65.
33 Sutherland, G. (1984) *Ability, Merit and Measurement. Mental Testing and English Education 1880–1940,* Oxford, Clarendon Press, p. 129.
34 Board of Education (1926) *The Education of the Adolescent,* p. xvii, and (1931) *The Primary School,* p. xii, both London, HMSO.
35 Simmons, J. (1955) *Leicester and its University College,* Leicester, Leicester University Press, p. 104.
36 Dent, H.C. (1977) *The Training of Teachers in England and Wales 1800–1975,* London, Hodder & Stoughton, p. 118.
37 Charles, D.C. (1976) 'A historical overview of educational psychology', *Contemporary Educational Psychology,* 1, pp. 76–88.
38 Willis Dixon, C. (1986) *The Institute. A History of the University of London Institute of Education, 1932–1972,* London, Institute of Education, p. 141.
39 Lester Smith, W.O. (1950) *The Teacher and the Community*, London, Evans Brothers, pp. 5–8.
40 Elvin, L. (1987) *Encounters With Education,* London, Institute of Education, p. 156ff.
41 Ford, B. (1964) 'The school of education and social work' in Daiches, D. (Ed) *The Idea of a New University,* London, Andre Deutsch, p. 138.
42 Ross, A.M. (1968) *Teaching and the Organization of Learning,* Lancaster, University of Lancaster, p. 13.
43 Musgrove, F. (1965) *Faith and Scepticism in English Education,* reproduced in Gordon, P. (Ed) (1980) *op. cit.*, pp. 24–41.
44 Browne, J.D. (1979) *Teachers of Teachers. A History of the Association of Teachers in Colleges and Departments of Education*, London, Hodder & Stoughton, p. 171. See the chapter by Alec Ross in the present volume on the development of BEd courses.
45 Land, F.W. (1963) *Educational Developments,* Hull, University of Hull, p. 7.
46 Lee, D.M. (1979) 'Perspectives in the education of teachers', *Bulletin of the Institute of Education,* 17, pp. 1–9.
47 Szreter, R. (1980) 'Landmarks in the institutionalization of sociology of education in Britain', *Educational Review,* 32, 3, p. 297.
48 Tizard, J. (1966) *Survey and Experiment in Special Education,* London, Harrap, pp. 5–17.
49 Bone, T.R. (1982) 'Educational administration', *British Journal of Educational Studies,* 30, 1, p. 36.
50 Gosden, P.H.J.H. (1984) 'The role of central government and its agencies, 1963–1982', in Alexander, R.J., Craft, M. and Lynch, J. (Eds) *Change in Teacher Education,* London, Holt, Rinehart & Winston, pp. 38–40.
51 Pedley, R. (1969) *The Comprehensive University,* Exeter, University of Exeter, pp. 20–1.
52 Entwistle, N.J. (1974) *Sylbs, Sylfs and Ambiverts: Labelling and Libelling Students*, and Williams, G. (1974) *Higher Education and the Stable State,* both Lancaster University.
53 See, for example, Stenhouse, L. (1975) *An Introduction to Curriculum Research and Development,* London, Heinemann Educational.

54 Wragg, T. (1979) *Teaching Teaching,* reproduced in Gordon, P. (Ed) (1988) *The Study of Education: A Collection of Inaugural Lectures,* 3, London, Woburn Press, pp. 143–65.
55 Dearden, R.F. (1979) *Theory Into Practice,* Birmingham, University of Birmingham, pp. 1–16.
56 Little, A.N. (1978) *Educational Policies For Multi-Racial Areas,* London, Goldsmith's College, p. 24.
57 Gulliford, R. (1977) *To Each According to His Needs,* reproduced in Gordon P. (Ed) (1988) *op. cit.*, 3, pp. 1–19.
58 Galton, M. (1984) 'Time to learn. The study of teaching and its implications for teachers', University of Leicester, unpublished.
59 Meiklejohn, J.M.D. (1876) *Inaugural Address*, reproduced in Gordon, P. (Ed) (1980) *op. cit.,* p. 4.

Chapter 11

Schools of Education — Their Work and Their Future

Tony Edwards

Introduction

'There is in public affairs no state so bad, provided it has age and stability on its side, that is not preferable to change and disturbance'. Montaigne's identification of change with trouble, quoted in Stephan Ball's *Micro-Politics of the School,* matches the mood of many who would normally consider themselves 'progressive' as they contemplate the current disturbances in education. In the macropolitics of schooling, of course, the entire 'progressive establishment' is regarded from the Right of being at best irrelevant to the new era, at worst a serious impediment to reform. It represents 'powerful bureaucratic interest groups' determined to defend their traditional privileges and 'strongly influenced by socialist ways of thinking.'[1] They include the local education authorities, whose complacency in the face of 'falling' educational standards is attributed by the Secretary of State to a virtual monopoly of educational provision which the Reform Act will end. They include HMI who, on GCSE and other matters, continue to show a regrettable 'progressivism', and the DES itself which persists in displaying that 'insolence of office' which claims to know better than the consumer what kind of education service should be provided (Cox and Marks, 1989). They may exclude the 'ordinary classroom teachers' as being more misled than sinning; but they certainly include the teacher unions for their defence of restrictive practices and other historical inefficiencies, and they include teacher educators for peddling the irrelevancies and errors of educational theory.

Any vigorous defence against such criticisms is liable to be dismissed out of hand as another display of vested interest by some part of the 'education business'. Certainly this chapter is being written at a time of unprecedented questioning of teacher education, and the questions extend to whether it has a future at all in anything like its present institutionalized forms. Earlier chapters have reviewed how it got to where it is. My task is to consider what might and should be left of it in universities when the present reappraisals have taken effect.

The Scope of the Present Enterprise

Of the 11,800 qualified teachers who in 1986 took up their first posts in maintained schools in England and Wales, 94 per cent came from training institutions in those two countries and about a third of those were trained in universities. The main university contribution is to the one-year postgraduate courses which, since the early 1970s, have become the main routes into teaching. Of those entering secondary schools by this route in 1988, nearly two-thirds came from universities. That predominance was especially marked in the shortage subjects of mathematics, science and modern languages.

Although the Secretary of State's first reaction to recent HMI reports on the quality of that training was to highlight the bad news (something which HMI itself was careful not to do), and although New Right publicists have used the reports with propagandist selectivity as evidence of pervasive failure, the main conclusions are more accurately summarized in such traditional terms as 'satisfactory but could do better' (HMI 1988a and 1988b). Briefly, there is still in HMI's view too much diversity between courses and too much autonomy for individual tutors, while 'disturbing proportions' of new teachers felt they had been poorly prepared for teaching less able (and more able) pupils, for the assessment of learning, and in some of the basic skills of classroom management. Nevertheless, over half those observed in their first year of teaching were already demonstrating a high level of professional competence, while the proportion of lessons judged to be 'excellent', 'good' or 'satisfactory' was so close to recent HMI judgments on experienced teachers as to suggest a considerable achievement from such 'tightly-packed' training. Since training for other professions rarely receives comparably close scrutiny, there is no way of judging relative quality; it might reasonably be asked, however, whether the proportion of 'satisfactory or better' lectures and seminars in other university courses would justify the belief of some recent critics of the PGCE that 'knowledge and love of subject' are sufficient to ensure good teaching.

The significant improvement which HMI noted since its previous (1982) survey of initial teacher training pre-dated the requirements and monitoring of the national Council for the Accreditation of Teacher Education (CATE). The Council's first five years of inquisition began amid considerable questioning of some of its criteria, doubts about a membership which seemed light in knowledge of what was being accredited, and more general concern that departments of education could become the channel along which other government interventions against university autonomy could flow. There has also been persistent concern that the heavy financial implications of meeting some criteria have been only partially recognized in university funding, while official advocacy of closer partnership with schools has not yet extended to considering the implications of that partnership for teachers' conditions of service or the resourcing of schools. The five years end, however, not only with general acceptance that national accreditation should continue, but also widespread agreement that the same criteria should be applied at the point of entry to qualified status and that a greater diversity of training routes should produce demonstrably comparable outcomes.

It is impossible to estimate what proportion of the present teaching force has participated in university-based in-service training, but that uncertain figure is relatively high among the 'leaders' of the education profession. In the 'final offer' year of the old INSET funding arrangements (1986/87), 3606 teachers followed award-bearing and full-time courses in universities, 60 per cent of them seconded by their LEAs. Another 4591 were studying part-time. Two years later, the full-time numbers had fallen to 2365, of whom fewer than 30 per cent were seconded. Part-time numbers had risen to 7036, many of those students being involved in new modular programmes brought rapidly into being in response to the decline in secondments. The increasing numbers of teachers paying for their own courses is worrying both to them and to the providers, however much it gratifies those who believe that employees should pay for enhancing their own human capital. The huge increase in non-award-bearing courses offered by universities (which involved over 45,000 teachers in 1988/89), and the now substantial contributions of university tutors to school-based staff development, are welcome because they extend to LEAs which previously made little use of the national INSET 'pool' and to many more teachers than followed the traditional routes. Even if these alternative forms of INSET also represent an expedient response to the decline in traditional markets, their prompt introduction at least demonstrates an adaptability, and an awareness of the 'real world' of market forces, which many critics of universities would deny.

Departments of education have tended to show quite strongly in the internal assessments of research performance which most universities have undertaken since the first selectivity exercises carried out by the University Grants Committee in 1984. They have done so despite a teaching year which is significantly longer than is normal in the university sector, teaching loads which are unusually heavy, diverse and fragmented, and the considerable upheavals in both initial and in-service training. Collectively, their academic 'productivity' is considerably higher in 1989 than it was when selective judgments were first made. Information submitted by thirty-two UDEs for the second selectivity exercise indicates about £40 million in new research grants and contracts over the five years ending in August 1988, and some 10,000 publications in books and academic journals. The scale and pervasiveness of such activity contradicts any notion of concentrating educational research in selected institutions. Instead, it demonstrates a commitment to that 'enriching' of teaching with research which HMI noted with approval[2], to providing a research base for schools and LEAs, and to maintaining opportunities for independent enquiry into educational policy and practice.

I have deliberately emphasized quantity in this opening section, aware that critics of UDEs are likely to regard such evidence as showing just how bad things are. Regarding this part of the 'education business' as a self-serving network, they see it as creating and justifying the very demands it claims to meet (Hillgate Group, 1989). From that perspective, both teacher education and educational research are regarded as largely useless, too often subversive, and certainly much more extensive than they need to be. In reviewing the three interrelated components of UDE activity, I hope to avoid giving some current polemical fashions more weight than they deserve, while recognizing that upheavals in and around the schools are certain to force the initial and continuing education of teachers in new directions. If I concentrate on what I believe to be the distinctive contributions of UDEs (and, of course, other parts of higher education), it is partly because some of these contributions are directly under attack, and partly because they may simply be lost sight of amid the clamant pressures and distractions of the new era.

Initial Teacher Training and the Study of Teaching

Implementing a National Curriculum of core and foundation subjects depends above all on 'a sufficient supply of suitably qualified and competent teachers' (HMI, 1989b). Predicted insufficiencies vary, but early government references to 'mismatches' which could be remedied simply by deploying specialist teachers more efficiently have now been replaced by estimates that some curriculum areas may be lacking up to a third of the teachers required by the mid-1990s. For it is one of the certain effects of a National Curriculum defined largely as a 'broad and balanced' range of subjects that it will make previously 'hidden' or 'repressed' shortages of specialist teachers much more visible. Indeed, the apparently egalitarian objective of setting common attainment targets for pupils 'wherever they live and go to school' constitutes an unprecedented means of holding the government to account for the consequences of its own policies because such a notion of pupil 'entitlement' is meaningless without an accompanying entitlement to the resources necessary to bring that common curriculum to life. Since the availability of 'sufficient' appropriately-qualified teachers is the most critical of these resources, teacher supply becomes a matter on which the government is highly vulnerable and on which it may be strongly tempted by expedient short-term 'solutions' to its difficulties.

It is in this context, with teacher shortages already severe in places, that support for alternative or non-traditional routes into teaching is growing. There is an understandable professional scepticism about crisis measures to change entry or training requirements when training has not been demonstrated to be an impediment, and when the real problems are rooted in pay, conditions of service, conditions of work, and status — indeed, when retention is becoming even more difficult than recruitment and both reflect the increasing uncompetitiveness of teaching in the graduate employment market. But it would not be a credible response for UDEs to hold rigidly to the old ways as the only source of 'suitable' initial qualifications. Imaginative initiatives are required, especially those intended to cast the recruiting net more widely. Some of those initiatives will require a more fundamental reappraisal of initial training because they will raise questions about how much of it is most usefully based in schools and made the responsibility of experienced teachers, and about the wider professional knowledge and understanding which should complement and support classroom competence. But a clear distinction has to be made between proposals which are primarily recruiting drives, proposals intended to improve the quality of training by strengthening the partnership with schools, and proposals intended to replace present forms of training by thorough-going apprenticeship. If this is not done, then 'emergency' measures may be transformed into a long-term cost-cutting model to the serious detriment of teachers and pupils. It is in this context that many UDE staff will be able to quote accurately at least one sentence from the Senior Chief Inspector's 1989 Report — 'Standards of learning are never improved by poor teachers, and there are no cheap, high quality routes into teaching'.[3]

Casting the net more widely to catch non-traditional entrants, especially from ethnic minorities and from those with technological qualifications and industrial experience, has already brought experiments in part-time and distance-learning courses which can be both adapted and expanded to fit particularly urgent specialist needs. There is now growing support from within teacher training for more salaried-entry opportunities for graduates especially in science and technology — for example, with proper part-time training as a necessary condition (as in the British Petroleum-funded experiment in Hertfordshire) or with immediate secondment to a full-time PGCE (as Surrey, for example, has been doing for mature graduates appointed to its teaching force). But greater diversity within the teaching force may not mean a larger teaching force, nor are the alternative routes likely to be cheaper unless training-on-the-job is largely sacrificed to the job and the trainee treated as a low-grade but indispensable member of a hard-pressed workforce.

It remains unclear whether the government's licensed teacher initiative will be mainly a tidying-up of unconventional routes, or a significant extension of a route already taken by 270 prospective entrants[4] in 1987/88, or the main highway which the Hillgate Group and others would like it to become. Attacks on it have been dismissed as protective reactions to a perceived threat to professional status. But as a training route, rather than as a prompt means of admitting teachers qualified in other countries, it rests on some dubious assumptions. For example, it assumes that 'mature' entrants need less training. If they are 'youthfully mature', they will resemble the quarter and more of entrants to traditional PGCE courses who are already older than the minimum licensee age of 26. If they have long experience in another occupation, they are likely to need unusual support from their tutors and their schools if they are not to revert under pressure to the didactic styles of teaching in which they were probably taught themselves. In so far as licensed teachers are most likely to be recruited to where vacancies are hardest to fill, they are likely to find themselves in the more difficult schools and in schools under too much pressure to provide the necessary support. As for the New Jersey model of on-the-job training, its enthusiastic promotion by the Secretary of State (despite the implicit but 'readable' reservations of HMI) exemplifies the dangers of eagerly transplanting initiatives from other countries without careful consideration of the particular circumstances which prompted them. For example, a main objective of the New Jersey scheme was to attract academically-able students into teaching, given the relatively low quality of those taking education degrees and the lack of any systematic training or induction for other graduates. HMI comments on the traditionally low academic quality of entrants to teaching in American schools have therefore to be set against the generally 'high calibre' of students on undergraduate and postgraduate initial teaching in this country[5]; in 1987, for example, 80 per cent of university PGCE students had higher, first-class or second-class degrees. The New Jersey Program embodies a sharp separation of theory from practice of a kind which UDEs have worked hard to overcome (and which HMI regularly criticize). It is also supported by considerable financial incentives for the provisional teachers, and by pupil-teacher ratios which allow mentor-teachers markedly more time for their supervisory responsibilities than their equivalents would normally have in this country. In brief, the 'lessons' learned in New Jersey are not easily applied in very different circumstances.

Close partnership with experienced teachers in initial training is certainly essential. Indeed, some of those who advocate it display an apparent and convenient ignorance of how extensive that partnership already is. The rapid development of various forms of IT-INSET reflect what is more generally true — that their participation challenges experienced teachers to reflect critically on their own practices, and so is itself a particularly powerful form of staff development where the necessary time and training have been made available. Organizationally, however, it is a partnership which has depended heavily on teachers' goodwill, and on contributions which their new conditions of service do not contractually require them to make. Where those contributions are particulary substantial, as for example in the long-established school-based model developed by Sussex University[6] or the internship model being tried in some Oxfordshire schools (HMI, 1989b), it raises questions about how the unit of resource for the students involved is distributed between the UDE, the LEA and the schools. It also raises fundamental questions about the scope of the school-based work, and about what is best done by tutors with a different if complementary frame of reference.

It is of course being argued, mainly from the political Right, that apprenticeship to 'a skilled and experienced practitioner' is all the training which many new teachers need. The arguments have been too consistent, and too systematically repeated, not to be regarded as a campaign (for example, Sexton 1987; O'Hear 1988a; Cox 1989; Hillgate Group 1989). The present focus of that campaign is to make the licensed teacher route into a main highway to professional recognition, initial training in its present form being dismissed as another restrictive practice constraining the free working of the market. It is also blamed for initiating, or at least supporting, many of those 'progressive' departures from traditional subjects traditionally taught and examined which these critics also deplore.

Borrowing the term from Cardinal Newman, O'Hear (1988b) defines 'newiness' as a tendency to parade uninformed opinions and suggests that university teachers should be armoured against it by their commitment to disciplined knowledge. Yet it is a main characteristic of his own and other highly opinionated attacks on teacher training that they are directed at a polemically-convenient but largely unrecognizable description. The attacks assume, for example, a continuing preoccupation with pseudo-academic 'studies', even though the Secretary of State himself recognized in his 1989 speech to the North of England Education Conference that 'the academic content of teacher training is now more rigorous, the professional content is much less theoretical, and much more directly related to classroom practice'. More fundamentally, it asserts an 'opposition' between 'theoretical studies of education' and 'the study and love of one's subject and teaching practice' as though the first excluded the second[7], and extols a 'large core of supervised practice' while disregarding the large core which already exists (Cox, 1989). 'Theory' is dismissed as being at best a pretentious and at worst a propagandist distraction from the real business of learning to teach, which is a 'practical skill' to be learned quickly and entirely through supervised practice. The criticisms reflect a contempt for teaching itself as well as for 'qualifications in teaching', not because of the examples of potentially valuable recruits which are cited — the literate wife of French extraction, the businessman with a degree in history who is 'happy to teach what he knows' or tell children 'the tricks of his profession', or the mechanic with 'a knack of explaining things to children' — but because of the reduction of the complexities of teaching and learning to a simple matter of knowing something and wanting to pass it on — or, more accurately, to pass it down.[8] It is perhaps worth noting that most of the provisional teachers whom HMI observed in New Jersey schools 'relied on a textbook for their information', and that most of their lessons 'involved the class in listening to an exposition by the teacher'.

Arguments that apprenticeship should now be the main route into teaching assume the availability of large numbers of demonstrably effective teachers, those 'masters of the craft of teaching'[9] who are able to provide conspicuous models for imitation and emulation. No reference is made to such teachers needing to be reflective about their practice as well as being so visibly and unarguably good at their job. No room is left for developing a wider professional understanding of the contexts within which teaching and learning occur. Apprenticeship has the advantage of direct and obvious relevance to coping with a particular set of circumstances. It encourages neither the questioning of established practices, nor reflection on how things might be done differently or better. It is the assumption that such opportunities are not needed, indeed that they merely get in the way of acquiring the 'practical skills' of teaching, which allows critics of what they call 'the theoretical study of teaching' to reduce it to a set of mere initiation rites which should now be abandoned.

Effective arguments against apprenticeship depend on clarifying the nature of the 'partnership' between higher education and the schools in developing professional skills and knowledge beyond a set of immediately useful classroom competencies. Partnership is not a matter of adding more of the same, but of bringing different but complementary strengths together. While it 'is now rare to find method tutors who do not work regularly with their students in classrooms[10], it would be surprising if their work with students was the same as that of the teachers with whom they cooperate. Teachers have a main responsibility for supervising serial or block practices because students need sustained experience of particular settings and guidance from those who know the settings best. What university tutors should offer is 'an analytic perspective that is fed by observation in a range of classrooms and sharpened by the evidence of research' (Ruddock, 1989). An analytical perspective may be provided by practising teachers, but they are likely to need explicit training for it because the complexities and pace of classroom life are much more likely to produce and reinforce a more intuitive, untheorized approach.[11] The 'practical skill' to which O'Hear and others reduce teaching is not readily made explicit, nor is it acquired simply by watching and imitating. This is why initial training needs the complement of explicitly reflective consideration of practice and the practical judgments involved, a complement which may be better provided 'in the security of temporarily distanced university-based parts of the course' (Maclennan and Seadon, 1988). It has to be conceded, of course, that 'there is no well-established and comprehensive body of theory covering teaching and learning' (O'Hear, 1988a), nor is it easy to conceive what such a 'covering' theory would be like. In any case, the notion of a body of rational knowledge about teaching which students could first acquire and then apply in particular classrooms has been largely abandoned in favour of 'reflective practice'. But reflection is not a matter of recollecting in the tranquillity of the university department the emotions, failures and successes of 'real' lessons; it involves disciplined inquiry into how learning is organized and assessed, and above all how the teacher can make his or her own methods an object for investigation. The responsibility which supervising teachers retain for their own classes is more likely to focus their attention on classroom organization and control, and so to give more prominence to basic skills than to more complex aspects of teaching and learning.[12]

Around the 'realities' of classroom life is a wider body of professionally relevant knowledge. Training too narrowly centred on the here-and-now is open to the charge of parochialism, leaving students under-prepared to cope with very different circumstances and under-informed about wider influences on their work. The 'general' courses which complement method work may themselves be confined to the most obviously 'relevant' issues and controversies, expecially since the rapid retreat from the disciplines of education has left UDEs uncertain what to do instead (Wilson, 1989). HMI advice on the matter is broadly consistent. The integration of 'theory' and 'practice' should not be left to the student; the best courses have already achieved a pervasive interaction between the various components of the course, with some challenging experiments to see how much 'general' work can also be school-based; and in distinguishing between 'essential professional training and optional academic study', departments have to keep firmly in mind what schools can 'reasonably expect' new teachers to 'know and be capable of doing when they take up their first posts'[13] (HMI, 1988b, 1.29 to 1.39 and 1989b). The conclusion to be drawn from such advice is now widely accepted within UDEs — that a profile of what a new teacher could be expected to know and be capable of doing would inhibit schools from imposing unreasonable tasks and giving too little support. It would also provide a clearer basis for that teacher's continuing professional education.

Continuing Professional Education and Research-based Knowledge

In the recent process of empowering the DES for a more interventionist role in educational policy and provision, greater central control over teacher supply and teacher training has been a conspicuous ingredient. The restructuring of in-service training can also be located with other moves against producer interests, since UDEs were often accused of relying on the 'diploma disease' to bring them students willing to accept whatever courses were offered on the providers' terms. The overt objectives of the funding arrangements which replaced the 'pool' in 1986 were intended to distribute opportunities for in-service training less erratically, and to focus them on policy priorities as these were defined by central and local government and by individual schools. INSET was also to be less credentialist in ways which were more directly and explicitly related to the improvement of practice.

Since that time, INSET has been considerably reshaped by the preferential funding of DES-designated priorities. Within and alongside those priorities, a great deal more is now initiated by LEA advisors or by individual schools so that it displays a much greater diversity of forms, and many more of the providers come from outside higher education. Indeed, it is notable that the recent DES (1989) guidance on how to get 'from policy to practice' omits higher education altogether in assigning responsibilities for the retraining required by the National Curriculum. The National Curriculum Council itself, however, is now actively seeking their cooperation after an initial period in which teacher training institutions generally were regarded with suspicion as being over-populated with unconstructive critics. It must now be evident to policy-makers, however, how quickly those institutions have diverted resources to the task of assisting schools to prepare for the tasks which the Reform Act has given them. It can also be claimed that as universities are drawn (or dragged) towards various forms of contract-funding, their education departments can claim to have had pioneering experience of the challenges, risks and tensions involved.

As they try to provide and plan marketable courses, UDEs face real dilemmas in managing their own resources apart from the uncertainties and short timescales involved. It is nice to feel useful; there is a commitment to offering as much support as possible to teachers and headteachers confronting unprecedented and simultaneous innovations in curriculum and testing and school management; there are exceptional opportunities in school-based or school-focused INSET for learning from experienced practitioners while demonstrating the usefulness of educational theory and knowledge in coping with 'real' problems; and there is a great deal of departmental money to be earned which can be used to offset the loss of traditionally-funded student numbers and to bring new blood into what might otherwise become a static, ageing staff. But the entrepreneurial and academic spirits are not always easily corked in the same bottle. There is an evident danger that with so much INSET about, some of it involving rather desperate buyers looking for sellers, UDEs might be drawn too far into replicating resources already available within schools and LEA advisory services at the expense of their more distinctive contributions.

From the time when the virtual disappearance of full-time secondments became probable except where an LEA had a specific task to be done, and as some LEAs became reluctant even to support teachers in part-time 'academic' study, the UCET Executive argued consistently in the DES and elsewhere for a necessary balance to be maintained between old and new forms of INSET. Critical reference to the irrelevance of the more 'academic' in-service courses ignored the extent to which teachers used the opportunity to reflect on and investigate their own practice or to study some matter of major professional concern to themselves and their schools. More generally, the separation of the academic from the practical reflects that dangerous reduction of teaching to a 'practical skill' which also endangers the quality of initial training. The 'historic neglect of pedagogy' which Brian Simon described in an earlier chapter is beginning to be remedied by research which recognizes the importance of developing ways of describing and interpreting classroom processes which teachers can use to examine their own work critically and exchange judgments with fellow-practitioners. Teachers were initially reassured by the National Curriculum Council that the new attainment targets and programmes of study did not 'necessarily involve changes in teaching style' as GCSE had certainly done. But the implementation of the National Curriculum will certainly direct attention as never before to how learning occurs and is assessed, and will require of many teachers an informed understanding of pedagogy and assessment which is unlikely to be acquired from brief instruction by outside experts or by their own colleagues returning from short courses with an obligation to disseminate what they have learned. Around these changes in the central business of schooling, there will be a continuing need for in-service opportunities which are not cut tightly to fit today's problems and which enable teachers to reconsider the nature of their tasks and the knowledge, skills and understanding which those tasks require. Room is needed for that critical questioning which requires a degree of detachment from immediate problems, and an independence from the preferred answers of policy-makers. In so far as higher education represents a 'capacity for critique and reflection as a basis for understanding', then it risks betraying that function if it runs too hard after short-term usefulness in a climate where 'commitment to the practical and an endorsement of the anti-theoretical are powerful imperatives' (Ruddock and Wilcox, 1988). It is not a matter of overlooking the 'realities' of the classroom in favour of academic abstractions but of exploring patiently and rigorously *which* realities are shaping and constraining practice.

The research base of UDEs is obviously vulnerable to the same utilitarian pressures. As expectations of high research productivity have risen, so opportunities have multiplied for often lavishly funded projects to produce (for example) training materials to support new curriculum or management initiatives, or to evaluate the initiatives themselves. Research money 'free' from obligations to pipe the payer's tune has correspondingly diminished. It is a powerful sign of the times that the Economic and Social Research Council's corporate plan emphasizes so strongly the disseminating of research findings to policymakers and practitioners, and that such a high proportion of Council money is now given to research centres and programmes which are able to display the relevance of their work to current problems. A great deal of educational research is now sponsored by bodies with a direct interest in the outcomes. The DES, or the Training Agency, or LEAs obliged to include a percentage for evaluation in their budget for TVEI or other initiatives, may not press hard for particular answers to the questions they pose, nor intervene directly in the process of investigation. But they are likely to shape the broad channels along which the research should run. Anticipating their displeasure at inconvenient findings may also be a significant 'hidden' constraint.

Mention was made earlier of the £40 million of new 'external' grants and contracts which UDEs received between 1984 and 1988. Of course, much more research was supported during that period by the research component of the UGC grant. UGC funding reflected the traditional belief that university teaching benefits from an environment in which new knowledge is being discovered. That belief is now being questioned, with teaching-only departments (or even entire universities) being justified on the grounds that while teaching in higher education needs 'scholarship', it does not need research. It was HMI's view, however, that students on initial training courses, and the same must be at least as true of those on advanced courses, 'benefited from the research expertise of the staff'.[14] That judgment seems to recognize not only the possible benefits of being in touch with 'new knowledge', but the wider relevance of those skills of investigation and that commitment to an open-minded questioning of received wisdom which the best research requires. What it produces are rarely confident solutions to practical problems — hence the frequent impatience of practitioners who want unambiguous answers to what are usually complex questions. Perhaps research in UDEs has been too fragmented and spasmodic, not systematic enough in making use of what is already known, and often reluctant to replicate studies so as to accumulate evidence. Yet it has also included some of the best work in curriculum development, the description of classroom processes, the assessment of pupils' learning, the socio-cultural explanation of marked and persistent differences in educational outcomes, and the evaluating of school effectiveness and of the impact on new policies on educational opportunity and quality. Such work depends on an environment which supports independent enquiry–research which will often question current policies or established practice, which may need time to produce results, and which may often have to insist that progress depends on first recognizing that some educational problems and issues are even more complicated than we had thought.

In the longer term, the future of university departments of education depends largely on how school-teaching itself is perceived and on how narrowly or broadly the professional knowledge of teachers is defined. More immediately, it depends on the quality and distinctiveness of their contributions to initial and in-service teacher education, and on their capacity to combine high research productivity with a willingness to confront research problems not amenable to quick or convenient results. Having cited O'Hear disapprovingly for his view of teacher apprentices, I will end by borrowing his justification for the academic freedom of universities. In relation to the work of university departments of education, it is a necessary condition for making 'specialist knowledge and training' available to teachers and to the education system at large, and for doing so in a spirit which is properly 'questioning, conversational, critical and collaborative'.

Notes

1 Quoted in Hillgate Group (1987) p. 1.
2 See Her Majesty's Inspectorate (1988a) pp. 4–5
3 Her Majesty's Inspectorate (1989b) para 70.
4 Department of Education and Science (1988) p. 2.
5 See Her Majesty's Inspectorate (1988a) pp. 7–10 and (1989a) pp. 2–3.
6 See Furlong *et.al.* (1988) pp. 65–119.
7 See O'Hear (1988a) p. 20.
8 See Hillgate Group (1987) p. 36; Hillgate Group (1989) p. 11; and O'Hear (1988a) p. 21.
9 Sexton (1987) p. 22.
10 Her Majesty's Inspectorate (1988a) p. 19.
11 See Edwards and Furlong (1978) p. 2–3; Hatton (1988).
12 See Booth *et al.* (1989) p. 40; and Furlong *et al.* (1988) pp. 88–9.
13 Her Majesty's Inspectorate (1989b) and (1988b) 1.29 to 1.39.
14 Her Majesty's Inspectorate (1988a) p. 4.

References

Booth, M., Furlong, J., Hargreaves, D., Reiss, M. and Ruthven, K. (1989)

Teacher Supply and Teacher Quality: Solving the Coming Crisis, Cambridge, Department of Education, University of Cambridge.

COX, C. (1989) 'Unqualified approval', *Times Educational Supplement,* 6 January.

COX, C. and MARKS, J. (1989) *The Insolence of Office,* London, Claridge Press.

DEPARTMENT OF EDUCATION AND SCIENCE (1988) *Qualified Teacher Status: A Discussion Document,* London, HMSO.

DEPARTMENT OF EDUCATION AND SCIENCE (1989) *National Curriculum: From Policy to Practice,* London, HMSO.

EDWARDS, A. and FURLONG, J. (1978) *The Language of Teaching,* London, Heinemann Educational Books.

FURLONG, V.J., HIRST, P., POCKLINGTON, K. and MILES, S. (1988) *Initial Teacher Training and the Role of the School,* Milton Keynes, Open University Press.

HATTON, E. (1988) 'Teachers' work as bricolage: Implications for teacher education', *British Journal of Sociology of Education,* 9, 3, pp. 337–57.

HER MAJESTY'S INSPECTORATE (1988a) *Education Observed 7: Initial Teacher Training in the Universities of England, Northern Ireland and Wales,* London, HMSO.

HER MAJESTY'S INSPECTORATE (1988b) *The New Teacher in School,* London, HMSO.

HER MAJESTY'S INSPECTORATE (1989a) *The Provisional Teacher Program In New Jersey,* London, HMSO.

HER MAJESTY'S INSPECTORATE (1989b) *Report by HMI on University of Oxford, Department of Educational Studies: Initial Teacher Training,* London, HMSO.

HER MAJESTY'S INSPECTORATE (1989c) *Standards in Education 1978–88,* London, HMSO.

HILLGATE GROUP (1987) *The Reform of British Education,* London, Claridge Press.

HILLGATE GROUP (1989) *Learning to Teach,* London, Claridge Press.

MACLENNAN, S. and SEADON, T. (1988) 'What price school-based work?', *Cambridge Journal of Education,* 18, 3, pp. 387–403.

O'HEAR, A. (1988a) *Who Teaches the Teachers?,* London, Social Affairs Unit.

O'HEAR, A. (1988b) 'Academic freedom and the university' in TIGHT, M. (Ed) *Academic Freedom and Responsibility,* London, Society for Research in Higher Education.

RUDDOCK, J. (1989) 'Accrediting teacher education courses: The new criteria', in HARGREAVES, A. and REYNOLDS, D. (Eds) *Education Policies: Controversies and Critiques,* Lewes, Falmer Press.

RUDDOCK, J. and WILCOX, B. (1988) 'Issues of ownership and partnership in school-centred innovation: The Sheffield experience', *Research Papers in Education,* 3, 3, pp. 157–79.

SEXTON, S. (1987) *Our Schools — A Radical Policy,* London, Institute of Economic Affairs.

WILSON, J. (1989) 'Topics, ideology and discipline in teacher education', *Educational Review,* 41, 1, pp. 29–37.

Appendix: Professors of Education in the United Kingdom.

(p/t = part-time; * = presently in post)

Aberdeen
J.D. Nisbet 1963–1988
Vacancy
L.B. Hendry* 1989

Aston in Birmingham
A.G. Joselin 1967–1973
Vacancy
R.C. Whitfield 1975–1983 (Educational Enquiry)
(Department closed)

Bath
K. Austwick 1966–1988
W.H. Dowdeswell 1972–1978
J.J. Thompson* 1979
I.M. Jamieson* 1989
J. Calderhead* 1990

Belfast
C.W. Valentine 1914–1919 (see *Birmingham*)
W.J. McCallister 1919–1946
S.D. Nisbet 1946–1951 (see *Glasgow*)
H.M. Knox 1951–1982
J.F. Fulton* 1977
H.R. Cathcart* 1977 (Educational Policy) (see *Ulster*)

Birmingham
A. Hughes 1903–1919
C.W. Valentine 1919–1946 (see *Belfast*)
M.V.C. Jeffreys 1946–1964 (see *Durham*)
F.J. Schonell 1947–1950 (see *Wales, Swansea*)

E.A. Peel 1950–1978 (Educational Psychology) (see *Durham*)
G.E.R. Burroughs 1966–1976
K. Charlton 1966–1972 (History and Philosophy) (see *London, Kings's*)
P.H. Taylor* 1966 (Curriculum Studies)
F.H. Hilliard 1968–1976
R.K. Elliott 1973–1977 (History and Philosophy)
M.G. Hughes 1977–1987 (Social and Administrative Studies)
R. Gulliford 1977–1988 (Special Education)
R.F. Dearden 1978–1987 (History and Philosophy)
M.M. Clark 1979–1984 (Educational Psychology)
G. Upton* 1988
S. Ranson* 1989

Bradford
F. Musgrove 1966–1970 (Research in Education) (see *Manchester*)
Vacancy
R. Beard 1973–1982 (Educational Studies)
(Department closed)

Bristol
H.M. Wodehouse 1920–1931
Vacancy
B.A. Fletcher 1942–1955 (see *Leeds; Southampton*)
R.C. Wilson 1951–1971 (Education and Social Development from 1964)
B.S. Morris 1956–1975
B. Ford 1973–1982 (see *Sheffield; Sussex*)
W. Taylor 1966–1973
E. Hoyle* 1971
W.P. Robinson 1977–1989
M. Beveridge* 1989

Brunel
W.D. Furneaux 1966–1981
Vacancy
N.D.C. Harris* 1986

Cambridge
G.R. Owst 1938–1959
W.A. Lloyd 1959–1971
P.H. Hirst 1971–1988 (see *London, King's*)
D.H. Hargreaves* 1988

Dundee
J.W.L. Adams 1966–1980 (Bell Chair, transfer from *St. Andrews)*
(Department closed)

Durham
A. Robinson 1923–1935 (Education joint with Psychology)
Rev. E.F. Braley 1935–1939
M.V.C. Jeffreys 1939–1946 (see *Birmingham*)
E.J.R. Eaglesham 1947–1966
B. Stanley 1948–1966 (joint Institute with *Newcastle*)
E.A. Peel 1948–1950 (Educational Psychology) (see *Birmingham*)
F.V. Smith 1951–1952 (Educational Psychology)
H.S.N. McFarland 1966–1974
Vacancy
G.R. Batho 1975–1988
F.J. Coffield* 1980
D.R. McNamara* 1986 (Primary Education)
G.R. Grace* 1989

East Anglia
L. Stenhouse 1978–1982 (Centre for Applied Research in Education)
H.T. Sockett 1980–1986 (see *Ulster*)
G. Brown* 1981
A.M. Wilkinson* 1981 (see *Exeter*)
B. MacDonald* 1984 (Centre for Applied Research in Education)
J. Elliott* 1987

Edinburgh (Bell Chair)
S.S. Laurie 1876–1903
A. Darroch 1903–1924
Vacancy
G.H. Thomson 1925–1951 (see *Newcastle*)
J.G. Pilley 1951–1966
Vacancy
L. Hudson 1968–1977 (Educational Sciences from 1969)
N.J. Entwistle* 1978 (see *Lancaster*)

Exeter
A.E. Dean 1913–1919 (Education joint with Philosophy)
Vacancy
S.H. Watkins 1923–1952 (Education joint with Philosophy, joint Psychology from 1935)
C.T.W. Curle 1952–1957 (Education joint with Psychology)
R. D'Aeth 1958–1977 (Education joint with Psychology, Education from 1963)
R. Pedley 1969–1972 (see *Southampton*)
A.M. Wilkinson 1972–1980 (see *East Anglia*)
R.A. Pring 1977–1989 (see *Oxford*)
M.G. Brock 1977–1978

E.C. Wragg* 1978 (see *Nottingham*)
J.C. Dancy 1978–1984
S.N. Bennett* 1985 (Primary Education) (see *Lancaster*)
D.N. Burghes* 1981
C.W. Desforges* 1988

Glasgow
S.D. Nisbet 1951–1977 (see *Belfast*)
N.D.C. Grant* 1978

Hull
R.W. Rich 1930–1934
A.V. Murray 1934–1945
W.R. Niblett 1945–1947 (see *Leeds; London Institute*)
E.B. Castle 1948–1961
F.W. Land 1961–1975
T.W. Bamford 1976–1977
V.A. McClelland* 1978
A. M. Clarke 1985–1987 (Educational Psychology)

Keele
W.A.C. Stewart 1950–1967
G.N. Brown 1967–1980
S.J. Eggleston 1967–1984 (see *Warwick*)
R.F. Kempa* 1974 (Science Education)
T.R.P. Brighouse* 1989

Lancaster
A.M. Ross 1967–1988 (Educational Research)
N.J. Entwistle 1970–1978 (see *Edinburgh*)
G.L. Williams 1973–1984 (Educational Planning) (see *London, Institute*)
S.N. Bennett 1978–1985 (Educational Research) (see *Exeter*)
S. Tomlinson* 1984
P. Mortimore* 1987

Leeds
J. Welton 1904–1916
Vacancy
J. Strong 1919–1933
F. Smith 1933–1947 (see *Newcastle*)
R.N. Armfelt 1949–1955
W.R. Niblett 1947–1959 (see *Hull; London Institute*)
B.A. Fletcher 1961–1967 (see *Bristol; Southampton*)
W. Walsh 1957–1972
T.H.B. Hollins 1967–1976

K. Lovell 1969–1981 (Educational Psychology)
D. Layton 1973–1989 (Science Education)
M.B. Sutherland 1973–1985
P.H.J.H. Gosden* 1978 (History of Education)
D. Child* 1981 (Educational Psychology) (see *Newcastle*)
R. Driver* 1989

Leicester
J.W. Tibble 1946–1966
G.H. Bantock 1964–1975
J.F. Kerr 1966–1977
B. Simon 1966–1980
G. Bernbaum 1974–1988
D.S. Wright 1975–1982
M.J. Galton* 1982
M. Mathieson* 1988
K. Fogelman* 1988

Liverpool
W.H. Woodward 1899–1907 (City of Liverpool Professor)
E.T. Campagnac 1908–1938
A.J.D. Porteous 1938–1963 (Sydney Jones Professor since 1953)
N.R. Tempest 1954–1972 (William Roscoe Professor)
W.A.L. Blyth 1964–1983 (Sydney Jones Professor)
E. Stones 1972–1982 (William Roscoe Professor)
Vacancy
Wynne Harlen* 1985 (Sydney Jones Professor of Science Education)
D. Hamilton* 1989

London, Chelsea
K.W. Keohane 1968–1976 (Science Education)
G. Matthews 1968–1977 (Shell Professor of Mathematics Education)
P.J. Kelly 1974–1977 (Biological Education) (see *Southampton*)
H. Silver 1974–1977 (Social History of Education)
P.J. Black* 1976 (Science Education)
D.C. Johnson* 1978 (Shell Professor of Mathematics Education)
W.B. Davies 1979–1988 (see *Wales, Cardiff*)
A.M. Lucas* 1980 (Science Curriculum Studies)

London, Goldsmith's
G. Whitty* 1989
A.V. Kelly* 1989

London, Institute of Education
J. Adams 1902–1922
Vacancy

T.P. Nunn 1913–1936
C.L. Burt 1926–1932
H.R. Hamley 1932–1949
F. Clarke 1936–1945
K. Mannheim 1946–1947
J.A. Lauwerys 1947–1970 (Comparative Education from 1953)
L.A. Reid 1947–1962 (Philosophy of Education from 1953)
B. Pattison 1948–1976
W.O. Lester Smith 1949–1953 (Sociology of Education from 1953)
P.E. Vernon 1949–1964 (Educational Psychology from 1953)
M. Read 1949–1955 (Education in Colonial Areas from 1953)
H.L. Elvin 1955–1958 (Education in Tropical Areas)
L.J. Lewis 1958–1973 (Education in Tropical Areas)
W.R. Niblett 1960–1973 (Higher Education from 1967) (see *Hull; Leeds*)
R.S. Peters 1962–1982 (Philosophy of Education)
J. Tizard 1964–1979 (Child Development)
B.M. Foss 1965–1968 (Educational Psychology)
D. M. Lee 1965–1971 (Education in Colleges of Education)
B.B. Bernstein* 1967 (Karl Mannheim Professor of Sociology of Education)
M. Blaug 1971–1984 (Economics of Education)
T. Veness 1968–1971 (Educational Psychology)
G. Baron 1972–1978 (Educational Administration)
J.N. Britton 1971–1975 (Goldsmith's Professor of Education)
W.D. Wall 1972–1978 (Educational Psychology)
C.B. Hindley 1972–1984 (Child Development)
G.W. Parkyn 1972–1977 (Comparative Education)
T. Blackstone 1978–1983 (Educational Administration)
M. Craft 1976–1980 (Goldsmith's Professor of Education) (see *Nottingham*)
H. Goldstein* 1976 (Statistical Methods)
B. Holmes 1975–1985 (Comparative Education)
D. Lawton* 1974 (Curriculum Studies)
H. Rosen 1976–1984 (English)
K. Swanwick* 1976 (Music Education)
H.G. Widdowson* 1977 (English as a Foreign Language)
P.R.C. Williams 1978–1984 (Education in Developing Countries)
H. Francis* 1978 (Educational Psychology)
N.J. Graves* 1978 (Robert Ogilvie Buchanan Professor of Geography)
R.M. Macleod 1978–1982 (Science Education)
M. Skilbeck 1981–1985 (Curriculum Studies) (see *Ulster*)
B. Tizard* 1982 (Thomas Coram Research Centre)
K.W. Wedell* 1979 (Educational Psychology: children with special needs)
P. Gordon* 1982 (Education)
G.L. Williams* 1984 (Educational Administration) (see *Lancaster*)
C.M. Hoyles* 1984 (Mathematical Education)
J.M. Ogborn* 1984 (Science Education)

M.W. Stubbs* 1985 (English)
G.R. Neave* 1986 (Comparative Education)
A. Little* 1987 (Education in Developing Countries)

London, King's College
J.W. Adamson 1903–1924
J. Dover Wilson 1924–1935
Vacancy
F.A. Cavanagh 1937–1946 (see *Reading; Swansea*)
Vacancy
A.V. Judges 1949–1965 (History of Education)
A.C.F. Beales 1965–1972 (History of Education)
P.H. Hirst 1965–1971 (see *Cambridge*)
L.R. Perry 1972–1978 (see *Warwick*)
K. Charlton 1972–1983 (History of Education) (see *Birmingham*)
E.J. King 1975–1979
D.N. Aspin 1978–1988

London, King's College London (KQC)
The amalgamation of King's College, London (K) and Chelsea College (C) established a new Department of Education as follows:
P.J. Black* 1976 (C)
D.C. Johnson* 1978 (C)
W.B. Davies 1979–1988 (C) (see *Wales, Cardiff*)
A.M. Lucas* 1980 (C)
D.N. Aspin 1978–1988 (K)
S. Ball* 1989

Loughborough
L.M. Cantor* 1969 (Schofield Professor of Education)
L. Cohen* 1977
J.R. Hough* 1988 (Economics of Education)

Manchester
H.L. Withers 1899–1902 (Sarah Fielden Professor of Education)
J.J. Findlay 1903–1925 (Sarah Fielden Professor of Education)
M.E. Sadler 1903–1911 (p/t Professor of History and Administration)
H. Bompas Smith 1912–1932
J.F. Duff 1932–1937 (Sarah Fielden Professor of Education)
R.A.C. Oliver 1938–1970 (Sarah Fielden Professor of Education)
A. Ewing 1949 – 1964 (Audiology and Education of the Deaf)
S. Wiseman 1961–1968
I.G. Taylor 1964–1988 (Audiology and Education of the Deaf)
F.W. Warburton 1965–1969 (Experimental Education)

H.J. Butcher 1967–1970 (Higher Education)
F. Musgrove 1971–1982 (Sarah Fielden Professor of Education) (see *Bradford*)
J.D. Turner* 1970 (Adult and Higher Education, Sarah Fielden Professor since 1985)
A.G. Smithers* 1977
P.J. Mittler* 1973 (Special Education)
J.M. Bamford* 1989 (Audiology and Education of the Deaf)
G.K. Verma*

Newcastle-upon-Tyne
M.R. Wright 1895–1920
G.H. Thomson 1920–1925 (see *Edinburgh*)
F. Smith 1925–1933 (see *Leeds*)
J.H. Nicholson 1933–1935
B. Stanley 1936–1972 (see *Durham*)
J.P. Tuck 1948–1976
D. Child 1976–1981 (see *Leeds*)
A.D. Edwards* 1979

Nottingham
A. Henderson 1905–1922
H.A.S. Wortley 1923–1935
C.M. Attlee 1935-1945
N. Haycocks 1945–1973
M.M. Lewis 1956–1973
H. Davies 1965–1972
E.C. Wragg 1973–1978 (see *Exeter*)
J.F. Eggleston 1973–1983
E.A. Lunzer 1969–1983 (Educational Psychology)
M. Craft 1980–1989 (see *London, Institute*)
P. Gammage* 1984
R.J. Murphy* 1989

Open
W. James 1969–1984
D.F. Swift 1970–1986
P. Williams 1970–1978 (see *Wales, Bangor*)
J.E. Merritt 1971–1985
G.T. Fowler 1972–1974
R. Glatter* 1977
T.R. Weaver 1976–1978
D.L. Nuttall 1979–1986
J.M. Raynor 1983–1986
J.M. Bynner 1985–1988
R. Moon* 1988
P. Woods* 1988

R. West* 1988
P.H. Light* 1989

Oxford
R.A. Pring* 1989 (see *Exeter*)

Reading
F.A. Cavanagh 1934—1937 (see *London, King's: Wales, Swansea*)
H.C. Barnard 1937-1951
C.H. Dobinson 1951-1968
V. Mallinson 1967-1975 (Comparative Education)
J. Wrigley 1967-1988 (Curriculum Research and Development until 1975) (see *Southampton*)
R. Wilson 1968-1989
J.K. Gilbert* 1988 (Science Education)
C. Adelman* 1989

St Andrews (Bell Chair)
J.M.D. Meiklejohn 1876-1902
J. Edgar 1902-1922
Vacancy
W.W. McClelland 1925-1941
A.F. Skinner 1941-1954
Vacancy
J.W.L. Adams 1956-1966 (see *Dundee*) (Department closed)

Sheffield
J.A. Green 1906-1922 (see *Wales, Bangor*)
G.H. Turnbull 1922-1954
W.H.G. Armytage 1954-1982
H.C. Dent 1956-1960
B. Ford 1960-1963 (see *Bristol: Sussex*)
J.P.C. Roach 1965-1982
N. Bolton* 1978
J. Ruddock* 1985
J. Gray* 1988

Southampton
C.R. Chapple 1901-1904 (see *Wales, Aberystwyth*)
F. Fletcher 1904-1906
F. Clark 1906-1911 (see *London, Institute*)
J.J. Maxwell 1911-1914 (Education joint with Philosophy)
J. Shelley 1914-1919 (Education joint with Philosophy)
A.A. Cock 1920-1939 (Education joint with Philosophy)
B.A. Fletcher 1939-1943 (see *Leeds; Bristol*)

G.C. Dudley 1943–1950
F.W. Wagner 1950–1971
J. Wrigley 1963–1967 (see *Reading*)
R. Pedley 1971–1979 (see *Exeter*)
J.G. Wallace 1976 (resigned same session)
P.J. Kelly* 1978 (see *London, Chelsea*)
C.J. Brumfit* 1984

Stirling
E. Perrott 1966–1974
B.T. Ruthven 1972–1974
Vacancy
A.T. Morrison 1975–1984
J.H. Duthie 1975–1989
Vacancy

Sussex
B. Ford 1963–1973 (see *Bristol, Sheffield*)
G.C. Allen 1966–1974
N.I. Mackenzie 1973–1983
R.A. Becher* 1975
C. Lacey* 1975
M.R. Eraut* 1986

Ulster
A. Milton 1967–1977
J. Hendry 1968–1970
J.E. Nesbitt 1971–1984
M. Skilbeck 1971–1977 (see *London, Institute*)
H.R. Cathcart 1972–1976 (see *Belfast*)
D.R. Jenkins 1976–1982 (see *Warwick*)
H.T. Sockett 1975–1980 (see *East Anglia*)
P.P. Daws* 1984
J. Rushton* 1984
E.D. Saunders* 1985

Wales, Aberystwyth
H. Holman 1893–1894
Vacancy
F. Watson 1896–1913
C.R. Chapple 1913–1939 (see *Southampton*)
I. Jones 1939–1960
Vacancy
J.L. Williams 1961–1977

J.R. Webster* 1978 (see *Wales, Bangor*)
C.J. Dodson 1981–1989

Wales, Bangor
J.A. Green 1894–1906 (see *Sheffield*)
R.L. Archer 1906–1942
W.M. Williams 1942–1947 (see *Wales, Swansea*)
D.W.T. Jenkins 1947–1966
J.R. Webster 1966–1978 (see *Wales, Aberystwyth*)
P. Williams 1978–1983 (see *Open*)
I.W. Williams* 1980

Wales, Cardiff
T. Raymont 1904–1905
W. Phillips 1905–1932
H.M. Mackenzie 1904–1915
B. Foxley 1915–1925
O. Wheeler 1925–1951
E. Evans 1951–1967
A. Taylor 1967–1988
R. Davie 1974–1981 (Educational Psychology)
J.G. Beetlestone 1974–1988 (Science Education)
W.B. Davies* 1988 (see *London, Chelsea*)

Wales, Swansea
F.A. Cavanagh 1921–1933 (see *London, King's; Reading*)
W.M. Williams 1934–1942 (see *Wales, Bangor*)
F.J. Schonell 1942–1946 (see *Birmingham*)
E.J. Jones 1947–1957
C.E. Gittins 1957–1970
Vacancy
D.G. Pritchard 1971–1981
M. Chazan 1977–1984
Vacancy
M. Williams* 1988

Warwick
L.R. Perry 1968–1972 (see *London, King's*)
R.R. Skemp 1973–1987
M.D. Shipman 1979–1984
J.G. Lawrence 1978–1984
R.L.E. Schwarzenberger* 1979 (Science Education)
D.R. Jenkins* 1983 (Arts Education) (see *Ulster*)
S.J. Eggleston* 1985 (see *Keele*)
J.R.G. Tomlinson* 1985

J.G. Woolhouse* 1987 (Education and Industry)
K. Robinson* 1988 (Arts Education)
K. Sylva* 1989 (Primary Education)

York
H. Ree 1963–1977
E.W. Hawkins 1965–1979 (from 1974, Language Teaching Centre)
I. Lister* 1977

Notes on Contributors

R.E. Bell is a Senior Lecturer in Educational Studies at the Open University. A former editor of *Scottish Educational Studies,* he was co-author (with Nigel Grant) of *A Mythology of British Education* (1974) and of *Patterns of Education in the British Isles* (1977). He has also edited a number of volumes on curriculum and higher education as well as contributing articles to books and journals not only in Britain but in Denmark, Ireland and Finland. Before joining the Open University he worked in Edinburgh University and was a member of the Scottish General Teaching Council.

Maurice Craft is Foundation Dean of Humanities and Social Science at the new University of Science and Technology established in Hong Kong. Until 1989 he was Professor of Education and Chairman of the School of Education at Nottingham University, where he was also Pro-Vice-Chancellor. He has held chairs of education at London University Institute of Education and at La Trobe University, Melbourne.

Tony Edwards has been Professor of Education at Newcastle University since 1979, and is Dean of the Faculty of Education. He is Vice-Chairman of UCET, and a member of the Human Behaviour and Development Group of the ESRC. He is currently investigating (with Geoff Whitty) the development of city technology colleges. Recent publications include *Investigating Classroom Talk* (with David Westgate, 1987) and *The State of Private Education: an investigation of the Assisted Places Scheme* (with John Fitz and Geoff Whitty, 1989).

Peter Gordon is Professor of Education and Head of the Department of History and Humanities at the University of London Institute of Education. He has published a number of books and articles on the history of education, including *The Victorian School Manager* (1974), *Selection for Secondary Education* (1980), and has edited three volumes of inaugural lectures, *The Study of Education* (1980 and 1988).

Peter Gosden is Professor of the History of Education and Chairman of the School of Education, University of Leeds. He is the author of a number of books on the history of the education system, including *The Development of Educational Administration in England and Wales* (1966), *Education in the Second*

World War (1976) and *The Education System since 1944* (1983). He is joint editor of the *Journal of Educational Administration and History.*

Professor Alec Ross is Academic Secretary of the Universities Council for the Education of Teachers. In 1988 he retired from the University of Lancaster where he founded the Department of Educational Research and the School of Education in 1967. He is the co-ordinating editor of *Higher Education: The International Journal of Higher Education and Educational Planning.*

Brian Simon is Emeritus Professor of Education at the University of Leicester. He has published three volumes of his *Studies in the History of Education* (1960, 1965 and 1974) and is completing a fourth (and final) volume covering the period 1940 to 1990. Other publications engage with contemporary educational issues. He has also been Chairperson of the International Standing Conference for the History of Education and Chairperson of the History of Education Society.

Margaret B. Sutherland is Emeritus Professor of Education at the University of Leeds and taught for many years in the Department of Education, Queen's University of Belfast. She is Vice-President of the World Association for Educational Research, Honorary Fellow of the Scottish Council for Research in Education, and a committee member in the Association Francophone d'Education Comparee. She was editor of the *British Journal of Educational Studies* 1974–1985. Her most recent book is *Theory of Education* (1988).

John B. Thomas is Reader in Education at Loughborough University of Technology and a Fellow of the British Psychological Society. Publications include *International Dictionary of Education* (with Terry Page and Alan Marshall, 1977), *The Self in Education* (1980), *Educational Research and Development in Britain 1970–1980* (with Louis Cohen and Lawrence Manion 1982) and a number of papers and reviews in educational, historical and psychological journals.

John D. Turner has extensive experience of teacher education both in Britain, where he served in the Institute of Education of the University of Exeter and as Director of the Colleges of Education Division of the University of Manchester, and in Africa, where he was a Professor of Education and spent three years as the Vice-Chancellor of the University of Botswana. He is at present Dean of the Faculty of Education and Director of the School of Education of the University of Manchester, and is the current Chairperson of the Universities Council for the Education of Teachers.

Author Index

Subject Index